Which Atlanta job gu should you buy?

Consider this:

• The *Atlanta Journal and Constitution* compared and reviewed all four Atlanta job guides *(Atlanta Jobs*, *Atlanta Job Bank, Atlanta Job Atlas,* and *How to Get a Job in Atlanta). Atlanta Jobs* was <u>the only</u> guide recommended![1]

• In a recent survey of career counselors and outplacement firms, those who were familiar with all four books recommended *Atlanta Jobs*.

• *Atlanta Jobs* is the only Atlanta job guide written by an experienced personnel professional with more than 20 years of personnel placement in Atlanta.

Still uncertain?

• Call the human resources departments at a few of Atlanta's major corporations and ask which book they recommend.

• Call the career placement department at any of the local colleges and ask their opinion.

Atlanta Jobs outsells all other local job search books!
The clear choice among those who know is . . .

ATLANTA JOBS

---

[1] For a copy of the entire review, write CareerSouth Publications, P O Box 52291, Atlanta, GA 30355.

YOUR INPUT IS VALUED,

AND WE WANT TO HEAR FROM YOU!

ATLANTA JOBS will be invaluable to you now, and we want future editions to be even more helpful! Your comments, suggestions and experiences help make that possible.

We appreciate your previous replies, and most of those are included in this edition. If your comments or suggestions are incorporated in future editions, you will receive a complimentary copy.

Some topics to consider:

• Which of the eight source groups described in the Career Search System were most helpful in finding your job?

• Which ultimately secured your job?

• Which personnel agencies were most helpful? Least helpful?

• Are there any additional companies or industries you would like to see represented here?

• Are there any professional/trade associations or network groups you know that offer job assistance, and that are not included here?

• Any comments in general?

Mail your information to
CAREERSOURCE PUBLICATIONS
P O Box 52291, Atlanta, GA 30355.

ATLANTA JOBS

featuring the

CAREER SEARCH SYSTEM . . .

Your source to Atlanta jobs!

Not just a vague, indiscriminate list of companies, but a **complete strategy** on how to uncover and utilize **every available source** to your advantage:

- Atlanta's primary hiring companies

- Personnel agencies

- Classified want ads

- Government positions

- Job fairs

- Professional and trade associations

- Network and support groups

- Free job assistance organizations

- Useful resources and publications

And more!

- Resume, cover letter, broadcast letters, and salary history preparation, with examples of each

- Interviewing strategies, including questions and answers

- Detailed company profiles, employment data and hiring procedures

Published by CareerSource Publications, P O Box 52291, Atlanta, GA 30355.

Manufactured in the United States of America.

Graphics and cover design by West Paces Publishing, Atlanta, GA.

All information herein is believed to be accurate and reliable. However, neither the author nor CareerSource Publications assumes any responsibility thereof. Correction requests should be mailed to CareerSource Publications.

ISBN: 0-929255-13-5

ATLANTA

JOBS

featuring the

CAREER SEARCH SYSTEM

Steve Hines

CareerSource Publications
Atlanta, Georgia

Also available from CareerSource Publications:

THE JOB HUNT by Steve Hines

All you need to conduct a successful job search! Completely explains every part of the job search, including resume preparation, securing interviews, job networking, locating free help organizations, interivew tips, and much, much more - even a self-analysis "What Am I Doing Wrong?" $12.95 + $2 postage/handling

THE CAREER SEARCH SYSTEM GUIDE TO
CHARLOTTE JOBS by Steve Hines

All-new second edition. Chosen one of *Inc.* magazine's best cities for growing a business, Charlotte continues to have one of the lowest unemployment rates in the nation. $13.95 + $2 postage/handling

JOBS SOUTHEAST

Quickly recovering from the recession, the Southeast offers innumerable employment opportunities. This guide pinpoints the 12 fastest growing cities in the SE and how to find employment in each one. Includes largest employers, network groups, local governments, etc. Available December, 1993.

JOB NETWORKING MADE EASY by Steve Hines

More job seekers find new employment through job networking than through all other sources combined! This step-by-step approach makes the process simple. $10.95 + $2 handling (ISBN #0-929255-14-3)

HOW TO GET A JOB ON A CRUISE SHIP By Don Kennedy

Make money and have fun! Learn step by step how to apply for and get one of the more than 30,000 jobs available every year on more than 100 cruise ships! Written by a former cruise staff member and officer for Royal Caribbean, Sitmar, Norwegian, and Carnival Cruise Lines. $10.95 + $2 handling (ISBN #0-929255-06-2)

THE JOYS OF JOB TRANSITION By C. J. Markos

A humorous and uplifting spoof at being "between jobs." You'll identify with the many cartoons designed by a job seeker laid off during the recent recession. A great gift to a friend "between jobs"! $4.95 + $1 handling (ISBN #0-929255-07-0)

For information and to order, contact
CAREERSOURCE PUBLICATIONS
P O Box 52291, Atlanta, GA 30355.
Or call (404) 262-7131; fax (404) 364-0253

TABLE OF CONTENTS

<u>Chapters</u>:

Appendices:

for Lynnsey Hines

CHAPTER I

INTRODUCING THE
CAREER SEARCH SYSTEM

CHAPTER I

INTRODUCING THE

CAREER SEARCH SYSTEM

Good news: Atlanta is a great place to live and has thousands of job vacancies!

Bad news: The word is out, and thousands of job seekers (latter-day carpet-baggers?) now have descended on Atlanta.

Good news: There is a job in Atlanta for you!

That's not just hype. Even in the current, extended recession, there are indeed innumerable career opportunities available in Atlanta, but the catch is how to find them. And that's not really a problem; it just takes knowledge, a plan of action, and the commitment to see the plan through.

In the summer of 1970, I moved to Atlanta, ready to seek fame and fortune in the business world. I had been teaching high school social studies for the previous three years, and thus coddled in the world of academia, I had no concept of what was in the "real world." I did not know what jobs were out there, or what companies offered them, and least of all, I didn't have the slightest idea how, where, or what to do to find my new career.

I wish I'd had a book like this!

In the years since that summer, I have worked in personnel recruiting and placement. I have seen thousands of applicants struggle and stumble, trying to advance their careers – expending too much time, energy, and money, and going in pointless directions. Finding a job is just not that hard – if you know what to do!

But of course, most people don't. They have limited knowledge and resources from which to draw. I am always surprised at how otherwise extremely capable executives often produce the worst resumes and go on to interview poorly! Even corporate personnel administrators, whom one would expect to know what to do, appear to be just as much in the dark as everyone else.

The purpose of the **CAREER SEARCH SYSTEM** is to fill this vacuum of misinformation and lack of information, and to provide job seekers with the knowledge needed to successfully conduct a job search. This System represents more than twenty years of knowledge, gained almost entirely from that best teacher, experience. I have compiled the arcana, simplified and methodized it, and the result is the **CAREER SEARCH SYSTEM.**

What is the **CAREER SEARCH SYSTEM?** It is a step-by-step, hand-in-hand, practical guide to finding employment. Whether your objective is finding a new career, advancing your present career, or rebounding from a lay-off, the **CAREER SEARCH SYSTEM** will guide you to the best job available.

Within these ten chapters, you will discover all the information needed to obtain the right job in Atlanta. Outlined in detail are the who's, what's, how's, and when's, that will result in the job you want. Many sources are revealed that you probably never considered or knew existed. Even if you were aware of them, you may not have understood how to benefit from them.

The **CAREER SEARCH SYSTEM** will give you the tools you need to apply in your job search. You have only to use them, following the guidelines and directions.

There is one requirement: the firm commitment to find the job best suited for you. And that requirement will include work. You may hear many times, "Finding a job is a job in itself," and that is so true.

But since most of us would rather play than work, let's get into the spirit of job hunting with a little game, on pages 16 and 17.

(Refer to pp. 16 - 17)

Now back to the real world! I hope this exercise has shown you what is ahead in your job search. As this is a practical guide, I cannot help you in assessing your abilities or needs and wants. Once you have finished that, my system definitely will get you the rest of the way!

The Career Search System

The **CAREER SEARCH SYSTEM** consists of five basic steps that will lead to job offers. Each step is discussed fully, describing in detail exactly what you should do.

Step #1 is organization. I am not a believer in creating work when none is required, but I have observed for many years that some basic organization is necessary for a successful job search. As your job hunt progresses, you will come to see the value of the systems and procedures I suggest and so I urge you not to rush into your campaign without this small amount of planning first.

Step #2 in your job search is to prepare your resume – not just a good resume, but a "better" resume: the "Power Resume." As you will read in the resume chapter, the first contact you make with a company is usually through your resume, and that first impression must be positive. Each section of the resume is discussed in detail, explaining how, when and why you use each, so that your resume will make the best first impression possible. Even if you plan to have a service prepare your resume, carefully read this chapter, so that you can give to the service the layout and standards you expect to be followed. Numerous examples are shown in Appendix A.

Start Here! Move 1 space.

ASSESS YOUR ABILITIES:
Objectively—Move 2 spaces.
Non-objectively—Move 1 space.

STAY HERE UNTIL YOU TRY ANOTHER SOURCE

MARKET RESUME:
Move 1 space for
each marketing tool you use.

MOVE BACK & FORTH A WHILE, THEN MOVE 1 SPACE

2 sources are better than one, but use another source, then move 1 space.

Getting the Idea?
Use another source
and keep moving.

DITTO DITTO DITTO DITTO DITTO DITTO DITTO

JOB OFFER
YOU WIN!

Go to church and pray no one
else has both good interview
and good follow-up!

GO BACK TO START. GET HELP AND TRY AGAIN.

ASSESS NEEDS & WANTS
Realistically—Move 2 spaces.
Unrealistically—Move 1 space.

Stay Here Until You Come to Your Senses!

ORGANIZE
Skip Organization—
Move Back 1 Space
Organize equipment, time, records & resources—
Move 1 Space
Organize emotional support systems—
Move 1 More Space!

PREPARE RESUME
Ordinary Resume—Move 1 space.
"Power" Resume—Move 2 spaces.

GET DEPRESSED
Wallow in self-pity!
Organize emotional support systems—
Then Move On—

CONGRATULATIONS!
You Got an Interview
Prepared for interview—move 1 space.
Unprepared for interview—move back 12 spaces.

PREPARATION
Research only—
Move 1 space.
Research & Rehearse—
Move 2 spaces.

CLOSE
but we're not playing horseshoes! Move back 1 space.

GOOD INTERVIEW!
FOLLOW-UP—Move 2 spaces.
NO FOLLOW-UP—Move 1 space.

In addition to your written resume, you need two additional items:

1) You must develop a short, oral resume to use when you want to quickly relate your background and objective. How to prepare this "30-Second Resume" is also discussed as part of Step #2.

2) You need business cards to hand out in your networking efforts, as well as other opportunities when you don't have your written resume available. This was discussed earlier and examples of good business cards are included in appendix A.

Now you are ready for *Step #3*, developing a marketing strategy to obtain interviews. If you have never been in sales and marketing before, you are now! Using a loose-leaf notebook to record your efforts and results, you will begin to develop contacts and sources in order to obtain interviews.

The System gives you far more sources from which to develop leads and interviews than you will probably use, but they are all there if you need them. Start with the ones that are the simplest and easiest for you, and if you are not satisfied with those results, use the others. The System even indicates which sources work best for different backgrounds, and so you can choose the one(s) best suited for you. A major part of this marketing plan will include job networking. You probably have heard of this concept, but lacked the knowledge to make it work for you. Since more applicants find their jobs through some form of job networking than through all other sources combined, this approach is vital to your search. The CAREER SEARCH SYSTEM explains several networking procedures in complete detail, outlining exactly what you should do and say.

Once your marketing efforts are into full swing, you will begin to be invited for interviews. *Step #4* contains information on the preparation you must do before an interview, as well as the interview itself. Numerous questions, suggested answers, and the reasoning behind the questions and answers are discussed fully. If the very thought of interviewing makes you break out in a cold sweat, then relax. The CAREER SEARCH SYSTEM will have you well-prepared and will carry you through the interview with flying colors!

If you have always thought that once you finished the interview, your work was over, then think again! *Step #5* covers the follow-up procedure you should do after the interview, to give you an extra push. The "thank-you note" is discussed, as well as additional research and sources you can employ.

In addition to the five basic steps outlined in Chapters II – VI, additional chapters cover other information you may need in your job search.

"Chapter VII: Salary Negotiating" explains how salaries most often are determined by companies. When you should and should not consider negotiating is explained, and if you do wish to negotiate your salary offer, several suggestions and procedures are outlined.

Job-related correspondence is covered in Chapter VIII. The basic format for cover letters is given here, followed by the variations used for specific instances. What to include in your "thank-you note" is clarified, with suggestions for making yours stand out. How to report your salary information or write a salary history is also detailed. In addition, you can find numerous examples of these correspondences in Appendix B.

"What am I doing wrong" is a question I frequently encounter, and I have the answers. Chapter IX discusses what to do should you find your job search at a standstill. I can help you evaluate your job search and pinpoint problems, then find the solutions. I have recommendations to energize your search and to help you avoid the common mistakes I so often observe.

Lastly, Chapter X concludes with a few more suggestions, even using rejection as an asset!

Conclusion

In the more than twenty years that I have been in personnel placement in Atlanta, I have dealt with hundreds of companies and their personnel representatives, interviewed thousands of applicants, and read tens of thousands of resumes. I stress my experience so you will understand that I know what is going on, in your mind and in the minds of companies, and to assure you that I know what I am talking about. I have encountered the problems you're facing many times, and I can help you find the solutions.

You need to read thoroughly every chapter in this book. You smugly may be thinking, "Not me!" but sooner or later you will realize I am right, and when you do, just remember, "I told you so!"

Step #1 in your job search is organization. Let's get started!

CHAPTER II

STEP ONE:

ORGANIZING YOUR JOB SEARCH

CHAPTER II:

Step One: Organizing Your Job Search

Getting Started

Every job will go smoother if you are organized, and this is definitely true of the job hunt. Before you write the first word on your resume or make your first phone call, you must be organized.

Organize your space. If at all possible, you should have a designated work area with a desk, phone, and the supplies you will need. Working off of the kitchen table is not satisfactory and you will quickly see why! Also, a small, two-drawer file cabinet and several file folders will be very helpful in keeping your information organized and easy to find. In other words, set up an in-house office, just as you would have at your job.

Organize your equipment. Have your phone convenient to your work area. Buy a telephone answering machine, if you don't already own one; they are relatively inexpensive, and using one will prevent you from missing any calls for information or interviews.[1] If you can afford one or have access to one, a fax machine also will be very useful;

---

[1] My pet peeve has become people who leave a message on my phone recorder, but speak so rapidly and/or enunciate so poorly that I cannot decipher the information, especially their phone number. When leaving messages, always repeat your name and phone number so that the receiver will have no difficulty returning your call.

I have observed that many companies are advertising that you can fax your resume instead of mailing it.[1]

A typewriter is a bare necessity, but you really need access to a computer and laser printer. With a computer, you easily can personalize your correspondence and resume to fit each situation, as well as store information for later reference. If you do not own a computer, try to locate a free source before you lease time or rent one. For example, many state employment offices have computers available for job seekers. Public libraries and college placement offices are other sources to check.[2]

Have business cards printed with your name, contact data, and your employment objective or expertise, but do not attempt to condense your resume onto this small card (see Appendix A for examples); you will use these cards extensively during your search, especially when job networking.

Organize your records. One of the complaints I often hear from job changers is that their present company requires too much paperwork. Companies don't require this work just to keep their employees busy, but rather they see the need to keep accurate and timely records, for use now and to refer to later. I personally do not enjoy keeping records, and yet I have learned over the years that I must.

I have kept the volume of paperwork you need for your job search to a minimum, so don't short-cut the little I have included. As your job search progresses, you will see the need for each item.

You will need a loose-leaf notebook with eight dividers and lots of paper to record your activities. Label the dividers with these topics:

- Time organizer

---

[1]If you do fax your resume, I urge you also to mail a copy, since many older fax machines use a coated paper that fades and disintegrates after a time.

[2] If you are not computer literate, now is an ideal time to learn at least the basics. Every company and every discipline is becoming more dependent on computers, and your lack of computer ability will severely hinder your career. Consider taking free or low cost classes through a local college or adult education program.

- Company "cold calls"

- Newspaper ads

- Personnel agency contacts

- Professional contacts

- Personal contacts

- Professional associations

- Information interviews

Organize your time. How much time can you spend on your job search? If you are currently employed, you must budget your time wisely, conducting your search in the evenings, weekends, and during the workday when possible. If you are unemployed, you should plan to spend at least 40 hours per week in your search, and you should plan your schedule just as effectively as you would in your employment. Use the example illustrated at the beginning of Chapter IV, called "Weekly Timetable," or some other time organizer.

During your unemployment, strive to maintain the same schedule to which you have become accustomed. Don't allow yourself to wallow in bed every morning, or you will be wasting valuable time. In addition, when you begin your new employment, you will have difficulty readjusting to the work regimen.

If you find yourself with extra time, use it constructively by establishing new contacts through volunteer work (see Job Networking in Chapter IV), enrolling in career enhancement classes, or acquiring certification in your field. Now is an excellent time to study up on new industry trends and advancements, especially computer-related developments. Include in your resume that you are currently attending these job-related classes; companies will be impressed that you are using your time wisely and learning additional skills.

If you have been a member of a health spa, continue your workouts just as before. Exercise is an excellent way to cope with stress.

Organize your resources. Files, phone books, and other reference materials should be within easy reach. Keep a copy of **Atlanta Jobs**

25

close at hand, since you will refer to it often. Think of this book as a workbook, similar to the ones you used in school. You should underline or highlight passages, write in the margins, fold down the edges of pages you want to refer to later – anything that will help you derive the most from the information contained here. In fact, by the end of your job search, this book should be thoroughly worn out.

Support Systems

There is one more item to organize, and this is by far the most important. If you learn nothing else from this book or only follow one of my suggestions, let it be this one: Don't attempt a job search at all until you have organized and have in place your psychological and emotional support systems.

I just spoke with an applicant who has 15 years experience in commercial real estate. Unfortunately, that field is very depressed currently and his job search has now stretched into seven months. His exact words to me were, "I sit across from my wife at breakfast every morning and I know she is thinking 'What is wrong with him?'." Of course, what he really meant was "What is wrong with me?"

Even in the best of economic times, conducting a job search is a highly traumatic and stressful endeavor. In the recent recession and slow recovery, the <u>average</u> length of time required to find new employment has stretched into many months. Even worse, in the past few months I have spoken with too many job seekers who have been looking for more than a year.

Maintaining a positive attitude through this most trying of times is painfully difficult, and you must recognize your need for the support of close friends and family, including your children. Let them know what you are doing every step of the way and what they can do to help you. Tell them of your frustrations and anxieties, fears and depression. Those are normal feelings and nothing to be ashamed of or suppressed.

Unfortunately, I have witnessed too many divorces and dissolutions of friendships that resulted from this stressful period. Open your lines of communication and keep them open at all times. You will be pleasantly surprised to discover how understanding and helpful your support systems can be.

26

In addition, you should keep them informed of the positive aspects of your job search – your progress and up-coming interviews, of your research and what you have learned. Many of these experiences will be very interesting and you will enjoy sharing them with your friends.

Join organizations, both those pertaining to your profession as well as non-profit charity associations. Become active and volunteer your time. This will give you needed diversions and new purposes, and also introduce you to another set of contacts, some of whom may be helpful in your job search.

Prepare yourself, too, by adjusting your attitude. Nothing can ruin a beautiful, sunny day faster than receiving a rejection letter in the mail. Accept the fact that you will be experiencing some let-downs and – yes – rejections, and don't be overwhelmed. When you begin to feel yourself slipping into a depression, that is the signal to pull out your emotional support systems and get back on track.

On the positive side, this time can be an opportunity for reflection, a time when you can sit back and evaluate your life and career direction. Are you really happy with your current occupation? What would you like to do differently? What are your goals? Most importantly, what are your priorities? What is important to you, in your personal life as well as your career?

Some churches in Atlanta sponsor programs for individuals and their families who are in employment transition, especially those whose job search has stretched into many months. Through prayer and community experience, these groups reach the spiritual aspects of job search trauma, as well as offering assistance in identifying practical resources. Some groups pair job seekers with other individuals who recently have experienced career transition themselves. Whatever your religious preference, you can benefit from the camaraderie that comes from discussing your job search with others who can identify with your experiences and problems. The groups of which I am aware are these:

Employment Transition Ministry
Cathedral of St. Phillip (Episcopal)
2744 Peachtree Road NW, Atlanta, GA
(404) 240-4764
Meets Wednesdays from 7:00 - 8:30 pm. After a short business agenda, attendees break into small groups lead by someone who also has experienced trauma recently.

Job Talk
Support group where participants share experiences of job transition. Spouses invited. Meets Wednesdays at 7:15 pm at Decatur Church of Christ,
1677 Scott Blvd, Room 215, Decatur, GA.
(404) 633-9242 for directions; for information, call Jeff Hendrick at 605-0690

59:59 Career Support Groups
Small groups of six to eight (half employed, half unemployed) covenant to meet once a week until all in the group are employed. Meets at different times and places, depending on need and availability. Call (404) 303-5959 or Jansen Chasanoff at 565-9775 for information.

Seekers Group
This coterie of men meets for coffee and doughnuts each Friday morning at 7:15 at TGI Friday restaurant located in the Prado shopping center at 5600 Roswell Road (near Roswell Rd x I-285) in Sandy Springs. An inspirational commentary begins the morning, followed by introduction of new attendees (good networking potential). Next comes practical information on job search, including job leads, and the session ends with a short Bible study. For information, call Gary Northcutt at 908-0822 (office) or 418-1056 (home).

All of this organization is vital to a successful job search, as you will come to see. Best of all, remember you are far ahead in the career search game already: You bought and are reading *Atlanta Jobs*!

CHAPTER III

STEP TWO:

PREPARING YOUR RESUMES AND BUSINESS CARDS

Part 1: The "Power Resume"

Part 2: The "30-Second Resume"

Part 3: Business Cards

CHAPTER III

Step Two: Preparing Your Resumes and Business Cards

Part 1: The Written Word – The "Power Resume"

It's not what you know, but how you present it. Let me explain.

I recently ran a small, classified ad in the local newspaper for a manufacturing plant manager. In response to that one short ad, I received more than 100 resumes; a larger ad would probably have elicited many more. Obviously, I did not have time to interview all of these applicants, or even to call them all. Many of them had the right background and experience, so what criteria did I use in deciding which to interview first? I used the same test that every other recruiter uses: the quality of the resume.

And what happens to the applicants with the poor resumes? I don't know, since I never call them!

Thus, you see that a resume has both positive and negative potential, and we can draw two conclusions regarding the resume:

1) A resume can get you an interview, which may ultimately result in a job.

2) But a resume also can *prevent* you from getting an interview, and thus you will never have the opportunity to show why you should be employed there.

The importance of a good resume cannot be overstressed. Even if you have exactly the right background the company is seeking; even if you can interview perfectly; and even if you would make an ideal employee for the company, you will never get in the door if the company's first impression of you is negative, based on a poorly prepared resume.

Wow! Did you ever think that one sheet of paper could have so much power over your life and career?

But not only does your resume need to be "good," it also needs to be "better," that is, better than your competition. Imagine reviewing 100 resumes for just one opening! In order to peruse that many resumes in a cost-effective time frame, I tend to scan through the pile and pull out the ones that look the most appealing and are able to grab my attention quickly . Since a positive impression of the applicant has already been established, these "better" resumes receive more attention and sooner. The others never even may get read.

This chapter will explain how to write a "better" resume and how to use its power to your advantage. In short, you will learn how to write the "Power Resume."

What makes up a "Power Resume"? There are many factors involved, and we will cover them in detail. In addition, numerous examples are given in Appendix A. First, however, let's discuss what a resume is.

Simply stated, a resume is

> "A short summary of your positive qualifications for employment."

Now let's analyze that definition.

Short: Most applicants need only a one-page resume, or two pages at the absolute most. And yet too many job-seekers feel that a short resume implies a lack of experience, and conversely, a long one suggests a well-qualified applicant. Nothing could be further from the truth. In fact, a lengthy resume suggests a verbose egoist, unable to discern the important from the irrelevant!

OK, maybe that's a bit severe. Truthfully, many job-seekers are probably not aware of what should and should not be in a resume. Perhaps that is why you are reading this. Bear in mind that personnel departments receive many, many resumes, and I assure you that from my own experience and from discussions with corporate recruiters, long resumes are seldom read. On the contrary, concise resumes get the most attention.

While on this subject, here's a bit of crazy logic: I recently interviewed a manager with a three-page resume. When I asked him if he ever read the three-page resumes he received, he immediately said "No!" He then went on to tell me that nevertheless, he was certain other managers would read his!

Summary: This is a resume, not your autobiography, and it should sum up only information germane to your job search. It should not include irrelevant information, such as your appointment to the college homecoming court or being selected "Most Eligible Bachelor," and do not include a photograph.

Your: This is *your* resume, not anyone else's. Do not mention the names and background of your family, spouse and children, or the name of your supervisor. (Incidentally, I once had an applicant rejected for an interview because his resume referred to "my lovely wife Lorain and our two adorable children, Mark and Susie.")

Positive: "Accentuate the positive," as the old song goes. A resume should emphasize achievements, accomplishments, honors, and awards, and omit any negatives. You may even wish to include a brief summary section, highlighting your best assets. Use positive wording, creating an up-beat image of yourself. If you were ever fired from a job, a resume is definitely not the place to reveal it.

Qualifications: Education, experience, personal data, references.

Employment: The finish line!

Preparation

Now that you understand what a resume is and what it can do, you can begin to assemble yours, by obtaining the necessary subjective and objective data. Objective data is listed below, but depending on your experience and job goal, you may not use all of it. In particular, the information on your college education will become less important as you gain more career-related work experience. Employment that occurred over ten years ago should be included only very briefly, in favor of your more recent experience, which should be discussed more fully.

In general, this is what you need to compile:

1) Address and phone number (permanent and temporary, if applicable)

2) College information, including

- graduation dates (month and year)

- grade point average (major and overall) and/or class ranking

- honors, achievements, elective offices, etc.

- percent of college expenses earned

- activities, including sports, clubs and professional organizations

- for recent grads, career-related courses taken or scheduled

3) Career-related seminars, courses and special training

4) Professional distinctions, honors, achievements, awards

5) Hobbies and interests

6) Activities, including membership in professional organizations and civic associations

7) Employment data, including

- brief description of your company(s) and its products/services, if not generally known to the public

- title or functional title

- dates of employment

- duties, responsibilities and descriptions

- accomplishments, awards, sales quotas, distinctions, etc.

8) Career-related experience, other than through direct employment.

Now is the time to plan whom you will use for references, and confirm with them. Three references are sufficient, probably one professional, one personal and one academic (for recent grads) or former employer. (Incidentally, we have further plans for using your references to aid in your job search. This will be discussed later in "Chapter IV: Marketing Strategies.")

In addition to that objective data, you need to assess your skills and qualifications, strengths and weaknesses. Be honest with yourself and answer the following:

- Why should XYZ Corporation interview (and maybe hire) me?

- What do I have that other applicants may not?

- What do I do best? Worst?

- What are my best developed talents (judgment, communications, work relationships, decision-making, etc.)?

- What are the most important achievements and accomplishments of my life and career?

These answers are important in understanding your employment assets. Start planning how you might incorporate them into your resume.

Format

There is no one universal format used by all job-seekers, but rather basic sections that can be worded and assembled to fit each person's background. The information I have outlined here is very general in nature, and will result in a functional/chronological resume, the type most commonly accepted. However, under certain circumstances, you may wish to use a topical format, which will be discussed later.

Most importantly, as you write your descriptions, keep in mind why you are writing this resume: to impress a potential employer and gain an interview. Thus, you want to include not only your basic qualifications, but also distinctions and achievements that put you ahead of your peers.

Name and address: At the top of your resume, place your name, address and phone number. Type your name in all capitals and use boldface in larger-size type, if available. Professional certifications, such as C.P.A., should be included on the line with your name (JOHN A. DOE, C.P.A.). If you have a temporary address (*e.g.*, a student) you can use that address and include a permanent address at the bottom or elsewhere, noting when it will be effective. If you are moving soon, you can use either your old or new address and phone number; just be certain that you always can be contacted by prospective employers. Needless to say, update your resume with the new address as soon as possible. If you feel comfortable receiving phone calls at work, you may include both your home and work phone numbers.

Objective: If you include an Objective, this will be the first section, after your name and address. If you are applying for a specific opening or in a specific industry, tailor your objective to fit. Remember, however, that if your resume states a specific objective (*e.g.*, sales) and you are applying for another (*e.g.*, management), you likely will not be considered. Thus, if you are not so sure about a specific objective, you can make it more open in nature. A better alternative used by many applicants is to prepare two or more resumes with different objectives, and use the one most appropriate. Or you can simply omit the objective all together, and open your resume with a Summary paragraph. In practice, I find that I tend to omit the Objective more and more often, in favor of a Summary section (described below) and a very personalized cover letter, and that is what I suggest you do also.

Summary: The purpose of a Summary section is twofold:

1) Summarize your abilities

2) Highlight your qualifications that propel you ahead of other applicants.

A summary paragraph is optional, but it can be very effective, especially if you have some short, important data you wish the reader to see first, as an enticement to read further. Do not defeat its purpose by making it too long and thus lose its impact.

The Summary can be used with or without an Objective, or you can incorporate the Objective within this section. It should be very positive and up-beat, with an emphasis on abilities and achievements. Here are three examples, and more are included on the sample resumes in Appendix A:

> Proven success in solution-oriented Sales and active Sales Management. Consistently promoted or recruited as a result of outstanding sales performance. Assembled highly effective and cohesive sales teams.

> Recent college graduate in Business Administration with proven record of initiative and accomplishment. Completely financed all education costs through full-time employment, thus gaining five years of business experience. Seeking Management Development Program utilizing practical experience and academics.

> Accounting/Finance graduate with more than four years accounting and auditing experience. Thorough knowledge of federal tax policies and procedures. Experienced with both manual and automated invoice systems, using Lotus 1-2-3 software. Seeking position as either Staff Accountant or Accounting Department Manager.

Whether you use an Objective or Summary section, or both or neither, be certain your resume has direction and focus. Don't try to make your resume so open that it seems as though you have no idea what career you are pursuing. Recruiters will assume that is exactly the case and will pass over your resume for one more focused.

Education: You can use either Education or Employment as your next section, depending on which is the stronger or more important. For example, recent grads with limited or no relevant experience will place the Education section first. However, if you were a co-op student or intern, or have some other good business experience, list that first and Education next. More experienced applicants will generally place the Employment section ahead. An exception to this is that experienced applicants with a degree from a highly regarded institution could list Education first. As you gain more experience, the Education section will continue to shrink, as the Employment section grows.

For the recent college graduate with limited career-related experience, academics will be paramount and thus will incorporate a large part of the resume. State the name of your college, the type of degree you will be receiving, major and minor concentrations, and month and year you expect to graduate. If you had a high Grade Point Average (above 3.0 on a 4.0 scale) and/or graduated in the top one-half of your class, include that information. Then list a few relevant courses that you have taken or plan to take. Earning a large part of your tuition and expenses shows initiative and should be mentioned. Definitely include honors, activities and elected positions. If you have more than one degree to include, list the most recent first.

Applicants with relevant work experience will list most of the same education information, eliminating less important data with each new job and subsequent resume. Course titles will be the first to be eliminated, followed by activities and minor honors. For about ten years, continue to include a good Grade Point Average, important honors and elected positions. By then, your recent achievements will be more indicative of your abilities.

If you are not a college graduate, I suggest you omit the Education section entirely, although you can include a reference to your academics in the Personal section, such as "Attended ABC University for three years, majoring in Business Administration," or "Currently enrolled at ABC University, pursuing a Bachelor's degree in Marketing. Graduation expected in June 1995."

After you have listed your academic institutions, then include relevant seminars and courses taken, and the dates. Also, include any professional certifications (C.P.A., Professional Engineer, etc.) or awards gained through additional studies, and the dates bestowed. However, do not include certifications from previous careers that are not germane to your current job search; for example, omit references to real estate courses, if you are no longer pursuing that career.

Employment: Note: You may call this section "Experience" if you wish, especially if you are including experience gained through non-employment (*e.g.*, volunteer work), temporary assignments or part-time jobs.

All potential employers want to see some work experience, even for recent grads, and the more successful and relevant it is to your job objective, the better your chances of securing employment. List your job title, company name, dates of employment and description of job duties. That seems simple enough, but since it is the most important part of your resume, it must be perfect. Follow these guidelines, and refer to Appendix A for examples:

1) Use reverse chronology (last job first).

2) Be concise, and thus hold your resume to one page, if possible, and never more than two.

3) Don't get bogged down in details and don't feel you must include everything you have done. Save something for the interview!

4) Titles can sometimes be misleading; use functional, descriptive titles when necessary. For example, I recently prepared a resume for an individual who was managing the company's entire personnel function, although his title was only Personnel Administrator; I used Personnel Director as his title, to emphasize the scope of his responsibilities.

5) Be certain to include management and supervisory responsibilities.

6) Emphasize accomplishments, awards and achievements. Underline and/or use boldface on the most important.

7) List your last or current job date as "present," even if you are no longer with the company, unless many months have passed since your departure. That may sound strange, but it is an accepted practice, since revealing your unemployment raises questions which probably could be explained best during an interview. However, you can explain your employment status in your cover letter, if you wish, or wait for your first contact with a company representative.

8) The most recent experience generally should have the longest description; experience more than ten years ago can be combined for brevity.

9) Percentages are usually more easily understood than exact figures, since the relevance of large and small amounts varies from industry to industry. Unless you are certain your readers will understand and/or be impressed with your figures, consider using percentages instead.

10) Do not list your reasons for leaving an employer, unless it makes a very positive point or explains several recent job changes.

11) Do not use acronyms or arcana that may be unfamiliar to most readers.

12) Include a brief description of your company(s) and its products/services, if most readers might not be familiar with it.

13) Numbers less than 10 should be written out.

14) Do not state your salary on the resume. However, some classified ads may request your current salary or a salary history, which can be included in your cover letter or on a separate page. (See "Chapter VIII: Correspondence.")

15) Since many companies shy away from individuals who have been self-employed, I suggest you avoid direct references to that. For example, you could describe your job title as "General Manager," rather than "Owner."

16) Use mostly "non-sentences" without a pronoun subject, and avoid using personal pronouns. Definitely do not write in the third person and avoid using the passive voice.

Personal: This section is optional and the current trend now is to omit it, especially for more experienced applicants. The reason is that your personal data should not effect your job performance, and therefore it should not be a consideration in your job application. In addition, some personal information could lend itself to possible discrimination, legal and illegal.[1]

---

[1] What is "legal discrimination"? You may be surprised to learn that not all discrimination is banned by federal statutes. In most states, including Georgia, you may be denied employment based on your appearance (height/weight), marital status,

Frankly, I prefer the resumes I receive to have a Personal section, since it often can yield a more complete picture of the candidate. Nevertheless, I generally do not include one on the resumes I prepare, in deference to the above reasoning.

However, if you have some special information to convey that you feel is relevant to your job objective, or if you simply feel that the information will yield a more thorough appraisal of you, you should include a Personal section.

If you do decide to add a Personal section to your resume, this is some of the information that may be included: birth date (not age, since that may change during your job search), marital status, height/weight and if you are available for travel. Unless there are absolutely, positively no circumstances under which you will consider relocation, I urge you to add that you are open for relocation; the reasons for including this are explained in "Chapter V: Interviewing Techniques."

Do not mention potential negatives (*e.g.*, obesity) or restrictions (*e.g.*, geographic). Some states restrict including age, and you may omit that if you feel it could be a handicap, and the same is true for marital status. Never state your race or religion, but do include citizenship status, if you sense it may be in question.

Next mention a few hobbies and interests (reading, sports, music, etc.), that you are actively pursuing and that can be used to "break the ice" during an interview. (Then be ready to discuss them; for example, if you list reading as an interest, be prepared for the question, "What have you read lately?") If you are multilingual, add that here; if you are not quite fluent, you can describe yourself as "proficient." If you have several years of college, but did not graduate, you may mention that here. If you have excellent career experience and have decided to stress that in lieu of a separate Education section, you should list your college degree here. Finally, include memberships in professional associations and your civic involvements; however, do not include more than three, lest your priorities be called into question.

References: You may end your resume with "References available on request." If you get to the bottom of your resume and will have to

---

sexual preference, foreign citizenship or geographic restrictions. Even discrimination addressed by law often has exceptions.

crowd to add this final sentence, either omit it or include it as the last sentence in your Personal section.

I recently read an article that described this closing line as "utterly useless" and suggested omitting it, and I have also discussed this with several professional resume writers whose opinions I respect. Frankly, I agree that it is stating the obvious – of course you will have references! – but it is also a good method of saying "The End" in more tactful terms, and it can be a good balance in your layout. Whether you include it or not is your decision; your resume will not rise or fall on that sentence.

Do not list your references on the resume, but do prepare a separate "References" page to have should they be requested of you; see Appendix A for examples.

Topical Format

As I stated earlier, the functional/chronological resume is the most widely used and accepted form because it is simple and easy to understand. Under certain circumstances, however, the topical format may be better suited for your use.

The topical format differs from the functional/chronological format in that it includes an Experience section, either in addition to or in lieu of the Employment section. It can be especially helpful when you are changing careers or re-entering the job market, and want to emphasize knowledge you have gained that is relevant to your new job objective. It also can be used to summarize what might otherwise be a very lengthy resume by combining many jobs into skill categories. And finally, it can be used simply to emphasize certain points or skills you feel important. Several examples of this format are shown in Appendix A.

I have begun to use more often a variation of this format, combining it with the functional/chronological. When doing so, I generally choose the two or three skills that best summarize my applicant's experiences or abilities, and include them under the heading "Qualifications." For example, I did a Communications Specialist's resume by summarizing her experiences in Marketing, Public Relations, and Copywriting, and then listing her employment and a very brief description of the responsibilities of each position.

Synopsis/Amplification Format

This resume version consists of a synopsis page that includes all the basic information and sections, but with no details. The details of employment and experience are placed on a separate page, called an "Amplification." I receive these occasionally, and they are acceptable. I really don't recommend them, however, because invariably they get too long and so bogged down in detail that they are difficult to read, not to mention boring. As I have stated before, save the details for an interview, when you have the opportunity to explain personally your experiences.

The Finished Product

In Appendix A, I have included many examples of excellent resumes, and I have tried to illustrate as many diverse situations and backgrounds as possible. But because each person's background is unique, do not try to copy too closely any example given. There are many acceptable variations of the basic format, and if you keep in mind your purpose in constructing a resume, you can vary the format to fit your needs.

In typing your resume, you should not use the old-model electric typewriter of many years ago. Much better results now can be obtained with an electronic typewriter/word processor with a laser or letter-quality printer. Better still, using a computer with a word processing program and a laser printer will give your resume the appearance of being professionally typeset. Do not use a dot-matrix printer.

As this is a resume, not a sales brochure, do not adopt any format that looks "gimmicky." Use separate sheets of standard size 8 1/2" x 11" paper, printed on one side only.

After you have finished typing, carefully proofread for errors and misspellings. Ask two or three friends to read it also, for suggestions and further proofreading.

When you are satisfied with your product, have copies made at a local quick-print shop; it's probably cheaper than you think and the copies generally will look better than those produced on the standard office photocopier. Choose a good quality of cream, light beige, or buff-colored paper for best results, although plain white is certainly acceptable. Do not use green, pink, or any other brightly colored paper. Also, do not use parchment paper, which does not photocopy well and because of its density, does not fax well either.

Your resume must <u>always</u> . . .

- Be focused
- Emphasize accomplishments and achievements
- Be concise and to-the-point
- Appear neat and clean

Your resume must <u>never</u> . . .

- Seem too vague or misdirected
- Run more than two pages
- Look like a brochure
- Include too much detail
- Be typed on an old manual typewriter

Buy extra blank pages to use for cover letters, and envelopes that match your stationery. Ask the printer (or your resume service, if you are having it prepared for you) if they can match your resume's letterhead (name and contact data) onto the blank, cover letter pages. That is an optional touch, but the matching letterhead on your resume and cover letter will appear more professional and appealing. Above all, be certain the resume is neat and clean; remember, it represents you.

And finally, here are a few common grammatical mistakes I have observed through the years on the resumes I have reviewed:

1) Without question, the most frequently misspelled word on resumes is "liaison," probably misspelled on a third of the resumes I receive. Another word often misspelled and misused is "Bachelor." It does not contain a "t" (batchelor), and the degree is a Bachelor of Whatever or a Bachelor's degree, not a Bachelor's of Whatever. The same is true of Master's degrees.

2) The most commonly misspelled (and overused!) abbreviation is "etc." (not ect.), and note the correct punctuation of the abbreviation "et al." (a period after "al," not "et").[2]

3) The most common punctuation errors I observe are in the misuse of periods, commas, semicolons, and colons, and the misplacement of quotation marks. The correct usage of these punctuation marks is generally misunderstood, and unless you are positive you have used them correctly, I advise you to check with a grammar reference book. Three primary examples are these:

- Commas and periods are always placed *inside* quotation marks, and the reverse is true for colons and semicolons. The placement of question marks and exclamation points varies, depending on the usage. (Now that you know this, notice how often it is done incorrectly!)

---

[2] Incidentally, the correct punctuation for foreign words used in print is to underline or italicize them. However, the Latin abbreviations "etc." and "et al." have become so commonly accepted that we no longer treat them differently. Other foreign words, such as *cum laude,* should continue to be underlined or italicized.

- The word "however" is preceded by a *semicolon*, not a comma, when used as a conjunctive adverb, separating clauses of a compound sentence; however, a comma is correct when using "however" as a simple conjunction or adverb. If this sounds confusing – and it does to me! – just notice how I have correctly used "however" throughout this book.

- Colons should be used at the end of a complete sentence, not a phrase.

4) Other frequent grammatical mistakes are inconsistencies in verb tense and in parallel structure.

If you still have questions regarding correct word usage, spelling or grammar, you can call Georgia State University's Grammar Hot Line at (404) 651-2906. This free service is staffed by professors who work the hot line on a volunteer basis between their regular schedule of classes. If your question cannot be immediately answered, the staffer will research the information and call you back.

Conclusion

Now let's go back to the question I posed earlier, "What makes up a 'Power Resume'?" The resumes in Appendix A are all good examples of "Power Resumes." Observe that they all follow these guidelines:

1) Proper layout

2) Concise, preferably one page and never more than two pages

3) Attention to detail, especially spelling, grammar and neatness

4) Emphasis on the positive (accomplishments, honors, awards and achievements)

5) Relevance to your job objective.

Thus the answer to the question is simple: Follow the outline and guidelines presented here, and you will have composed your own "Power Resume." My knowledge on the subject is first-hand, having read many thousands of resumes, written at least a thousand more, and consulted with other personnel recruiters to obtain their input as well.

Thus, you can rest assured that your better and more powerful resume will get the best results possible.

P. S.

Now that you know what is involved in preparing your own resume, you may be concerned that it is too difficult and time-consuming for you, and you may be planning to have a professional resume service prepare it for you. Considering some of the home-made products I receive, I might encourage that also – but with definite reservations and qualifications.

In the past, I have been hesitant to recommend the use of resume services, because I have seen so many poor results. In fact, I recently discussed this with the former Director of Employment for a major Atlanta corporation, and who is now a training consultant. We were talking about resumes – specifically, the bad ones – and we agreed that some of the worst were "professionally" prepared.

Let me quickly add, however, that although I most remember those bad examples, I have also reviewed many excellent resumes that were prepared by resume services. A good, experienced resume service can be extremely helpful; just be careful with your choice. Insist on editorial approval and be certain it meets our standards before you accept it. Ask the background and experience of the person who will be preparing your resume, and request to see actual copies of recent work. Show them some of the samples I have included in Appendix A, to use as a pattern for your resume.

The best of these services will have a personal computer with a laser printer that can do italics, boldface and variable-size type. Excellent results can be obtained, however, using an electronic typewriter or word processor with proportional pitch and the ability to justify right and left margins. You should not pay to have your resume printed on the standard electric typewriter of many years ago.

Although the layout and appearance are important, the paramount factor is the content of your resume. You can help in this preparation (and probably save money) by composing most of the content of your resume beforehand, and simply have the service do the re-typing and lay-out correctly.

Whatever you decide, remember that this resume represents *you*. If you have the time and feel competent, use the information I have outlined and make your own resume. It's really not as difficult as you might imagine. Otherwise, pay to have it prepared for you, but be satisfied that it is an accurate depiction of you, and that it does you justice.

Part 2

The Oral Synopsis:

The "30-Second Resume"

How many times have you been at a party, seminar, or other meeting when someone turned to you and said, "Tell me about yourself," or "What do you do?" or "What is your background?" What did you answer?

"Well, I was an accountant, but now I'm between jobs," or "I used to be an accountant, but was laid off. Do you know of any job openings?" Worse yet, did you ramble on for several minutes and bore your listener so badly that he/she was wishing to be in another room, another place, another time?

Wouldn't it be great if you had a short, prepared answer that covered your background highlights and job objective, and still kept your listener's attention?

During your job search, you will encounter many networking opportunities when you will be called upon to relate your qualifications and objectives. Some of these situations you will have created through your specific networking efforts, but there also will be other times when someone simply will turn to you and ask, "What do you do?"

You should be prepared for these opportunities with a short, oral synopsis of your background and career objective. Since you may have only a few moments of your listener's time, you need an answer that will quickly stress the most important factors you want your listener to know while you have his/her undivided attention. You cannot hope to relate all of your background, experiences, and achievements at once, but rather you will reveal just enough of your background to hold your listener's interest and hopefully lead to further dialogue.

What you need is a "30-Second Resume."

I recently attended a seminar in which the speaker commented that the average American executive has an attention span of approximately thirty seconds! I do not know the accuracy of his source, but that generally confirmed my suspicions and experiences. Perhaps if you will be honest about it, that may be true for you too!

When I receive phone calls from job seekers asking for advice, I always ask, "What is your background?" or "Tell me about yourself," and their answer reveals much of what is right or wrong in their job search. If they are unable to relay quickly and concisely their background, or if they ramble on until I cut them off, then I know what they should do first: they must compose their "30-second resume."

Composing your "30-Second Resume"

When writing your "30-second resume," bear in mind when and how you will use it, remembering its two primary purposes:

1) to relay only the most important facets of your background

2) to arouse enough interest to lead to further dialogue.

Note that its purpose is not to include all the information you want to relate, and since you want to involve your listener in dialogue, you should keep your discourse upbeat and non-technical.

What should you include? First answer these questions:

1) What are the requirements for the job I am seeking?

2) What in my background fits those requirements?

Armed with that information, you can begin to separate relevant material from information that can be discussed later. Then plan how you will capsulate the most relevant material into a very short time span

– approximately 30 seconds. If your listener seems interested in hearing more, you can elaborate and give details then. But first, you must get his/her attention with your "30-second resume."

Preparing this oral resume may take as much time as your written one, and it is equally as important. Probably the worst mistake job seekers make with their written resume is making it too long and detailed, boring the reader and losing his/her attention. I assume you already know that the purpose of a resume is not to get you a job, but to arouse just enough interest to obtain an interview.

The same is true regarding your oral resume. Keep it short and relevant to your job objective, saying just enough to show you are qualified and to keep your listener's attention. What would you want to hear if you were the listener? What can you say that will arouse interest and perhaps lead to further discussion?

Most importantly, plan this well in advance and then rehearse it aloud or with a friend. Here are some factors to consider:

> ***Job objective:*** In as few words as possible, explain the field or type of job you are seeking. Probably this should be the first item in your oral resume, but you also can explain your qualifications first and then show how it fits into your career plans.

> ***Education and training:*** Some professions emphasize academics, and if you have the right degree, you should mention it. (For example, a science degree may be helpful in a pharmaceutical or chemical sales position; a degree in industrial management is good preparation for a manufacturing management position; a marketing MBA is usually vital to a staff marketing position; etc.) Familiarity with computer hardware and software programs is becoming a necessity in most professions, and you probably will want to indicate your proficiency. Certification is nearly always an important asset and should be stressed. Career-related seminars and training programs also may be added, if they are well-known.

> ***Skills:*** Some examples are good communicator, self-motivated, well-organized, aggressive, etc. Keep in mind that you may be called upon to give specific instances showing how you exemplify these characteristics, so be prepared with some good illustrations.

Accomplishments and achievements: This is an integral part of both your written and oral resumes, and must always be included. Of what in your life and career are you the proudest? Choose the most important one or two and mention them. Remembering that corporations are all "bottom-line"-oriented, you should also stress any increases in revenue or decreases in expenses due to your efforts.

Prior employment: If you seek to advance your current career path, then your past and current employment may be the most important information to stress. Condense it into a few sentences, stating job titles or descriptive titles and the responsibilities you have had.

Other experience: If your objective is to change careers, mention specific experiences that relate to your new field. For example, if outside sales is your objective, stress your familiarity with the product line, through experience, academics, or whatever. Volunteer experience and civic involvement may have given you some experience relevant to your new career. Prior employment could have given you some transferable skills or knowledge.

I realize that this may be an enormous amount of information to condense into thirty-or-so seconds, but you must.

If you still are having difficulty filtering down enough material to reach the 30-second point, try this exercise: Take fifteen pieces of paper and write on each piece an item of information you would want to relay if you had all the time you wanted and could hold your party's attention level. Then remove the four least important, then another three, another two, and finally one more. The remaining five items probably will be the core of your oral resume.

Then organize your information into a clear, concise "30-second resume." Practice it aloud many times until you are comfortable repeating it and then try it with a friend for critique.

You may wish to end your oral resume with a "tickler," such as "What more would you like to know?" or "Is there something you would like for me to explain further?" This also has the advantage of beginning a dialogue and allows you to add information you may have wanted to include earlier.

In an informal or social setting, you also could ask, "Are you familiar with that industry?" or "Do you know someone who does that type of work?" If your listener does know someone, you are off to a fast start in your information gathering!

Just as you can vary your "tickler," you also may need to develop variations of your "30-second resume" to fit specific situations. For example, should you be talking with an authority in your industry, you could be more technical in your description than you would at a social gathering. In your "cold calling," you might wish to stress your ability to reduce costs or increase profits.

As your job search progresses, you undoubtedly will be surprised how often you will need this oral resume. Not only will it form the foundation of your networking campaign, but you also will use it on many other occasions. When you contact companies for the first time, when you attend network meetings, when you are asked the standard interview question, "Tell me about yourself" – these are only a few of the many times you will use your "30-second resume," so take the time to prepare it well.

Part 3

Business Cards

Why do you need business cards, even when you are unemployed?

There will be many occasions, especially in your networking efforts, when you will have the opportunity to discuss your job search with someone. Many of these meetings will be planned, but more often they will occur simply by chance. You want to leave your listener with contact data as well as a short summary of your expertise or job objective, and you cannot possibly carry copies of your resume at all times.

Oftentimes you will want to leave information with several persons, but when a full resume would be inappropriate. For example, when attending a professional association meeting, passing out your resume to many members would be viewed as obnoxious and criticized severely. Certainly you would not want to distribute your resume at a party or other social gathering. However, exchanging business cards is an accepted practice on nearly all occasions.

There are other, more practical reasons, too. Resumes cost more to print than business cards, and business cards are far easier to carry than an 8 1/2" x 11" pile of resumes. You can keep your business card in your pockets, wallet, purse, attaché case, car, or virtually anywhere. Furthermore, business cards are not only easier for you to handle, but your recipients are more likely to keep this small card than a bulky resume.

In order to give a longer lasting impression when exchanging your business card, a good practice is to personalize your card when possible. For example, write your nickname or most recent employer on the card when you hand it out.

In Appendix A, I have included some sample business cards. Note their simplicity, with only name, contact data, and employment objective, experience summary, or expertise. Do not attempt to condense your resume onto this small card, lest it look crowded and messy. As with your resume, do not design a flashy format or use colored paper. Again, this card is a reflection of you.

Business cards are inexpensive to have printed, as low as $10 for 1,000, depending on how much information you want to include.

Keep your business cards in an easily accessible place (*e.g.*, pocket or purse) and don't hesitate to give one out whenever you feel there is a possibility of developing a lead. Offering your business card will usually elicit a card in return, and you may wish to contact that person later.

CHAPTER IV

STEP THREE:

GET THAT INTERVIEW!

Part 1: The "Visible Market"

Part 2: Job Networking

Part 3: Useful Resources

CHAPTER IV

Step Three: Get That Interview!

Plan your attack!

I hesitate for this to sound like a battle plan, but maybe that is a good analogy. At any rate, this must be as well-planned and organized as any military assault. Get out the armaments – that is, the supplies I listed in Chapter II; you will need them now.

In our case, the military assault becomes a marketing assault. Every company develops a strategy for positioning its product or service in front of its buying public. Likewise, you will plan how to get yourself and/or your resume enough exposure to obtain interviews, the next step toward your new job.

The **CAREER SEARCH SYSTEM** includes thirteen marketing tools with which to develop your marketing plan. Depending on your background, you most likely will not need all thirteen, but if you do, the System is here to help. Each tool works best for certain types or levels of applicants, and I have indicated that information at the beginning of the discussion of each tool under *"Pro's"* and *"Con's."* In addition, each tool also has certain advantages and disadvantages, and those also are discussed.

Correctly utilized, these marketing tools will provide as many interviews as you can handle. You may even find yourself in the enviable position of having too many interviews! In that case, be careful not to tire yourself and interview poorly. Two interviews per day is all most individuals can handle successfully.

Before you begin your marketing assault, you must have your business cards and resumes prepared, especially your oral, "30-second resume." Chapter III detailed why you need these documents and how to prepare them, and examples of written resumes and business cards are included in Appendix A. All three are vital to the success of your efforts throughout the job hunt, so prepare them well.

Beginning your job search

There are essentially two approaches to conducting a job search, depending on which "job market" you utilize:

    1) the "Visible Job Market"

    2) the "Hidden Job Market"

The "Visible Job Market"

Career counselors generally agree that approximately 25% of all job vacancies fall into the first category, the "visible job market," which consists of those jobs that are
- advertised in classified want ads,
- recruited for by personnel agencies,
- available through job fairs,
- sought by corporate human resources departments, or
- available with federal, state, and local governments.

Locating these openings is the fastest and easiest course of action, and depending on your background, it may be all you will need to do. Individuals with experience in health care, computer science, or food service, for example, will find countless openings in their field through these sources. Applicants with between two and four years of career-related experience are always the most marketable, and they too may need only to tap into the "visible job market."

Nearly all job seekers will utilize these sources, and since they are easy and inexpensive, you too should use them. The CAREER SEARCH

SYSTEM describes fully how to obtain the best results from each source, and you need only follow the instructions.

The first six sources described in this chapter address the correct procedure you should follow in order to

• mass-mail your resume or background data to companies

• establish direct contact with companies, either through their personnel department or with a department manager,

• utilize personnel agencies and the services they offer,

• stand out from the crowd at job fairs,

• respond to classified want ads (Cover letters, salary histories, and other correspondences are discussed later in "Chapter VIII: Correspondence" and examples are given in Appendix B.), and

• apply for government positions.

The procedure for locating and applying for government openings is not as difficult as you may believe, and I even have found some shortcuts. Also, as the demand for government services increases in high-growth cities, the government payroll there also increases significantly.

Job Networking

In addition to this "visible job market," there are many other jobs available with companies, but as yet unadvertised and generally unknown, even within the company. There may be a planned addition, promotion, retirement, or replacement for which management has not yet begun a search. These plans may be only in the consideration stage now, awaiting further developments. In addition, companies often will create a new position if and when they find the "right" person.

These unpublicized openings are referred to as the **"Hidden Job Market,"** and experts generally agree that at least three-fourths of the jobs available at any time are part of this gray area. The primary way to locate them is through job networking, and Part 2 of this chapter details four methods to uncover them:

- Establishing a Job Network

- Attending networking clubs and meetings

- Networking through professional associations

- Using the "Information Interview"

Job networking is the most time-consuming and laborious method of job search, and to most job seekers, the most mysterious. Few job seekers understand the importance of job networking, and even those who do, have little knowledge of how or where to begin. *And yet more applicants find their job through some form of job networking than all other sources combined!*

The importance of job networking cannot be over-stressed. At least 70% (and I have read articles suggesting 85%) of all applicants will obtain new employment through this method, and thus you must incorporate it into your job search. The CAREER SEARCH SYSTEM leads you through it step-by-step, and you will be surprised how easily your networking progresses.

The sooner you begin developing your job network the sooner you will be employed!

Other useful resources

Part 3 of this chapter describes three more tools and how to use them in your search:

- Public agencies

- Privately funded organizations

- Useful publications

Atlanta is fortunate to have available a number of free job search services, both public and privately funded, and I have included information regarding several. Most job seekers are not aware of these

Atlanta Jobs has grown tremendously in size and scope since the first edition in 1989, which had only 150 pages! I have located many more free or non-profit job-help organizations and in addition, many new groups have formed. To help you track them, I have organized this chart with references to the appropriate page number where you will find detailed information.

- Job networking groups
    - Atlanta Job Network (St. Jude, St. Ann, Peachtree Presbyterian, Corpus Christi, *et al.*) - p 110
    - Atlanta Exchange p 112
    - SAMS p 112

- Job assistance/spiritual support groups
    (Employment Transition Ministry, Seekers, Job Talk, 59:59 Job Support Group) p 27

- Public job assistance (Professional Placement Network, GA State Univ., Vereran's, *et al.*) p 129

- Privately funded groups (Jewish Vocational Center, Latin American Association, Mature Workers Support, Urban League, Seniors for Seniors, *et al.*) p 132

- National Career Networking Group of Georgia (non-profit outplacement) p 135

- Resume database banks
    - SE Employment Network p 134
    - Matchmaker p 71
    - GSU p 131

organizations and the extensive assistance they offer. Since they are free or inexpensive, you must incorporate them into your search.

I also have included a description of useful publications you may wish to add to your job search. Some of these will be helpful in locating companies to contact and others can be used in preparing for interviews. Most of these publications are free or low cost, or readily available at your local library.

Organizing your job search

If you have not yet organized according to the suggestions I outlined in Chapter II, you should do so now.

Next, plan your time. This is especially important if you are currently employed, since you will be limited in the amount of time you will have available for job search, and you must prioritize your efforts to maximize your results.[1]

If you are currently unemployed, how much time do you plan to spend job hunting? If your answer is other than at least 40 hours/week, think again! Perhaps being unemployed is an advantage here, since you will have enough time to conduct a thorough campaign. Continue to conduct your work-week as though you were still employed – which you are, only now your new job is finding a job.

Set up your notebook, using the forms illustrated on the next few pages, especially the weekly timetable form. Then read through all the sections on marketing tools and decide which ones you will use and in what time frame. Using your weekly timetable, schedule your time. This organization is more important than you may think, so don't shortcut.

You now are ready to begin your marketing assault! Read through every tool at least once, and then decide when and how you will use each one.

---

[1] For several reasons, companies prefer to hire individuals who are currently employed, and so I urge you not to resign your position in order to job hunt. Even if you are very unhappy with your job, I suggest you stick with it as long as possible, unless it becomes too difficult to conduct your job search effectively.

PROFESSIONAL NETWORK CONTACTS

Name	Phone	Company	Title
(results)			
1. Steve Reinking 568-7213 ABC Corp. Controller			
Referred me to Linder Mfg. Co., whose controller is Retiring.			
2. Bill Johns 377-6430 Quik Corp Treasurer			
Very friendly, may have leads, set up Info Interview for Tuesday			
3. Susan Hope 761-3100 NC Financial Acctg Mgr			
Very busy, no suggestions			
4.			

PERSONAL NETWORK CONTACTS

Name	Phone	Results
1. Bryan Smith 568-7213 Neighbor is VP of H.R. w/ Mycorp. Will call + introduce me.		
2. Joy Baer 721-3601 Her company is expanding their Acctg staff. Will arrange i'view!		
3. Harry Pitts 231-9556 No help now, but will think about it.		
4.		

Networking forms

Sunday	Monday	Tuesday	Wednesday	Thursday	Friday	Saturday	Next week
Read Ads	Call Personnel Agencies	Personnel Agency interview 8:30 A.M.	Research ABC Corp.	Practise interview w/ friend	OPEN	Network w/ friends	ABC Corp interview Tuesday 10:00
Mail Ad Responses	Network w/ business Associates	Association meeting 6:30 p.m.			Catch-up!		

Sample — Weekly Timetable

COMPANY "COLD CALLING"

Company (results)	Phone	Contact/title	Nothing	Sent + Resume
1. Matt. Mfg. Co.	847-1000	Katie Beam / Personnel	7/21	
2. Rob'ts Co.	768-3400	Sam Rush / Treas.		7/22
3. Stephens & Collins Has opening! Call back 7/25.	471-1234	Sue Hummer / Acctg Mgr		7/22
4. ABC Corp Referred me to XYZ Supply Co.	231-9565	Bob Roe / Controller	7/21	
5.				
6.				
7.				
8.				
9.				
10.				

Sample   direct   contact   form

PART 1:

THE "VISIBLE JOB MARKET"

Tool #1:   Mass Mailing

Tool #2:   Direct Contact

Tool #3:   Classified Advertising

Tool #4:   Personnel Agencies

Tool #5:   Job Fairs

Tool #6:   Government Jobs

Tool #1: Mass-Mailing

Pro's: Contacts a large number of companies, easy to do, minimal expense, can be done during non-business hours.

Con's: Least effective job search method, time and labor intensive.

This is the oldest and simplest method of job search, and undoubtedly the most popular. It can be done at your convenience during evenings, weekends, or at any time you are not busy with other activities. Since it requires no face-to-face or verbal contact, it feels comfortable or at least non-threatening. Thus, this approach is tried by almost every job seeker.

The down side is that it is also the least productive method, probably securing fewer than 2% of all job offers. Nevertheless, since some applicants will find it successful and since you can plan it around your other job tools, you can use it also.

There are two approaches to this method:

1) a selective mailing, in which you target companies more likely to have a need for your background, and

2) a "resume blizzard," when you attempt to reach as many companies as possible.

Of course, your percentage of success will be much higher with the selective mailing, but that also may require time researching which companies you should contact. The other approach, obtaining a list of hundreds (maybe thousands!) of companies and blindly sending data to each one, generally results in an avalanche of rejection letters and very few promising leads.

Resume with cover letter vs. "broadcast letter"

Most mass mailings include a resume with cover letter. This cover letter mentions information not included in your resume (*e.g.*, why you have chosen to contact them, salary requirements, geographic

69

restrictions, etc.) and emphasizes highlights in your background that will encourage the reader to peruse your resume. (See "Chapter VIII: Correspondence" for a full description and Appendix B for examples.)

An alternative method, the "broadcast letter," has gained popularity recently. Essentially, the broadcast letter is a one page merger of the cover letter and the highlights of your resume. It tends to be more "reader friendly" by not including all of your experiences, but just the parts most likely to catch the reader's attention. It emphasizes accomplishments and achievements, and stresses what you can offer the company. Contact data is readily found and the reader is encouraged to call you for more information or an interview. Examples are included in "Appendix B: Correspondence."

The advantages to the broadcast letter are obvious. Since only one page is involved, it is simpler to handle and less expensive to mail. The primary disadvantage is of course that the reader has only limited information presented.

In speaking with applicants who have tried both methods, I have observed that for most mass-mailing, the broadcast letter is equally as successful as the resume with cover letter. Thus, I suggest that you use the broadcast letter with most of your mass-mailing, but use the resume/cover letter approach when you have reason to believe the company may have an opening for your experience.

Procedure

In planning to whom you will send your resume or other background information, imagine a series of concentric circles. At the center will be the companies most likely to be interested (*i.e.*, those that hire regularly in your field or for your discipline); the following ring will include companies you're not sure about but have reason to think might be interested; the next ring will be less certain; and the last ring will be the long shots.

• *Begin your mass-mailing with the center core* and expand outward as time permits. Determining which companies fall into each circle will require some research on your part, but the pay-off will be worth the effort. You probably already know many companies that will fall into the center, and the detailed company profiles I have included in Appendix C will provide more. Using the reference materials in the last section of this chapter will help you identify still more. After you have contacted those companies, you can spread into the outer rings.

• *Keep accurate, well-organized records.* As part of your overall organization, you should maintain a record of every company you contact and the results. You can make a list if you wish, but the simplest method is to keep a copy of your correspondence. This copy will include the date and the person you contacted, and you can write notes on the page regarding your activity there. Keep the pages in alphabetical order in a folder in your desk so that you can refer to it quickly when (not *if* – think positively!) a representative of the company calls. To help further with your organization, you may wish to separate the "core companies" correspondence from the others.

• *To whom should you address your correspondence?* Most job seekers will send it to the generic "personnel department," where it will be added to the pile of resumes already received. The more enterprising job seekers will send it to a specific department that will be more likely to need their background. But the job seekers who will be employed first will seek out the name or at least the title of the person responsible for hiring their experience.

However, if you don't know the name or title and don't have the time or ability to research the data, send your letter to "Human Resources." Later when you have more time or better information, you can re-contact the company, directing your information to a more appropriate source.

While you are mailing your resumes, also send one to "Matchmaker," a free resume bank sponsored by National Career Network of Georgia, a non-profit outplacement association (see Tool #12: Privately Funded Organizations). This resume database is accessible by companies through their computer modems and is used by hundreds of local companies. And it's free.

MatchMaker, c/o National Career Network of Georgia
2110 Powers Ferry Road, Suite 310, Atlanta, GA 30339

Conclusion

I have included this job search technique as Tool #1 because it is the most popular approach and the one most job seekers try first. That is unfortunate, since it really should be your last effort, to be used only after you have tried other more productive tools.

Why is a "resume blizzard" generally so unproductive? There are several reasons:

• I would be willing to wager any amount of money that at least 95% of the job seekers in Cincinnati have sent their resume to Proctor & Gamble and the Kroger Company, two of the largest companies headquartered there. Likewise, in Atlanta, everyone contacts Coca-Cola and BellSouth. Can you imagine the number of unsolicited resumes these large companies receive?

• Determining to whom you will direct your information is very difficult. There may be several persons within the company who sometimes seek your expertise, and you cannot hope to contact each of them. Human Resources should know of all job vacancies, but that is often not the case. And unless you indicate some person or department on your envelope, your resume could end up anywhere in the organization.

• Most of the new jobs being created in today's economy are not with major corporations. In fact, one reads daily about massive downsizing and lay-offs at the Fortune 500-type corporations. The growing job markets are in small- to medium-size companies, generally not included on any list of companies you may locate.

Mass mailings work best for only certain types of job applicants, generally those with highly desirable experience. Otherwise, the more years of experience you have, the more frustrating you will find this method.

Nevertheless, if you have the time and inclination, I suggest that you go ahead and send your resume to companies in which you have a strong interest or feel that they often may have needs for your background. Most of all, it will make you feel good that you are doing something constructive toward your job search, and there is a definite possibility you might uncover an opportunity, either for an interview now or for a networking source later. However, be prepared for the downside – the rejection letters – and don't slip into depression because of them.

And relax. The CAREER SEARCH SYSTEM describes twelve other sources. If this one is not the right one for you, several of the others will be.

Tool #2: Direct Contact

Pro's: Works best for entry- and mid-level positions, especially for applicants with less than six or seven years of experience. Ideally suited for recent grads, first job changers, and persons seeking a specific industry or company. Good approach for individuals with experience and knowledge in one industry.

Con's: Labor intensive, especially in locating hiring authorities. Less effective for applicants with extensive experience that is not in one industry.

There are two reasons for directly contacting a company without prior knowledge of their current job needs:

1) They may have a job opening for your background, and you can arrange an interview with them.

2) You can obtain some useful information and/or job leads.

This section discusses the first reason; the second reason is discussed in Part 2 of this chapter on Job Networking.

Most importantly, don't waste your time and money by blindly contacting companies that you know little about. That "shotgun" approach generally is not effective, in time, cost, or results. There are other sources to those companies, such as personnel agencies, newspaper ads, networking, etc. Use your time wisely, and concentrate your direct contact efforts on the companies that regularly hire for your specialty or an industry that can use your specific experience. Unlike other books that are hardly more useful than the Yellow Pages, the CAREER SEARCH SYSTEM has researched the hiring practices of hundreds of companies. The result of this research is a selected list of companies (Appendix C) that omits companies that seldom have personnel needs, in favor of targeting firms that do the most professional-level hiring – which incidentally, are not necessarily the companies with the largest numbers of employees.

From my personal experiences and through research, I have compiled a list of approximately 300 of Atlanta's most active employers, found in Appendix C. These companies were selected for diversity and for the number of applicants hired each year (most hire between 25 and 100+ professional-level employees). I have tried to include examples from as many industries and professions as possible, and you probably will be interested in many. My associates or I spoke with each of these companies personally, and thus, the information is current and accurate, according to their staffing specialists.

Mounting a Direct Contact Campaign

Scan through the list of companies in Appendix C and then using a highlighting marking pen, mark those in which you have an interest and those that hire in your specialty. I have included a thorough description of their operations and hiring procedures, as well as the types of applicants frequently sought and whether the company seeks entry-level and/or experienced personnel. Read through the company profiles and you will find practically any and every job description included many times. I doubt there is any discipline for which I have not included at least a dozen major hiring sources.

Next, add several pages in your notebook to record your efforts. Use the sample form "Company Cold Calling," or one similar, and list the companies you plan to contact. (When you call, be sure to include the date, as I illustrated.) In addition to the large corporations detailed in Appendix C, you may know of other companies who hire in your field or for your specialty and that you wish to contact.

Be selective and don't make your list too long, since making a personal contact is time consuming. Long shots generally are not productive and definitely will expend time you otherwise might use more productively. Choose companies that you have reason to think may have openings in your field or that may be expanding their general work force.

Whom should I contact?[1]

---

[1]Although the vogue designation for the generic term "Personnel Department" is now "Human Resources," not all companies use that name. In addition, larger companies will also have a separate Recruiting or Staffing specialty within Human Resources. Although there can be definite distinctions, I have used these terms fairly interchangeably, and for our purposes here, that is adequate.

This is a debatable question, with many career counselors giving one answer and personnel managers another. As with most debates, there are good reasons to support both sides.

Most, if not all, career counselors would suggest that you should make your initial company contact with a "hiring authority," that is, a department manager who has control over the personnel requirements in his/her department. One reason is that this person may have current or projected personnel needs that have not been requisitioned from Human Resources or Personnel Recruiting. Secondly, this manager will most likely be the ultimate decision-maker with whom you would eventually interview, and thus you are a step ahead by starting here. This logic concludes that Personnel Departments are often another hurdle and should be by-passed when possible.

There are many reasons why Personnel Departments may not be aware of all the needs within their companies. A manager often will have plans to add to or alter the department in the future, and if your background fits the need, he/she may consider going ahead with the change now. Also, some department heads prefer to hire direct, rather than using their recruiting staff, who may be busy with other assignments. Furthermore, some companies are very decentralized and encourage managers to conduct their own personnel search and hiring. There are many other reasons, too, more than we can discuss here.

Most personnel managers would disagree with those assumptions, and strongly feel that you should contact them first. It is their function within the company to interview and screen applicants, following federal and local statutes, as well as company policies and procedures; these guidelines may be unknown to executives attempting to conduct their own hiring. These personnel professionals have been trained to interview carefully and thoroughly, and they should be more in tune to the overall needs of the company, not just one department.

In addition, some department managers may find your contact a nuisance, and you will be off to a bad start. Personnel may feel you are trying to short-circuit them, and they too will be annoyed. And finally, some companies have a firm policy that all initial contacts with applicants must be through Personnel.

But perhaps the best reason for contacting Personnel is simply expedience. Large companies will have many department managers over your specialty, and you cannot expect to contact all of them. Also, you may not have the time or resources to trace all the hiring authorities within a company. In these cases, you must utilize the company's Personnel Department.

Although in my practice I generally work with Personnel, I adhere more to the former reasoning. I understand Personnel's concerns, but tend to agree that it is better to contact a hiring authority, especially when you have a friend or contact within the company who can tell you whom to contact. (Of course, this person may also tell you that the company requires you to start with Personnel.) However, you can assuage Personnel by also sending them a resume, noting whom you have already contacted.

"Cold Calling"

Now comes the laborious part: "cold calling" each company. In your "cold calling" section, list the companies you plan to contact, using a form similar to the one illustrated earlier in this chapter. Ideally, you should speak by phone personally with an official at each company, but that is not always possible. The company representative may not be available, or you may not have the time or facility, especially if you are currently employed. In these cases, you should mail a resume and include a cover letter. (The cover letter is explained in Chapter VIII.)

Many people have a fear of the phone, and if you are one of them, you need to get over it. Preparing and rehearsing what you plan to say on the phone will help, as well as having your "30-Second Resume" prepared and ready to use. I mentioned earlier that you would be using this oral resume often, and now is one of those times. If you missed the discussion of this topic, it was described in Part 2 of "Chapter III: Preparing Your Resumes."

Procedure to follow

Regardless of whether you contact Personnel or a department manager, the procedure is the same. In Appendix C I have listed most of Atlanta's largest hiring companies, and the procedure to follow if you go through Personnel. Note that in the company list, I have indicated the Personnel contact by job title or department, not by name. This is because the interviewing authority frequently changes and you will lose valuable time trying to contact or sending a resume to the wrong person. It is useful, however, to know the name of the interviewing authority, and that is one of the purposes in calling the companies directly.

When the company receptionist answers your call, ask for the Whomever (the department or job title I indicated as the contact, or the department manager you are seeking). When Whomever's secretary answers, say, "Hello. My name is Whatever, and I am seeking a position in _____(or as a _____). May I speak with Whomever?" Most likely at this point, you will be instructed to send your resume, in which case ask for the name of the person to whom you should address it, and record the name in your notebook. Don't be upset, however, if you are not given the name; some companies have a policy forbidding the disclosure of employee names.

If you actually do get the opportunity to speak with Whomever, you must be prepared. This is your chance to make a positive impression, have a brief telephone interview, and schedule a personal interview also. Fortunately, you are a tempo ahead, because you already have composed and rehearsed a brief summary of your qualifications – the "30-second resume"! You may have only one shot here, so make it count.

If it appears that they do have an interest or need for your background, offer to come for a personal interview, if this is possible for you. If you are talking with the company's interviewer, you must be ready for this telephone interview. Prepare and practice your interviewing techniques in advance, and don't be caught by surprise. (See "Chapter V: Interviewing Techniques.")

If your contact states that there are no job opportunities available there, try to turn the call into a networking or information call. Ask for suggestions in your job search. Is he/she aware of openings with other companies for your background? Even better, would he/she consider spending a few minutes with you in an "information interview." This "information interview" is discussed later in the chapter as "Tool #9" and you should have read that section before beginning your "cold calling." (Actually, you should read this entire book at least once before beginning any part of your job search!)

Assuming you were instructed to mail your resume, you will also need to include a cover letter. Having already written your resume, writing this will be easy. Chapter VIII is a thorough discussion of correspondence, especially cover letters and their different purposes and forms. Several examples are included in Appendix B.

In the closing paragraph of your cover letter, you will have said that you plan to telephone them in a few days. Definitely do so. You want to know if your resume was received or lost along the way, and if it has been reviewed. Does the company have an opening for someone with your credentials? Is it being routed to another department or department manager? Are there any questions they would like to ask or additional information they need? As always, record the results of your phone call in your notebook.

Finally, you will recall that I suggested you contact department managers whenever possible; but this is not to say that you should ignore Human Resources or Recruiting. In fact, if you are told by the department manager that no opening currently exists, I suggest you also contact Personnel. Individual departments and their managers seldom keep a resume file, but Human Resources usually will, and another need for your background may arise later.

Even if the department manager does request your resume, you may wish to send one to Personnel as well, especially if you do not hear back from this manager within a reasonable time period. This is because the manager may be too busy with other projects to consider you now, but there may be another opening somewhere else within the company. Also, just as the Personnel Department may not be aware of projected needs within other departments, those department managers may not be aware of upper management's plans.

In summary, don't look upon personnel departments as just another hurdle to be avoided whenever possible, but rather utilize them when necessary or expedient. They have a purpose within their companies, and you should make use of it.

Telephone Etiquette

In today's high-tech world, on many of your phone calls, you may be connected with your party's answering machine, "voice mail," or some other answering device, and you will be asked to leave your name, phone number, and "a brief message." I nearly always do leave a message and have been pleasantly surprised at the high rate of times I have had my call returned.

I too have an answering machine, to cover the times when I am out of my office or otherwise unavailable to receive calls. My pet peeve has become the callers who leave an incoherent or inaudible message, and I am forced to replay the message several times. For example,

- they speak so rapidly that I cannot understand, especially in relaying their phone number;

- they have an unusual name or a foreign name that is difficult to understand or spell;

- their message is garbled or their thoughts are unorganized.

On those occasions when you are referred to an answering service, I suggest you do leave a message, but with the knowledge that a poor message will have created a poor impression, and that may result in your call not being returned. Speak your name and phone number clearly, leave your prepared message (short and well-enunciated), then repeat your name and phone number. End your message with "Thank you and I look forward to speaking with you soon." Unless your name is a very common name like Smith or Jones, you should spell it. Most importantly, say your phone number slowly and clearly.

Conclusion

The **CAREER SEARCH SYSTEM** outlines many different and effective sources for obtaining interviews and job offers, and not all of them will apply to you. Quite frankly, the direct contact source has limited success unless you fit one of these categories:

1) You have extensive experience within one industry or discipline, and that experience would be useful to most companies within that industry or discipline.

2) You have less than five years experience and can still be cross-trained into other functions within your discipline.

3) You have highly desirable experience or academic background. For example, most medical specialties, restaurant managers or computer science professionals are very much in demand and have no difficulty in finding employment with any number of companies.

If you do not fit into one of those descriptions, the direct contact source is not the one where you should be concentrating your efforts. That is my major complaint with books that list hundreds (thousands?)

of companies, and suggest that you call, contact, or send your resume to as many as possible. There are other sources in the **CAREER SEARCH SYSTEM** that will benefit you more.

Tool #3: Classified Advertisements

Pro's: Cheap and easy source of many listings, covering all disciplines and levels. Good place to start. Good source to locate personnel agencies, as well as companies not using agencies, and small companies with infrequent needs. Often quotes salary. Local companies can be quick interviews.

Con's: You can get lost in the crowd of responses. May be difficult to discern good opportunities.

For obtaining employment in Atlanta, the largest source of announced openings is contained in the classified ads section of the Sunday edition of *The Atlanta Journal-Constitution*. It is a "must" in your job search. If you are currently living in Atlanta, you probably already receive it; if not, here is the procedure to order a subscription:

- In Atlanta, call 522-4141. You will be billed or you can charge the fee on a credit card.

- Out of Atlanta, but in Georgia, call (800) 282-8790. Same procedure as above.

- Out of Georgia, call (800) 241-1164, and ask for extension 5868. Subscription rate varies by location and you must pay in advance or charge to a credit card.

This Sunday section is by far the largest in the Southeast. Within the fifty or so pages of ads will be up to 10,000 job openings, advertised by both companies and personnel agencies. These openings are listed alphabetically, by job category (accountants, data processing, engineers, sales, etc.).

In addition to locating current job openings, perusing these ads can yield other information. You can determine which disciplines and industries are growing, because these will be mentioned most often. Conversely, shrinking job categories will be conspicuous by their absence. If you are contemplating a career change or undecided on which career to pursue (as so many recent college grads are!), reviewing these ads can help you decide. Further, if there is a retailer near you who sells many newspapers from across the country, you can compare the size of the want ads from several cities to get an idea of the job prospects in each city. Not surprisingly, you will find that Atlanta's want ads are among the largest in the country.

In choosing which ads to consider, keep in mind that if the ad sounds too good to be true, it probably is. The newspaper tries to screen its clients, but bogus or misleading ads sometimes slip by. Here is one clue: if you call a company, and someone answers with the phone number and then refuses to reveal the company's name, hang up!

In addition to newspapers, another excellent source of classified ads is professional and trade magazines. If you have access to any periodicals in your field, review them and answer any classified ads that seem fruitful; these ads are usually on the last few pages of the publication. Respond to them as you would a newspaper ad. This source is especially helpful in determining which personnel agencies specialize in your field, since they are the ones that would place advertisements in specific journals.

Procedure

Peruse the job categories that apply to you and circle in red the openings, both company and personnel agency, for which you plan to apply. After you have finished scrutinizing the ads, cut out the company (not agency) ads you circled and tape them onto blank pages to put in your notebook, in the section you labeled "Classified Ads." Leave lots of empty space beside the ads, to record your activity with them, including dates contacted and results.

Now, cut out the personnel agency ads. You may notice that one agency is advertising several jobs for which you will want to apply. Write the name of each agency at the top of a page and then tape the corresponding ads to the page, and include it in your "Personnel Agencies" section. Leave space on the page to record activity with that agency.

Now go back to the company ads and contact each one. If the company included its phone number or did not specifically forbid phone calls, I suggest you call them and ask if you can speak with someone regarding the opening. If you do get through to the recruiter, you must be prepared for an interview then, so before calling, you should study

"Chapter V: Interviewing Techniques." Also, here is another opportunity to use your "30-second resume"!

Most likely, however, you will be instructed to mail your resume before you speak with anyone personally regarding the position. Politely ask to whom you should address the resume, and record the information in your notebook. Including that person's name on your envelop and cover letter is an optional but personal touch, and some recruiters will note it. Don't be surprised, however, if the receptionist has been instructed not to give out that information.

Along with your resume, you will include a cover letter. Refer to Chapter VIII for a description and to Appendix B for illustrations. In your notebook, record the date you sent your resume, when you called to follow-up, and the results.

Responding to personnel agency advertisements will be slightly different, and after reading the next section on Personnel Agencies, you will better understand the distinctions. Whenever possible, call them before sending a resume. By talking with them first, you can ascertain if you fit their available openings and whether or not that particular agency will be able to help you. Operating procedures vary from agency to agency, some requiring that you send a resume first, others requesting you to come in for a personal interview and bring your resume. If you are instructed to mail your resume, ask to whom you should address it and record that name in your notebook on the page for that agency. Some agencies will have several persons handling the same opening, and so there may not be a specific contact person.

A formal cover letter is not necessary to send to agencies, although you may if that is convenient. Just a short typed or handwritten note with your salary requirements and restrictions (if any) is sufficient. Keep in mind, however, that this note is the agency's first impression of you and you must impress them in order to be referred to their client. Additional information on the use of this interview source is contained in the next section of this chapter.

"Blind Ads"

Oftentimes companies advertise their job vacancies without identifying themselves, and you are instructed to mail your resume to a post office box number. These are called "blind ads," since they do not reveal the name of the employer. You may be interested in the openings but hesitant to reveal your name and information without knowing whom you are contacting. I have heard of individuals who responded to a blind ad, only to learn that the ad was submitted by their own company! Unfortunately, their employment was terminated as a result.

If the company is using their own post office box, you can obtain the company name before sending your resume by calling the post office branch that handles the zip code in the address listed. Ask who rents that specific box number, and if the box is rented to a company or someone who conducts business through that mail box, the post office will give you the name.

Electronic Classified Ads

In the past few years, several attempts have been made to establish classified advertising databases that can be accessed either by phone or computer. Each year, I include information about them and it seems that the following year I remove them, since none have been financially successful.

The latest of these is called The Job Connection and uses a cute beagle dog with a British accent as its mascot. Using a touch-tone phone, you can activate their database and receive information about job openings listed with them. The service is free to job seekers, so I urge you to try it. Call (404) 353-JOBS.

If you have mailed your resume to a company, plan to call them in a few days to confirm that your resume was received. Ask if there are questions or additional information needed to complete your application. And, of course, offer to come for an interview at their convenience.

Just as you would prepare for a face-to-face interview, be ready for a phone screening also. Telephone interviews are usually short and cover only basic information. Typical questions will revolve around why you are seeking new employment and if you have the background needed for the job. If you pass this quick test, you will be invited for an interview.

Here's a final word on classified ads, and this applies to direct contact and personnel agencies as well. A personal, face-to-face interview is always preferable to indirect contact, regardless of how good your resume looks. Thus, whenever possible, try to be seen, rather than just heard. If you are very interested in a specific position and have been able to speak with a company interviewer on the phone, press for an interview time or at least offer to bring by your resume in person. And if you do deliver your resume in person, ask to simply meet the interviewer, if he/she is available.

Tool #3: Personnel Agencies

Pro's: Probably the largest source of job openings. Easy and convenient. Good agencies will supply you not only with interviews, but also information on the company, the job, and the interviewer. Can work well at all levels and fields. Usually free. Good source for quick interviews.

Con's: Not usually successful for hard-to-place applicants. Not easy to find most useful agencies. Fee sometimes involved, especially at lower-level openings.

The number of job openings represented collectively by the various personnel agencies in Atlanta can be numbered in the tens of thousands. There are literally hundreds of these agencies in Atlanta – more than twenty pages in the Southern Bell Yellow Pages and in at least three different listing categories. Because they represent so many companies and opportunities, they should be an invaluable source for you.

Oftentimes, this industry receives a lot of bad press, much of it deservedly so. Some of these firms are excellent and do a very creditable job, and thus they are highly regarded and utilized by their client companies. But unfortunately, some agencies are downright awful. How do you select one?

First of all, don't select one; select several. Every agency would like to have you as its exclusive applicant, but "putting all your eggs in one basket" is not in your best interest. Rather, make yourself available to whichever ones can offer you exposure to the best companies and positions.

Understand, too, that every agency specializes in a certain level (entry, middle management, executive, etc.) or areas (clerical, management, engineering, etc.), and there are probably personnel agencies or individuals within an agency that specialize in your field. Your task is to zero in on the ones that handle applicants at your level and in your field of specialty, without trying to call every personnel agency listed in the phone book.

Selecting your agencies

The best method for locating older, more established agencies is to call the personnel department (or a specific department manager) of a few major Atlanta companies and ask which agencies they use for your discipline and if they would recommend a specific recruiter there. This has the advantage of not only finding an agency, but also talking with a corporate personnel professional who may have other suggestions as well. In addition, when you then call the agencies that were recommended, be certain to mention the company and/or the individual who recommended them, and I guarantee you will get a warm reception!

You also should contact newer agencies, since they often are more aggressive and may give you more attention. These agencies probably will advertise in the Sunday classified section of the local newspapers, especially *The Atlanta Journal and Constitution.* Pick out the agencies that are advertising for positions that interest you and contact two or three.

Another good source is to network. Ask friends and business associates which agencies they have used and would recommend. When attending job networking or professional association meetings, ask several people if they have used an agency or recommend one; this is especially helpful if the person to whom you ask has a background similar to your own.

If you graduated from a local college, check with the Career Placement Department and ask for recommendations. In addition, you can call a university's academic department that covers your background, and ask if they are aware of agencies that specialize in your field.

Although you should not waste your time calling every agency in the phone book, nevertheless you should peruse the Yellow Pages under the headings "Employment Agencies" and "Executive Search Consultants" to see if there are agencies who specialize in your field. Oftentimes these agencies will have your industry as part of their name (*e.g.*, "Restaurant Recruiters" or "Insurance Personnel Search") or they may have a box ad that mentions your specialty.

Still another excellent source is the back pages of trade newspapers and magazines. Agencies who advertise in these specialized journals usually concentrate on that discipline in their recruiting.

The Georgia Association of Personnel Services publishes a directory of their membership, including the specialties of each member, which you can order for $6. However, I have included most of their information in Appendix D. In addition, there are excellent agencies who are not members, and thus I still suggest you use the criteria listed above.

Lastly, to inquire if there are complaints about any agencies in general or specifically about the one(s) you are considering, call the Atlanta Better Business Bureau at (404) 688-4910.

Contacting your agencies

Once you have selected the agencies that you plan to use, here is the procedure to follow. If you are in Atlanta, you should visit them personally for two reasons:

1) to determine if they can adequately represent you or if you want them to represent you, and

2) to make a personal impression on them, so they can better present you to their clients.

If you are not local, call them to see if they can help you. If you are asked to send in a resume, do so, and then call back in a few days to check on the activity in your behalf. Ask them frankly if they will be able to arrange interviews and in what time frame. Be polite, but persistent. Can they help you or are you wasting your time? When would they like for you to call again? Do they have any suggestions for you? Since they have reviewed your resume, ask for their opinion of it.

Types of Personnel Agencies

Understanding the nature of personnel agencies and how they work will enable you to better utilize their services. Most importantly, realize that they are not philanthropic organizations; they are in business to make a profit. Their income is derived entirely from fees collected through their efforts at matching applicants with client companies.

Agencies can be broadly categorized into three groups, related to the sources of their income:

- Executive search firms

- Temporary agencies

- Contingency agencies

Executive search firms, sometimes called "headhunters," are retained by companies to search for specific personnel needs and are paid in advance by the retaining company. Since they work on a limited number of specific cases, they generally are not a good source for entry- and mid-level positions. Senior-level executives, however, may benefit from search firms that specialize in their area of expertise.

Temporary agencies derive their income from providing companies with contract labor, for which the company pays the agency and the agency in turn pays the laborers. Usually this is for hourly or clerical work, but some firms offer long-term contracts, especially for engineers and other specialized work. There are also temporary agencies specializing in short-term professional-level openings, especially in accounting and data processing.

Since many times these temporary positions will become permanent, you should consider applying to these agencies if you are unemployed or have extra time. Ask if they have any "temp-to-perm" positions available.

Even if the position is only temporary, you can network with the employees there. I know of an accountant whose supervisor on a temporary assignment referred him to the company's CPA firm for placement. Also, we recently hired a temporary receptionist who was seeking a sales position in the hospitality industry; I happened to know the personnel manager with a major hotel here and referred her to them.

By far the largest number of agencies falls into the third group, called "**contingency agencies**," and these will be your best source to call. These firms are paid only when one of their applicants accepts employment through their efforts with one of their client companies, and thus, their fee is contingent upon making the placement. These agencies will have many job openings in many diverse industries and with many different companies, and some of these companies also may have listed the same opening with other agencies.

Remember that since they are paid only when they make a job placement, they are most interested in applicants who fit the current needs of their clients, and if you are more difficult to place than another applicant, you will not get as much attention. When talking with them, state your employment objective, but be as flexible as possible and listen to their suggestions. However, you are under no obligation to accept any interview that does not meet your standards.

Interview with the agency as though it is the company with whom you hope to be employed. Many companies have established a strong rapport with the agency(s) they use and have great confidence in the agency's opinion. Thus, you must impress the agency enough to be referred on to these key clients.

At the end of your interview, ask how soon you can expect to hear from them and when you will be sent on an interview. Also, seek their frank appraisal of your resume and interviewing skills, and ask if they have any suggestions or recommendations for you to consider.

During this interview, you should ask questions that will help you to evaluate the agency, the agency interviewer, and the assistance they can offer you. Personnel agencies have notoriously high employee turnover, and it is not unlikely that this interviewer has been at the job for only a very short while. If this is the case, an opinion of your resume and interviewing skills may be totally useless. In addition, this trainee may not understand your background and experience, and will not be able to present you to potential clients.

Working with Agencies

You have every reason to expect the agencies your select to treat you honestly and fairly. They should never send you on interviews for which you are not qualified[1] or refer you to positions in which you have

---

[1] Over the years, I have had many candidates insist that if I would just set the interview for them, they would "sell themselves" enough to get the job, regardless of their lack of qualifications. I never would waste their time or my clients' time in such a fruitless arrangement, and they often could not understand why. Believe me, an agency that somehow finagles an interview for you for which you are not at all

no interest. You should be briefed before each interview regarding the nature of the position, promotional potential, salary range, and company background. The best agencies will maintain files in their office of company literature for you to peruse, including annual reports and recruiting information, especially for their best clients. Many agencies also know their client's interviewers and interviewing techniques.

In return, you should treat your agencies with the same respect you expect from them. If you are not interested in a specific interview, tell the agency why; this will help your recruiter to be more selective for future interviews. Always show up for your interviews or advise the agency well in advance to cancel; most agencies will not work with you once you have failed to show for an scheduled interview. Call your agency recruiter immediately after each interview to relay your impressions of the interview.

Your personnel agencies and recruiters can become good, professional friends, and you should treat them as you would other professionals. I still talk with applicants I placed more than twenty years ago!

Agency Contracts and Fees

If the agency requires you to sign a contract, read it carefully before you sign and be sure to get a copy. Agency contracts are fairly standard, and generally speaking, you need not worry about signing one. The important facts to know are these:

> 1) You do not have to accept any offer extended unless you are sure it is what you are seeking. Do not allow the agency to pressure you into accepting a position you do not want.

> 2) No fee is involved until you do accept employment as a result of their service.[1]

---

qualified is not doing you any favors. They are wasting your time and their (soon-to-be-former) clients' patience.

[1] There is one extenuating circumstance of which you should be aware. In the past, I have seen agency contracts that required a portion of your salary increase, should you accept a counter-offer from your present company. The basis for this is that your increase is a direct result of their efforts in obtaining you other employment, which then forced your present company to make you the counter-offer. Thus, before

However, before you accept a position through a personnel agency, be certain you understand your legal liability, if any, to the agency. For example, are there any circumstances under which you may be held responsible for all or part of the fee? Are you required to remain with the company for a period of time before your liability to the agency expires? If the company defaults on the fee, are you obligated for it? If you are uncomfortable with any part of the contract, get a written waiver from the agency before you accept the position.

When I first began agency recruiting twenty years ago, most personnel agencies accepted job openings that were both "fee paid" (*i.e.*, the hiring company pays the agency fee) and "non-fee paid" (*i.e.*, the applicant pays the fee). Salaries were lower then and since the agency's fee is based on a percentage of their placement's first-year's income, consequently so were agency fees. In addition, the concept of companies paying an agency fee was not so well accepted.

Times have changed, and the reverse is currently true. Most professional-level personnel agencies now handle only positions in which the hiring company pays the agency's fee, and these "fee paid" positions cost you nothing. I strongly recommend that you restrict your initial agency contacts to those handling only "fee paid" openings, and if necessary, you can call the other agencies later.

However, if you have limited qualifications (and this often happens to trainees), you may find yourself in the uncomfortable position of considering a position that requires you to pay a fee. I personally have a strong disdain for companies that will not pay an agency fee and yet willingly hire through personnel agencies, knowing that the high expense of the agency fee will be passed on to their new employee. Nevertheless, if you find yourself in this situation, be absolutely, 100% certain you want that job before you saddle yourself with the large financial burden of an agency fee. Try to negotiate with the agency for a lesser amount or with the company for a reimbursement later. Better still, stay away from this situation to begin with.

Agency Scams

There is one more situation you unfortunately may encounter: the "up-front fee" agency or some other business that requires you to pay a

---

accepting a counter-offer, confirm that you are under no contractual obligation to the agency or that your present company will pay the fee.

fee in advance of any job assistance. This fee may be only $75 or $100 for a list of job openings (usually copied from the newspaper), or they can soar up to several thousand dollars for "counseling" or resume distribution. Outlawed in many states, some of these scams will pose as personnel agencies, and sell you lists of alleged job openings, guarantee you employment after their fee is paid, or some other useless "service."

Atlanta has had its share of these operations. Just this morning I read of an FBI sting on a business here that guaranteed overseas employment for a fee of $295, but in fact had no jobs to offer and kept the money. Beware of these crooks and before you hand over your money, ask for references or call the Better Business Bureau.[1]

Summary

Personnel agencies can be an excellent source and you should use them when possible, but recognize they do have limitations. If you are seeking employment in a very narrow field (*e.g.*, public relations or staff marketing), they likely will be of little help. If there is something in your background that makes you less marketable than their other applicants, you will not have good results with them. As I stated before, the best approach with agencies is to ask for a frank analysis of the help they can offer you.

I mentioned earlier about "temp-to-perm" positions, *i.e.*, jobs that are classified by the company as temporary, but may become permanent within a short period. In today's economy, many companies are reluctant to commit to full-time, permanent employees, but nevertheless need additional help. Temporary employment offers several benefits to the company, as well as to you. I have spoken recently with job seekers who have accepted temporary or contract employment as part of their total job search, and I suggest you consider that also. It provides you with income, skill and knowledge development, networking potential, and could become permanent. Best of all, you can continue your job search in your time off, showing that you are currently employed.

I frequently speak with applicants who have been offended by a personnel agency – not that they were really mistreated, but rather they

---

[1] I must make a distinction between these shams and legitimate "outplacement" firms. Those latter firms can be very helpful and are often part of a severance package offered by employers. If you have doubts as to a firm's legitimacy, check their references.

were made to feel like one of the herd, impersonal and dehumanized. Instead of "good-bye," they wanted to say "moo" or "baa." Perhaps their interview was cold, short, and perfunctory, or frequently interrupted. Another major complaint I often hear is that phone calls were not returned promptly, or even at all.

I won't make excuses for this behavior on the part of agencies, but I will explain why it happens, and I even will admit some guilt myself. Remember back to the resume chapter when I stated that I often receive up to 100 or so responses per advertisement. Then you must understand that each personnel agent will be handling many, many applicants at all times. Unfortunately, we often do not have enough time to appease everyone and still do our work.

So don't let yourself be offended to the point of cutting yourself off from any possible source of leads and interviews. Your purpose is to use the agencies for your benefit, and don't lose sight of that objective, regardless of how you may feel toward the agency. I assure you that they mean no personal affront.

And remember, this source is only one of the many you have available. Don't make the mistake of waiting for an agency to find you a job when you have other sources to tap.

Tool #5: Job Fairs

Pro's: Exposure to multiple companies and/or job vacancies, free or low cost, good networking possibilities

Con's: Can get lost in crowd, some job fairs have poor company representation, visibility may be a problem if currently employed

Job fairs are large scale recruiting events. Their objective is to bring together qualified applicants and company recruiters at one time and in one location, hopefully leading to job offers. These gatherings often attract hundreds, even thousands, of job seekers and may have fifty or more companies represented.

For companies, this method could be cheaper than advertising expenses or personnel agency fees, and more time-efficient as well, since they can screen many applicants in a short period. For you, the job seeker, it offers the advantage of gaining exposure to a number of companies at one time, also saving time and money. In addition, you may encounter companies of which you were not aware or with whom you were unable to make contact.

In the past few years, I have noticed an increase in the number of job fairs offered in Atlanta. Since most of these are free or low cost, you should plan to attend some. The Sunday edition of *The Atlanta Journal-Constitution*'s Help Wanted classified advertising will include time and location in the Career Calendar section and there likely will be more information and details in a display ad further in the Help Wanted section.

Sponsors for these events may be non-profit or for-profit. Typical non-profit sponsors include professional associations, college alumni groups, professional service organizations, industry associations, and local media. Companies that have a large number of positions to fill often will conduct their own "open house" or job fair. In addition to these groups, there are many for-profit firms that conduct job fairs, often for specific target groups (*e.g.*, sales, engineering, ex-military, or computer backgrounds).

95

Preparation

Much of your preparation will be like preparing for an interview, which of course, is exactly what you are doing. Refer to "Chapter V: Interviewing Techniques" for a full discussion. As with interviewing, your success at the job fair will be largely determined by your planning and preparation. Take time to develop a game plan and start your planning early.

If possible, determine in advance which companies will be present, select the ones with whom you want to interview, and conduct some research into those companies. Rank them in order of importance to you and plan to visit them approximately in that order. The names of the companies planning to attend is usually listed in the display ad in *The Atlanta Journal-Constitution* or other advance notice, but if not, call the sponsor and request the information.

Check ahead for registration requirements or qualifications screening. You may be asked to send in your resume beforehand so that companies can peruse it prior to the event.

Have available many copies of your resume, at least 25. This is one occasion where you will be expected to distribute your resume freely. Of course, be certain it conforms with the principles we discussed earlier in "Chapter III: Preparing Your Resumes."

Carry an attaché case, which will keep your resume neat and clean, as well as have room to store the company literature you will receive. Include a notebook to record your activities or carry a small note pad in your coat pocket.

At the Fair

When you arrive at the fair, you will be given a program of participating companies. In addition to the ones you planned to contact, you may wish to seek out others as well.

Use your time wisely. You may have all day or just a few hours, but either way, you will be at your peak performance for only a few hours at best. Allow time for a short break and to recompose.

Many job fairs also offer seminars on job search techniques, but most of these classes are offered by other groups at other times. (See "Tool

#8: Job Network Groups.") Your focus should be to make company contacts, and thus I suggest you attend the seminars only after you have completed your mission or as a rest break between interviews.

Make notes regarding each company and their representative with whom you spoke personally, so that you will remember them later. You need not take complete notes, just enough to jog your memory later. You can use this note-taking time as a rest break or when you are waiting in line.

After the Job Fair

Send a thank-you note to the companies with whom you spoke and include some bit of information that will help them remember who you are. They will have spoken with many, many applicants and thus you will need to refresh their memory. In this note, you will indicate that you plan to recontact them in a few days.

In speaking with some company recruiters who have worked at these fairs, a common comment is that applicants must take the initiative in recontacting companies with whom they left their resume or interviewed. If you have mailed a thank-you note, you will have said that you will recontact them; definitely do so.

Evaluate your results from the fair. What did you gain from the experience? What could you have done differently that might have produced better payoff?

Review your notes. What companies should you be recontacting? What actions should you take as a consequence of the fair? What follow-up needs tending? Do you have new leads to check?

Networking at Job Fairs

Job fairs offer an excellent opportunity to job network with other job seekers. For example, while standing in line, you can compare job search techniques and information with the people around you. Anyone you happen to meet is a potential source for leads. Use your "30-second resume" whenever you have the chance.

Save your resumes for the companies, but hand out your business cards freely and solicit others as well; you may wish to contact later some people that you meet. Don't just mill around waiting for an interview; use all of your time constructively.

Standing Out

As I stated earlier, there may be hundreds or thousands of job seekers at a job fair. How can you stand out from the crowd?

• Develop a game plan for what you plan to do at the fair and proceed accordingly. Not only will you accomplish more, but you also will feel less stressed and more relaxed with this preparation. Not surprisingly, you also will reflect that feeling and attitude.

• Be appropriately attired, with a professional, business image. Since you may be there several hours, plan to "freshen up" while there. For example, men should carry an electric shaver in their attaché case and women who wear make-up should also check their appearance often. Carry and use breath mints.

• Be organized. Don't fumble for papers or a resume, but have your materials readily accessible. Keep your business cards in a pocket easy to reach.

• Be prepared. If you know which companies you will be seeing, compile and learn information about them and be certain to relate it during your interview. Prepare for the interview, following all of the suggestions I have outlined in the next chapter on interviewing techniques.

• Take an occasional rest break, so that you will not seem tired.

Conclusion

Why attend job fairs? Depending on the size of the fair, several hundred participants may receive offers then or later from the companies they met or interviewed. Since these events are inexpensive and closeby, you have every reason to attend! This tool is still one more of the many you have learned about through the CAREER SEARCH SYSTEM.

Tool #6: Government

Pro's: Generally stable and secure. Local and many state jobs are generally permanent Atlanta. Many openings for recent grads.

Con's: Can be very long and complex procedures. Not good source if you need a job quickly, although efforts are underway to streamline federal hiring.

There are more than 225,000 government employees in metro-Atlanta, and that figure is growing annually. Even during the recent recession, government employment in Atlanta increased, much of it at the local level. The approximate numbers are these[1]:

Federal - 47,700 (including 5,900 in defense-related, non-military)

State - 46,000 (18,000 in education)

Local (18-county MSA) - 132,100 (including 72,500 in education).

Appendix F includes addresses and contact data divided into the above three groups.

If at all possible, I suggest you go to a Georgia State Employment Office, especially one of the five metro-Atlanta offices listed below, where you will find not only Georgia openings, but many federal and local job lists as well. Call if you need directions.
• Clayton County: 1193 Forest Pkwy, Lake City, GA; (404) 363-7643

---

[1] Source: *Georgia Labor Market Trends*, 6/93 issue, published by the Georgia Department of Labor, Labor Information Systems. Estimates include all full- and part-time wage and salary workers. Proprietors, domestic servants, self-employed persons, unpaid family workers, and personnel of the armed forces are excluded.

- North Atlanta/Fulton County: 2943 N. Druid Hills Rd NE (in Toco Hills Shopping Center); (404) 679-5200
- South Atlanta/Fulton County: 2636 Martin Luther King Jr Ave (across from MARTA's Hightower station); 656-6000 (auto phone info)
- Dekalb County: 1275 Clarendon Ave, Avondale Estates, GA; (404) 288-1345
- Cobb County: 2972 Ask Kay Dr SE, Smyrna, GA; (404) 434-3865
- Gwinnett County: 1535 Atkinson Rd, Lawrenceville, GA (404) 995-6913

If you are not in Atlanta or unable to go to one of the above offices, then

(1) go to your local US Office of Personnel Management (or in smaller cities, the State Employment Services Office) and request the Federal Job Opportunities List for Atlanta (out of state, ask for Georgia and peruse for Atlanta openings);

(2) write the Georgia State Merit System and request the pamphlet, "The State Employment Process" (Their address is included in the Merit System discussion in this chapter);

(3) contact the local government offices listed in Appendix F.

U. S. (Federal) Government

The process for obtaining a federal job is somewhat complex, and that is why I urge you to go to your local State Employment Services Office, including the ones in Atlanta. They should be able to explain the procedures involved and help you with the applications.

Most federal government agencies hire through the Office of Personnel Management (OPM), formerly known as the civil service commission, and a competitive exam is required. This exam may be all written, all experience-oriented, or a combination of both. You can obtain information on application procedures, application forms, and the Federal Job Opportunities List for Atlanta at many locations, including the employment offices in all states, college placement departments, and the offices of all members of Congress. These sources will be the fastest methods of obtaining the information, but if none of these sources is available to you, you can write the OPM Atlanta Area Office and request application information and the Federal Job Opportunities List to be mailed to you. I am told this office is extremely busy, and thus use the alternate sources when possible. Their address here is

U S Office of Personnel Management
Atlanta Area Office
75 Spring St SW, Suite 956
Atlanta, GA 30303-3309.

Do *not* call. All requests for information must be in writing.

If you are in Atlanta, the fastest and simplest method to learn of the application procedures and job openings is to visit the self-service Federal Job Information Center, open Monday through Friday, from 9 - 4. They are located at 75 Spring St SW, and you can review the job list in Room 960.

US Postal Service: Certain federal organizations fill their job vacancies through their own hiring systems and have no contact with OPM. The largest of these in Atlanta is the US Postal Service (USPS), with more than 7,000 employees here, including some 3,000 at the managerial level. Interestingly, nearly all USPS employees start as clerks or carriers, and only the highest levels and technical positions (attorneys, engineers, etc.) are hired from outside the system. Thus, one would start entry-level, and then bid for higher-level positions after one year of employment. Numerous college grads are hired each year into this program. Call (404) 765-7234 for information on job vacancies, then fill out an application and you will be notified when to take the exam required of all applicants.

General Accounting Office: Another federal agency conducting its own hiring is the General Accounting Office (GAO), a Congressional agency and not under the Executive Branch. Most of their hiring is for economics, public administration, accounting/finance, and computer-related degrees, both entry-level and experienced. A job announcement is published each fall, and applications are taken from September through April. They also offer several co-op programs and summer internships. Call (404) 332-1900 for information.

Administrative Careers with America: In addition to the above organizations and procedures, the Federal Government's new program Administrative Careers With America (ACWA) is an alternative and usually faster method for obtaining entry-level federal employment,

GS 5 - 7 levels. About 100 different types of occupations are filled through this program, and you may apply for these jobs when you are within nine months of graduation, or upon completion of the qualifying academic courses or three years' work experience.

There are two options for applying:

• You may take a written examination. Based on your exam rating, your name will be placed on a list of eligible applicants and referred to Federal agencies with vacancies.

• You may apply based on your college grade-point average (GPA) or scholastic record, without having to take a written exam. To do this, you must be a college graduate and have a GPA of 3.5 (4.0 scale) or higher, for all completed undergraduate course work; or have graduated in the upper ten percent of your class.

Outstanding Scholar Authority: Federal agencies with vacancies can hire recent graduates with a GPA of 3.5+ (on a 4.0 scale) or who have graduated in the top 10% of their class, directly from the outside, bypassing OPM. This can happen when a government recruiter interviews you on campus or you can apply directly to federal agencies for employment consideration. The OPM is establishing an Applicant Referral List, which will contain the names of candidates who meet the GPA/scholastic requirements, but usage of the Referral List by individual agencies is strictly optional. Thus, your best bet is to contact each agency directly, and Appendix F lists the recruiting information for the largest government agencies in Atlanta.

For more information regarding ACWA, call the Career America College Hotline at 900-990-9200. By calling this number, you can obtain current employment and career information, application forms, and materials relating to ACWA. There is a charge of 40¢ per minute for this call.

My contact at OPM also suggests that you first write OPM, indicating your objectives and qualifications, and they will send you information regarding the agencies that may have openings for you.

Incidentally, the federal government offers its employees alternate work schedules, one of which allows an employee to work nine-hour days, Monday - Thursday, and then have Friday afternoon free. It's still a 40-hour week, but the half-day can make a nice, long weekend!

This schedule is also finding favor within the private sector as well, and I have noted in Appendix C (the list of companies) some of those that also offer this benefit.

State of Georgia

The vast majority of state job vacancies are filled through the Georgia Merit System, which last year hired more than 5,000. If you are in Atlanta, again I refer you to the state employment offices for information on current openings. A list of available openings is published each Friday and is available at all Georgia state agencies and colleges, as well as the labor departments of all states. It cannot be obtained by writing or calling; rather, you must go in person to an employment office or to the merit system office, located in the same building as the MARTA Georgia State station. However, you can call (404) 656-2724 for a recorded announcement of the hiring procedure. Their address is

State of Georgia Merit System
200 Piedmont Ave, Suite 418, West Tower, Atlanta, GA 30334.

The merit system office is open Monday - Friday, 8 - 4:30, but you are encouraged to arrive by 3:00.

One of the larger non-merit system agencies is the Department of Audits. It is divided into two sections, financial and performance, whose addresses are listed in Appendix F.

Local Governments

Appendix F lists the contact data and procedure followed by the five major metro counties, plus the City of Atlanta.

PART 2:

JOB NETWORKING

Tool #7:   Developing a Job Network

Pro's: Most effective source overall. Works well for all experience levels, especially middle level. Best source for individuals changing fields, re-entering work force, or other difficult-to-place situations.

Con's: Slow, time-consuming, labor intensive, lots of "dead-end" leads.

I am often asked what is the most important part of a job search. The answer is easy: Job Networking!

Looking at all the "con's" to job networking might make you want to skip it, in favor of the easier and simpler methods. Before you do, consider this: More people find their jobs through networking than through any other source, at least 70%, and I have heard estimates of up to 85%! Perhaps this is a good example of the old adage, "You get what you pay for," because even though it is the most difficult, it is the most fruitful.

In addition, twice as many new jobs are generated by smaller businesses than by the large, major companies. In fact, the "Fortune 500" are projected to decrease employment during the current decade, and a recent report by Dun & Bradstreet Corp. indicates that companies with fewer than 100 employees will account for almost 80% of the new jobs. Further, firms with fewer than 20 employees are expected to add 57% of the new positions. As I stated earlier in this chapter, simply mailing your resume to the biggest companies will not find enough openings. Networking, however, will help you locate these smaller firms.

There are several approaches to job networking, all of which can generate many leads and interviews. This and the following three sections detail the most successful methods that you can incorporate in your job search.

Before starting to network, you already must have developed your "30-Second Resume," described in Part 2 of Chapter III. If for some reason, you skipped that discussion, refer back to it now. I stated that you will be using this oral resume often, and now is still another of those times. The "30-second resume" is just as important as your written one, so spend enough time to make it the best possible.

Developing A Job Network

Since job networking can be so productive, you should spend at least half of your time developing this source. I know what you are thinking: that it's too difficult or that you lack the skills or contacts from which to establish your base. Not true – once you get started, you will be surprised how well it goes. As with so much of your job search, it simply requires planning and organization. Even if you are new to Atlanta, you can cultivate a network system; the procedure is the same.

First, let me emphasize what job networking is <u>not</u>. It is not an excuse to abuse your friends and relatives by bombarding them with constant calls for contacts or by pressuring them to use their influence when you sense their reluctance. Certainly you will want to include them in your job networking, but there are so many potential networking sources at your disposal that you should not test the patience of any person. If you find yourself calling the same people, then you are not conducting a correct job search.

Start developing your job network by compiling a list of individuals you want to contact. Begin with friends and relatives, who should be the most sympathetic and supportive, and this will get you off to a good start. Expand this list to include business associates, then social, professional, civic, and church contacts, and anyone else you think could help. However, if you are currently employed and discretion is utmost, you may wish to contact only close, trusted associates.

In compiling this list you also should predetermine why you are including each person. How can they help you? What information do you think they may be able to share with you?

Now phone each one and let them know that you are actively seeking new employment. Conduct your calls seated at the desk of the new "job search area" you have set up, so you can record all of the information you are given and keep it organized. Here are some questions to ask:

• "Do you have any job search suggestions?" They may have just completed a job search themselves and will have some good advice.

Or they may know of someone else who has, and you can contact that person to ask what he/she learned during the job search.

• "Do you have any contacts that could be of assistance?" Perhaps your contact may be friends with a Director of Human Resources that could be a good lead, or a department manager in the field you are seeking, or some other person who might be helpful.

• "Is there a career consultant, personnel agent, or advisor you know and would recommend?"

• "Are you aware of any organized professional or job network groups that I should contact?" In addition to the local chapters of national trade and professional associations, Atlanta is fortunate to have several job networking groups. Atlanta also is headquarters for the National Career Networking Group of Georgia, a non-profit, but fee-based networking group that has received much positive publicity lately. (Networking groups, professional associations, and privately funded job-search organizations are all discussed later in this chapter.)

In addition to your initial list, there are many other networking sources. When at social gatherings, listen out for people who might be able to lead you to a source. Call the appropriate academic department head at a local college and ask for suggestions. If possible, discuss your situation with current or former clients.

When you prepared your written resume, you secured at least three persons who agreed to be your references. Definitely include them in your network list, and since they are familiar with the quality of your work, they likely will be able to suggest other persons to contact.

College alumni groups are an outstanding source, and you should locate the local chapter president of your alumni association and attend the meetings, planning to job network there. If you don't know who the local officers are, call the alumni office or the president's office at your alma mater and ask for the local contact.

Many college alumni associations sponsor career seminars and job fairs, and they often have "young alumni" sub-groups. Try to locate alumni with backgrounds similar to yours and ask for career and job search advice. You also should discuss your job search with the chapter president and perhaps arrange an "information interview."[1] In fact, I just spoke with an applicant who expects a job offer from Coca-Cola and whose interview was arranged through the president of his alumni association.

Still another valuable source of leads and contacts can be found through professional and trade associations. If you are already a member of a society that covers your field, you should contact the president or job coordinator. If you are contemplating a career change, these groups can be a tremendous help. Search out the one(s) that pertain to your newly chosen field, contact them and attend their meetings. In researching this subject, I encountered many persons who obtained their jobs by networking at these monthly meetings, and thus I strongly urge you to try it also. This source is discussed in more detail in the next section, "Tool #9: Professional and Trade Associations," and Appendix E includes information on many of the most active of these groups locally.

Volunteer your time with a professional association, church, civic group, favorite charity, or any other organization where you will meet people. As you get to know these new friends, they may have suggestions or contacts, and you likely will find persons who recently conducted their own job search. This is especially helpful if you are unemployed, since it keeps you active and involved, as well as adding to your emotional support systems and avoiding depression.

As you see, networking has infinite possibilities. Think about it, and you surely will come up with many more potential sources for contacts.

Conclusion

Don't expect instant results or that all of your efforts will be productive. Accept the fact that although most of your leads will not be useful, you must follow through on all of them anyway. That is the slow, time-consuming part of job networking.

But since networking is the most effective source overall, you should plan to spend much of your time cultivating leads and contacts, and then following through on them. Don't let all the dead ends depress you; sooner or later, one or more of your leads will bear fruit. It only takes the one "right" lead to land you your new job!

---

[1] The "information interview" is discussed later in this chapter as Tool #9.

Thus, approach each network contact as though an opening were available for you. You never know when there really might be.

Tool #8: Job Network Groups

Pros: Most are free or little expense; offer emotional support, job search seminars, and sometimes job openings; excellent networking opportunity; good source for recent grads through middle-management.

Con's: Some volunteer instructors are not well-qualified; not best source for senior executives; very open and thus may not be good if you are currently employed.

Atlanta is fortunate to have several network groups specifically aimed for job searchers. The largest of these, the **Atlanta Job Network**, is a loosely federated system of at least twelve member groups who meet weekly and welcome anyone seeking a job, regardless of experience or background. At any given weekly meeting, you may be introduced to top executives, blue-collar workers, recent college graduates, and everything in between. There are no charges and no reservations. Although they all meet in churches, they are non-sectarian.

While their primary purpose is to help job seekers through job networking, they also offer seminars on the practical aspects of getting a job (*e.g.*, interviewing, resume preparation, focusing your job objective, planning a job search, job networking, etc.). In addition, they maintain files of job openings sent to them by many metro employers, and these files can be perused at the weekly meetings.

In the past few years, I have spoken with many job-seekers who were very pleased with the assistance they received from this organization, and so I urge you to attend one or several of the meetings. There are more than twelve Job Network groups in the metro-Atlanta area, and you can meet with any one or more that you choose. Telephone ahead for directions and to confirm times. You may also wish to inquire what topics are being discussed, and plan to attend the one(s) that would be most helpful to you.

  • St. Jude's Catholic Church in Sandy Springs, 7171 Glenridge Drive NE. Meets every Monday at 7:30 pm, and you must arrive early. For directions, call the rectory at 394-3896; for information, call Jim and Trudy Knocke at 393-4578. Oldest and largest of the Job Network groups; often has 200 attendees.

• Peachtree Presbyterian Church in Buckhead. (Note: With 10,000 members, this is the largest Presbyterian church in the US.) Meets every Thursday at 7:30 pm, and you are encouraged to arrive early for sign-in. Easy to find at 3434 Roswell Rd NW (a different "Roswell Road" from St. Ann's.), but if you need directions, call the church office at 842-5800; for information on monthly topics, call Tim Lane at 434-0471.

• Catholic Church of St. Ann at 4905 Roswell Rd, Marietta, GA. (Note: If you are not familiar with the Atlanta area, there is more than one "Roswell Road"; be certain you are on the right one!) Meets every Tuesday at 7:45 pm. For directions, call 998-1373; for information ask for Sue Deering.

• Corpus Christi Catholic Church in Stone Mountain at 600 Mountain View Drive. Meets every Monday at 7:15 pm. For directions, call 469-0395; for information, call Joe Humphries at 294-8377.

• Roswell United Methodist Church, 814 Mimosa Blvd, Roswell, GA. Meets every Monday from 7:30 - 9:00 pm. Also has Job Opportunity Bulletin Board, which lists current job openings; last year they had more than 300! For directions, call 993-6218; for information recording, call 642-7943.

• Christ Our Shepherd Lutheran Church, located in Peachtree City at the intersection of Highway 54 at Peachtree Parkway. Meets biweekly on first and third Thursdays at 7:25. For information and directions, call the church at 487-8717.

• Southern Crescent Job Network, an association of several church and non-profit assistance groups that meets weekly at Riverdale Presbyterian Church on Monday from 7:15 - 9:30 pm. Located in Riverdale at 6611 Church Street. For information or directions call the church secretary at 997-5909.

• Embry Hills United Methodist Church, 3304 Henderson Mill Road, Atlanta. Meets Tuesdays at 7:30 in the church Fellowship

Hall. For information, call Greg Felty at 491-7679; for directions, call 938-0661.

The Atlanta Exchange is a predominantly African-American referral network, with 26 member organizations, representing many industries and professions. (Several of these are included in the appendix on Professional and Trade Associations.) They sponsor social gatherings, especially networking parties, plus business and career enhancement seminars.

An individual does not join the Exchange; instead, you call them, relay your background and experience, and they will refer you to a member organization that represents your industry or need. Occasionally they may have a job requisition from a local corporation, but direct referral to companies is not their primary focus. They do have a book of current job openings that you can peruse at their office.

It is important to remember that the Exchange is a networking group, not a public job agency. They will not find you a job, nor will their member organizations, so do not call and expect them to have a job waiting for you. However, they do offer an outstanding opportunity to network as part of your job search, and I am certain many applicants have found employment through their services. For more information or for the date of their next meeting, call William Ware at 876-0490.

Sales and Marketing Seekers (SAMS) is a networking and support group, comprised mostly of career salespersons seeking employment. They meet Friday mornings at 7:00 for coffee and doughnuts at Roswell United Methodist Church. For information, call the church office at 993-6218 or Richard Card at 971-0848.

Other job networking groups are listed in the earlier chapter on organization (Chapter II) and later in this chapter in the section called "Tool #12: Privately Funded Organizations." Especially helpful is the National Career Networking Group of Georgia, a non-profit association relying heavily on its members for networking tips. These bodies have a more specific purpose and constituency, as well as offering an opportunity for networking. The ones I listed in Chapter II are more spiritually based, and the privately funded organizations are targeted to special need groups.

Procedure for attending networking meetings

A little preparation before the meetings and some understanding of the networking opportunities they offer will help you derive the most from these groups.

Plan ahead. Carry a few copies of your resume, but you should give one only to persons who request it. Far better is to pass out your business card, which will show your job objective or expertise and your contact data. This small card is easier to keep and less likely to be tossed in the trash. Although many attendees will be casually attired, I suggest you dress in a business suit, since you may receive more and better information if you project a professional image. Needless to say, be certain you know the time, date, and location.

Arrive early. Remember that the primary focus of these groups is to encourage job networking. Arriving 20 minutes early will allow more time to meet other job seekers and exchange information.

Set goals. A easy goal is to meet at least ten attendees and exchange business cards. Discuss what you have learned and ask for suggestions from them. An even better plan is to locate at least two attendees with backgrounds or objectives similar to your own. Trading job hunting tips with them will be especially helpful to your own search, as well as to theirs. Ask for suggestions in selecting personnel agencies.

Don't waste time. Don't spend too much time with one person. Keep moving and try to locate other participants who can address your needs. However, you should always exchange business cards and perhaps phone those persons later. Should you locate someone with very good information relative to your job search, get their name and contact data (a business card, for example) and ask if you can call or meet with them later, when there are fewer distractions and you can continue your dialogue.

Actively participate. Converse with as many people as you have time. If you are researching a specific company and seeking information or a contact there, mention it often. You likely will encounter someone who can help. Many of the classes allot time for this exchange of information and you should mention it then also. If you have questions or comments during the classes, speak up. The facilitators are glad to hear from you, if you don't monopolize their time.

Identify yourself. Each group has a sign-in table and you are given a name tag on which to write your name. Under your name and in only a few words, include your job objective or expertise in letters large enough for other attendees to read. If someone with a background or objective similar to yours sees this tag, you likely will have identified a useful source. For variety, you occasionally might write in your alma mater, home state, former emloyer, etc.

Take notes. The classes are generally informative, and you should take notes. You also will want to jot down details about some of the participants you meet and the information you obtain from them.

Exchange information. If everyone at these meetings only selfishly soaked up information from other attendees, there would be no purpose in participating. Offer your own ideas and experiences, and any other information helpful to others. Some weeks you may feel that you have given more than you have received, but it will all balance out later. However, don't allow yourself to be trapped by someone seeking too much information for the short period you have at the meeting. Should this be developing, ask if you can call them later when you both have more time for discussion.

Follow-up. All of the knowledge you obtained at the meeting will be useless, unless you incorporate it into your search. In addition, keep in contact with some of the participants you meet, especially those with backgrounds or objectives similar to your own. If someone provided you with information that resulted in some positive step in your search, send them a thank you note.

Conclusion

Although your results will vary from week to week, you will always come away with a boost in morale from commiserating with other job seekers like yourself. I also suggest you occasionally take your spouse or best friend with you, so that they will better understand what you are doing and feel more personally involved.

These groups perform an outstanding service to Atlanta and their sponsors are much to be commended. Since they offer so much and are also free, you should include them in your job search.

A word of caution: I have observed that many attendees seem to be hooked on the seminars offered and ignore the opportunity for networking. Although the seminars offered are very helpful indeed, that is only part of your reason for being there. If you only attend the seminars or only speak with your friends there, you will not be profiting from all you should.

Tool #9: Trade and Professional Associations

Pro's: Works well for middle- and upper-level executives, and somewhat for entry-level. Good source for changing careers.

Con's: May be costly if you must join first or pay to attend meetings. Can be slow and time-consuming getting to the source.

Too few job seekers are aware of the excellent job search potential found in their professional associations. Not only do these groups offer excellent opportunities for networking, but also they frequently have well-developed career placement and career enhancement programs, and some even sponsor job fairs. Although not all associations offer these services, those that do can provide a significant boost to your career search.

Association help comes in many ways, including monthly newsletters listing both job seekers and job openings, a resume bank retained for companies to peruse, a job information "hot line," annual job fairs, and direct matching of jobs and applicants. Smaller organizations may have a less formal, yet very effective networking system. In addition, many associations sponsor career development seminars, covering such topics as job search within their industry, career planning, industry innovations, etc.

There is an organization covering virtually every conceivable job description, industry or academic discipline. Although you already may be a member of one or more of these associations, there likely are other associations of which you may not be aware, but from which you could benefit. *National Trade and Professional Associations of the United States* (published by Columbia Books, Inc., Washington, DC) is a catalogue that lists thousands of trade and professional associations and labor unions with national memberships. Even more complete is the *Encyclopedia of Associations*, a multi-volume work that includes detailed information.

Available at most public libraries, these books include not only addresses and descriptions of each organization, but also a cross reference section to access associations by subject. You likely will be surprised to learn that many disciplines are represented by numerous associations, some of which specialize in specific industries. For example, under the Subject Index heading "Marketing," there are 75+ specialty associations, in addition to the 52,000-member American Marketing Association. In the same section, there are many organizations listed for specific ethic or minority groups, such as "black," "women," "handicapped," etc. Thus, I urge you to incorporate these publications in your job search. (If you are not able to obtain these through a local public library, mail order information is included in "Tool #13: Publications.")

Nearly all of the largest associations offer job assistance on the national level. Moreover, I have researched a large number of these groups that offer some sort of job assistance locally, either formal or informal, and included them in Appendix E. If your association is not listed, I suggest that you contact the national headquarters of your association and ask for the local Atlanta chapter president, and then inquire about their direct career assistance, if any. In future editions, I hope to add still more associations, and I would appreciate hearing from you if you have information on others that are not included in my current list.

In some cases, you must be a member of the association offering employment assistance before they will help you. However, I was pleased to find that many organizations are interested in helping an applicant secure employment now, assuming he/she will join the association later. Since membership dues can be expensive – prohibitively so if you are unemployed – I suggest you call the association contact I have listed to inquire if membership is a prerequisite.

Some associations require a small fee to cover costs, especially if their services are extensive or staffed by volunteers. In some cases, the fee is waived for members. I have noted these charges and other requirements when applicable.

If your association does not offer any formal job assistance, remember that you can attend their meetings and network there; in fact, I have recently spoken with several persons who obtained their current jobs that way. And if the associations do offer job search assistance that you plan to use, you have even more reason for attending their meetings.

Most associations meet monthly and welcome visitors and potential members, in addition to their current members. Since there may be a fee involved or reservations required, you should check ahead. Appendix E also includes information on monthly meeting dates. If you are strapped for cash and don't want to stay for the meal, you can leave after the social hour or the business meeting.

Networking at Association Meetings

A close friend of mine recently moved to Atlanta in search of an audit/accounting position. I suggested that he attend a meeting of the Institute of Internal Auditors, which he did, and he even sat beside a woman who had just found her job the previous month by networking at the I. I. A. meetings. Unfortunately, however, Ray is somewhat shy and felt uncomfortable in an unfamiliar setting where he knew no one. He spent the entire evening alone and gained nothing from the experience, except a fear of ever returning!

Many job seekers are like Ray, and you may be one of them. With a little preparation beforehand, however, you can overcome your reticence and successfully job network at any meeting – professional association, alumni group, business meeting or whatever. The key word here is "preparation."

I included the name and phone number of at least two members (the president, job coordinator, and/or membership chairman) of every association listed in Appendix E. You should call one of those officers to confirm the meeting date, place, fee and program of the next meeting, and then indicate that you would like to attend. Ask if you can meet him/her at the meeting and if he/she will introduce you to a few members. If you are unable to stay for the meal, tell your new contact so that the association is not charged for it.

Now set your objectives for the meeting. What do you hope to accomplish? You will want to meet some officers, certainly the president and/or the job coordinator. Ask if there are members who recently completed a job search, and then try to locate them to discuss your current search and to ask for suggestions. Are there other specific members you want to meet, department managers with certain companies, etc.?

Plan what you will wear – business attire, of course. You should dress as though you were going on an interview, which is exactly what you are doing! Carry enough business cards to hand out, as well as a few resumes to give to key people. Take a small, pocket-size notebook to record quick information. Remember your "30-Second Resume"? You will use it often at the meeting, so rehearse it some more.

At the meeting, remember your objectives. Don't spend too much time with one person, or you may run out of time. Ask open-ended questions, and then listen; people are always more impressed with good listeners than they are with good talkers! Do not pass out too many resumes, three at the most, or you will seem too opportunistic. Record names and information in your notebook, but don't waste time recording too much now; you can do that later.

If you have the inclination and the time available, volunteer to help out on a committee or such. You will make some valuable contacts and begin to feel more comfortable at the meetings.

Immediately after the meeting, record your results. Whom did you meet (name, company, job title, association function, etc.)? What follow-up do you plan? Is there someone you met and with whom you would like to schedule an "information interview"? What would you want to do differently at the next meeting?

You should send a thank-you note to the person who introduced you at the meeting and enclose your business card. Are there others you need to write and/or send a resume?

Planning what you will do at these meetings will make you less nervous and self-conscious, plus you will accomplish more. You can use this procedure to network at other meetings as well (*e.g.*, college alumni groups, social gatherings, etc.) As with so much of your job search, it only takes organization and preparation.

Conclusion

In reviewing "Appendix E: Trade and Professional Associations," you will note that I have included specific names to contact, rather than only titles, as I did in the company list. This is because many organizations are mostly volunteer and not listed in the phone book, and the fastest way to reach them is through a member or officer. However, since these officials are usually elected for one year only, you may be referred to the current slate of officers for help.

I personally know of many people who found their jobs through associations, and so I am positive it works. Definitely plan to incorporate them in your search. In the "Professional Associations" section of your notebook, record the names of the associations you contact, the people with whom you speak, when you attended meetings, and the results. These contacts will be helpful now and later.

After you are employed, I strongly urge you to become active in your association, not only attending the meetings but also volunteering for committees and signing up for professional seminars. The knowledge you will gain from the meetings, programs, and classes will be very helpful in advancing your career, as will the professional contacts you make. Drawing from your own experiences will enable you to be very helpful to other job seekers – and then too, you never know when you might need their services again!

Tool #10: The Information Interview

Pro's: Especially helpful to change careers or re-enter the job market. Good way to re-energize a stale job search campaign. Provides more useful information than can be obtained in informal settings.

Con's: Very time consuming. Can be difficult to find right sources to contact. May not be feasible if you are not in the city where you are attempting to relocate.

The information interview is the current rage among career counselors, and for a good reason: it works!

Essentially, the information interview is contacting successful and knowledgeable business associates or authorities in your field, and arranging a meeting time to discuss your job search face-to-face, rather than over the phone or at some other informal setting. During this interview, you attempt to obtain much of the same information you would have asked on the phone, but now in more depth and with more details.

The primary reason for using this approach is that you are likely to get more and better information in a formal interview setting than you would simply by phone. It is especially helpful if you are contemplating the possibility of changing careers or re-entering the job market, and you want some ideas and information to help you with your decision. It is also useful if you are having a difficult time with your search and need some fresh input and suggestions to get you going again. Even if you don't fit either of those categories, you likely will find this method profitable.

You also can "cold call" a department manager or other executive and request an interview time to discuss your career search. Some managers will be flattered that you consider them an authority and will be glad to talk with you; others, however, may consider it a nuisance.

I even know someone who was able to create his current job with a company that he "cold called" for an information interview! That, however, is the exception and you should not mislead your contact by saying you are seeking help when in fact you want a job interview. Your objective is to gain information – suggestions, names, etc. – and trying to turn your information interview into a job interview will offend your source.

Nevertheless, if you do sense during your discussion that your source is asking questions that suggest you may be considered for a position within the company, be prepared for a full job interview. You should have read "Chapter V: Interviewing Techniques" and thus are ready for this pleasant turn of events!

Although you may think that a luncheon is a good location for an information interview, it really is not. There are too many distractions and the setting is too informal. Try to conduct your interviews in your source's office where you will have his/her undivided attention.

The main disadvantage to the information interview is that it is far more time-consuming than a phone call. If you are currently employed or not living in the same city as your potential sources, you may not be able to utilize this method. In addition, some of your contacts may feel inconvenienced, particularly if they are often called upon for this type of interview. Nevertheless, it is a good networking technique, and I suggest you consider it.

Procedure

To derive the most from this technique, you must – guess what? – organize and prepare. To facilitate this, I have designated six steps to follow.

Step 1: Compile a list. First make a list of persons to contact and why. Or you may need to use the reverse approach, and decide what information you want and then research the name of a specific authority who might have that knowledge.

Since information interviews are time-consuming, you should be selective in planning your list. What possible information can you obtain from each person on your list and how can you use it in your job search? Having answered that, you are ready to call your first authority.

Step 2: Contact your authorities. Unless you are contacting a personal friend, you should phone your sources at their place of employment. During the conversation, you will state why you are calling (You are seeking information as part of a job search.) and why you are targeting him/her (You consider him/her to be an authority on some subject related to your job search.). Immediately state that you are not calling for a job interview, but only for information that will be helpful in your job search. Then ask for a fifteen minute interview time at his/her convenience.

In attempting to reach your sources, you may encounter problems getting through the secretary or receptionist. Remember that part of these employees' job is to screen unwanted calls for their bosses, so don't be upset if you are quizzed on the purpose of your call. On the contrary, these assistants can be your ally if approached correctly.

You likely will be asked, "May I say who is calling?" and/or "May I ask to what this is in reference." Instead of trying all sorts of devious end runs, try to enlist his/her support and tell the truth, stressing that you are not seeking a job interview and that you will take up only a minute or two of the boss's time on the phone. If you have been referred to this authority by someone, say that so-and-so said you should call. If you are told that your authority is not available now, ask when a convenient time will be to call back. Be polite, ask the secretary's name, and then thank him/her for the information. When you do call later, be certain you refer to the secretary by name.

If after several attempts you cannot bypass this roadblock, try calling early in the morning, before normal business hours, or late in the afternoon, after business hours.

Step 3: Prepare for the interview. After you have established an interview time, the next step is to plan what you will do in the interview, and understanding your respective roles will help. Even though you will be seated in the small chair in front of the big desk, nevertheless you are the interviewer now and your victim is the "interviewee." Thus, you will have prepared just as thoroughly as you would expect from one of your interviewers.

What questions should you ask? This will depend on why you have arranged the interview and what your objectives are. Decide what general and specific information you hope to learn, and then develop questions which may lead to that information.

For example, if you are considering a new career, you should ask questions such as these:
- Why did you pursue this career?
- What qualifications did you have for this career?
- What do you like most about your industry? What do you dislike?
- Would you encourage others to pursue this career? Why?
- To what do you attribute your success here? (A nice compliment!)

If you are attempting to further your established career path, these questions could be helpful:
- What do you feel are the future trends in our industry?
- Which companies are experiencing the strongest growth in our field? Who are the "winners" and the "losers"?
- Of which professional associations are you a member? Who are the officers?
- If you were considering a job change, what companies or individuals would you contact?
- Why have you and your company been successful? (Again, a compliment!)

Although you should not carry a notebook and take notes during a job interview, you will do so here, since you are the interviewer. Write your questions in a place that will be easily accessible during the interview (the first page of your notebook, on a separate note card, etc.). During the interview, you also will have spontaneous questions that arise from the conversation.

A day or so before the interview, plan what you will wear – professional attire, of course. Check out the location and be certain you know how to get there. Even still, on the day of the interview, allow extra travel time; there is no excuse for being late.

Step 4: Take charge of the interview. Remember your objective for the interview (to get as much information as possible) and don't waste too much time in incidental conversation. Thank your source for allowing you this time and for sharing his/her knowledge with you. Then get straight to the point. Your contact will appreciate your time concern and the interview will be off to a good start.

During the interview, don't feel that you must write down every bit of information now. Make the most of this short interview and record just enough information to jog your memory later, realizing your time constraints.

After your allotted time is over, thank your source for the time and information, and then end the interview. Let me repeat this: after your allotted time is over, thank your source and then end the interview. If you overextend and wear out your welcome, your source will be irritated and you will lose any empathy and support you may have developed. However, if your source offers to continue your time, you can accept if you wish.

Step 5: Review the interview. Immediately after the interview is concluded, record the information you did not have time to write during the interview. Then critique your performance. What would you like to have done differently if you had the opportunity? What will you do differently on your next information interview? Did you obtain the information you needed?

Step 6: Plan your follow-up. Now analyze the information you garnered and plan what you will do with it. Do you have new sources to contact? Did your source mention companies you now wish to call? Are there organizations and/or associations you plan to contact and meetings you plan to attend?

Don't forget to send your source a thank-you note as soon as possible. A hand-written note is fine, if that is more convenient. If you have some item of information that you feel would be of interest, enclose it with your note. Be certain to include your address and phone number or a business card, should he/she recall some information later for you.

You may wish to stay in touch with your source periodically. If so, note on your calendar when you should call back, probably in a few weeks. Needless to say, don't become a pest!

Carrying your resume

Should you carry your resume to an information interview? There are two theories on this, and since both have merit, use the approach that suits you.

You may have a copy of your resume, in case your source asks for it, but do not offer it yourself. Remember that you are there to obtain information to use in your job search, and offering your resume will both waste time that you could better use asking questions, as well as possibly offend your source who is expecting an information interview only.

Nevertheless, if during the interview, your source is impressed with your preparation, thoroughness, and/or subject knowledge, you may be considered for possible employment. Having your resume then allows you to seize this opportunity.

The other approach is *not* to carry a resume with you. If asked for it, state that you did not bring one, since you are only conducting an information interview. Then offer to bring one by later. This way, you may be able to have two interviews, one for information and another for possible employment.

Conclusion

How successful this technique works for you will be determined by

1) how successful you are in selecting good sources to interview,

2) how well you prepare for the interview, and

3) how much use you make from the information you are given.

I am often called for an information interview, and I know from these experiences that the information I recall during the session is much better than that I would have given on the phone. People generally like to be helpful (especially when there is no tangible cost involved!), and I think you will be pleasantly surprised with the reception you receive. Even if your source is reluctant to have a personal interview, you will probably be given helpful information on the phone.

PART 3:

OTHER RESOURCES

Tool #11: Public Agencies

Tool #12: Privately Funded Organizations

Tool #13: Useful Publications

Tool #11: Public Agencies

Pro's: Free and easy source. Free testing and counseling available. Listings at all levels of experience. Includes jobs available in the public and private sectors.

Con's: Companies tend to shy away from public agencies, since there is limited applicant screening or matching.

Georgia Employment Service

The state-operated employment service has several offices in metro Atlanta and maintains lists of job openings from corporations, the Georgia State Merit System and many federal agencies. In addition, they offer information on the procedure to follow in applying for state and federal government positions.

I recently attended the opening of their new location in north Atlanta and was very impressed with all that they offer. Computers are available for writing or revising you resume (BYOD: bring your own disk). Their computerized job bank is very user friendly and includes listings from all over the Southeast. They offer seminars on every facet of the job search process and have a large amount of free job search literature. Whatever your preconceived ideas of this public agency are, you will be pleasantly surprised with their state-of-the-art equipment and assistance. Incidentially, you will also see several copies of *Atlanta Jobs*, as they use it extensively!

You must go to an office in person (do not mail a resume) and have your Social Security card and valid driver's license to use for identification. Office hours are 9 a.m. - 4:30 p.m., Monday thru Friday. A brief orientation session is required first and is given at several different times during the day at each location; call and ask the times before you go to an office. Here are six metro branches, so pick the one closest to you, although I suggest you go to the North Atlanta office if at all convenient. Call if you need directions.

- North Atlanta/Fulton County: 2943 N. Druid Hills Rd NE (in Toco Hills Shopping Center); (404) 679-5200
- South Atlanta/Fulton County: 2636 Martin Luther King Jr Ave (across from MARTA's Hightower station); 656-6000 (auto phone info)
- DeKalb County: 1275 Clarendon Ave, Avondale Estates, GA; (404) 288-1345
- Cobb County: 2972 Ask Kay SE, Smyrna, GA; (404) 434-3865
- Gwinnett County: 1535 Atkinson Rd, Lawrenceville, GA; (404) 995-6913
- Clayton County: 1193 Forest Pkwy, Lake City, GA; (404) 363-7643

Claimant Assistance Program

The Georgia employment service also offers a specialized job placement program called the Claimant Assistance Program (CAP), which includes a wealth of free information, seminars, and publications on finding employment. I have reviewed the information and generally recommend it highly. In addition, the offices in Cobb and Gwinnett tend to have mostly professional-level claimants, and thus the classes could be very relevant to your job search.

You cannot request to be included in CAP; rather, you are assigned to participate when you file for your unemployment benefits. (Incidentally, you can file at any of the state offices, regardless of the county in which you reside.) There are two criteria:
  (1) you must have been terminated as a result of a lay-off or reduction-in-force, and
  (2) your prior company must have been in Georgia.

Professional Placement Network

The Georgia Department of Labor has offered this service since 1986, but I suspect it is still not as well-known as it should be. The Professional Placement Network (PPN) publishes a monthly newsletter which is circulated to more than 600 active Atlanta employers, and includes resume synopses of 130 job-seekers, divided into job categories (accounting, engineering, advertising, etc.). The newsletter includes only college graduates with at least two years experience, although a few recent grads are sometimes included (3.0 GPA required). The synopses published are assigned a code number for anonymity, and interested employers can contact the PPN to get a full resume, with the approval of the applicant.

This service is becoming more recognized and utilized, and currently the PPN receives requests for more than 350 resumes each month from employers responding to the newsletter. In addition to the newsletter, they maintain a resume file for employers to peruse or call for potential applicants. Their goal is to find employment for ten applicants monthly.

Unfortunately, the newsletter has room for only approximately 130 synopses, although they receive many more than that number of applicants. They screen out the synopses that are poorly written or unqualified, and they look for advanced degrees and other examples of over-achievement. (All resumes received are kept in the resume file, however.) Thus, the quality of your synopsis is important.

To obtain an application form, call or write
Mr. Clancy W. Murphy,
Georgia Department of Labor
2943 N. Druid Hills Road NE
Atlanta, GA 30329.
(404) 679-5200

Veterans' Placement Unit

Federal law mandates that each state must have a special job assistance program for veterans. Here in Georgia, each state employment office has at least one veteran (usually a disabled veteran) on staff responsible for administering this program.

If you are a veteran and wish to participate in this service, you must visit one of the many state employment offices (no appointment necessary) and complete an veteran's application form. Then you will be assigned to a job counselor, who will offer job-search advice, make job development phone calls in your behalf, and attempt to arrange employment interviews. This group also conducts monthly job-related seminars at Fort McPherson.

Georgia State University

The state-supported colleges and universities of Georgia have Career Placement Departments that are open to the public, with certain restrictions. Atlanta's largest university, Georgia State University, maintains an extensive computerized file of applicants that is available to interested employers. Although most of these applicants are recent grads, I am told that they also receive calls almost daily from prospective employers seeking experienced personnel.

If you are enrolled at Georgia State or if you are an alumnus(a), call 651-2380 to be included in their placement services. If you are neither, then you must have a letter from your college, stating job placement reciprocity. Send that letter, your resume and a cover letter requesting that a "Placement File" be opened for you in a certain field (accounting, sales, engineering, etc.). Once you are approved, usually within three days, you are entered into their computer, to be notified of positions available in your field. Further, your resume will be kept on file for prospective employers to peruse. Send the required information to
Mr. Ben Upchurch, Director of Placement
Georgia State University, University Plaza
Atlanta, GA 30303.
Or for more information, call (404) 651-3617.

Tool #11: Privately Funded Organizations[1]

Pro's: Specialized help for specific target groups. Will more closely empathize with your problems. Often acts as non-profit personnel agency, arranging interviews, counseling, etc.

Con's: Often must be "minority" group member. Companies tend to shy away from non-selective referrals.

Atlanta has several privately funded groups that offer many forms of job assistance to their specific constituency. I have included nine here, and I suspect there may be more.

Atlanta Urban League

The Atlanta Urban League sponsors a free service called the "Employment Referral Program," which operates as a sort of non-profit training center and personnel agency. They place up to 500 applicants annually in Atlanta, from hourly personnel to recent college grads to top-level executives. Although the service is open for all, 98% of their applicants are African-American.

The Urban League requires all applicants to come to their offices for a personal interview and evaluation with one of their counselors before they will refer you to companies. They also offer assistance on the standardized tests that many companies administer for new hires.

For more information and to arrange an interview, contact Martin Cook, Director of the Employment Referral Program. If possible, call rather than write.
>   100 Edgewood Avenue
>   Suite 600
>   Atlanta, GA 30303
>   (404) 659-1150

---

[1] See also "Tool #8: Job Network Groups," discussed earlier in this chapter, and emotional support groups, included at the end of Chapter II.

Jewish Vocational Service

JVS is a non-profit agency offering employment counseling, resume assistance, interview coaching, vocational testing, and other general career help, including video recording and critique of your interviewing skills. There are nominal fees based on one's ability to pay, but I am told that no one is turned away for lack of funds. They maintain a Job Bank of current openings referred to them, and when appropriate, they make direct referrals of applicants to companies and arrange interviews.

Call for an appointment.
1100 Spring Street NE, Suite 700
Atlanta, GA 30309
(404) 876-5872

Employment Resource Center for Mature Workers

Funded by the YWCA of Metropolitan Atlanta with several grants, including the United Way, the ERC is a free service, targeted for applicants age 45 and older, especially women re-entering the job market and others needing job resources and counseling. They sponsor a Job Bank for perusal by job-seekers and employers, workshops and seminars on job-related issues, and referral to employment training resources. In addition, they maintain an on-going dialogue with businesses on the hiring of mid-life and older workers, and they strongly encourage employers to notify them of job vacancies.

The Center is open Monday through Thursday from 10:00 am to 3:00 pm, and you must phone first for an appointment with a coordinator.
957 North Highland Avenue NE
Atlanta, GA 30306
(404) 872-2231

Priority Two

Established in Pittsburgh, this organization now has chapters in several other cities, including Atlanta. It operates as a sort of non-profit outplacement service with a definite Christian perspective. The seven-week program consists of a lecture followed by smaller group workshops on specific issues. The tuition is based on one's ability to pay, up to $50, which includes the workbook and exercises; "scholarships" are available. Meets Wednesday at 6:30 (7:00 in the summer) in room 323 at North Avenue Presbyterian Church, located in Midtown at 607 Peachtree St (the corner of Peachtree Street and North Avenue). For information, call the church office at 875-0431.

Latin American Association

Funded by the United Way, this association offers job assistance to Hispanics and other Spanish bilingual applicants, both for professional and non-professional positions. Primarily, they serve as a referral agency, accepting job openings and referring applicants for employment. In addition, they conduct seminars on the basics of job search, including resume preparation, interviewing techniques, etc. There is no charge for their services.

For more information or to schedule an appointment, contact Patricia Rincon, Employment Director, at
    2581 Piedmont Road NE, Suite C1145
    Atlanta, GA 30324.
    (404) 231-0940; fax 231-1566

Southeast Employment Network

Unlike the other network groups I discussed as "Tool #8," this is not an "applicant-oriented" network. Rather, it is a private group of 80± technical recruiters representing mostly high tech companies, who meet monthly to discuss the personnel needs of their individual companies and to share resumes they have received, as well as any other helpful recruiting information. There is no charge to applicants for this service, or to attend the semi-annual job fairs they sponsor. If your background is in MIS, high-tech engineering or telecommunications, or your objective is computer systems-oriented, or you have a non-technical background but have worked in a technical environment (*e.g.*, human resources for a high tech company), you can have your resume circulated to all 80± member companies simply by mailing one copy to

    Barry Jones
    P O Box 2404, Lilburn, GA 30247
    (404) 921-0751

National Career Networking Group of Georgia

Established as an organization to encourage networking among members, this is a non-profit, fee-based association that offers members weekly information packets containing job openings referred to the association by companies and other members. They do not list openings from newspapers or other publicized sources; rather, they encourage members to pass on information they cannot use but could be helpful to other members. They also offer resume services, career counseling, access to an office, reference materials, phone, fax, computers, and other office equipment.

The one-time membership fee is $395, which can be paid monthly; no one is rejected for financial problems. For more information, call Mike Castardi at (404) 955-9114, or write 2110 Powers Ferry Road, Suite 310, Atlanta, GA 30339.

They also sponsor a free resume bank for corporations to access through computer modem. Mail your resume to the above address and it will be included in their database.

USO of Georgia

For military members and their families, this organization offers free booklets and guides to Georgia job search and job training resources, job search tips, and other career transition information you should know. They also maintain a career resource library and hold career transition seminars. Call (404) 761-8061 and the information will be mailed to you.

A-Crew

A Seniors for Seniors-sponsored organization, the Atlanta Center for the Re-Employment of Experienced Workers is for middle-age and older unemployed white-collar workers. Meets several times weekly at First Presbyterian Church of Atlanta in Midtown (Peachtree St x 16th St). Call 333-5088 for a recording of specifics.

Career Calendar

The Sunday edition of _The Atlanta Journal and Constitution_ includes a column called "Career Calendar," that lists many other privately funded or public job search assistance that is free or at a small cost. This column includes upcoming job fairs, job network groups, low-cost aptitude and intelligence testing offered by local colleges, free resume consultation, and other helpful assistance sponsored by non-profit agencies. "Career Calendar" is located at the beginning of the "Job Guide," which is generally one of the first pages of the classified want-ads.

Tool #12: Useful Resources and Publications

Pro's: Sources smaller, specialized companies for specific industry experience, as well as larger corporations and employers. Most helpful for experienced applicants searching for companies in their industry.

Con's: Moderate expense or travel to a public library, some duplication from other sources.

I am including information on reference materials that you may order, although many are available at public libraries, and some comments regarding each. In contacting the companies that are included in these publications, treat them as a Direct Contact.

Atlanta Chamber of Commerce

Several helpful publications are available from the Atlanta Chamber of Commerce. You can order by phone and charge to Visa or MasterCard. You can also order by mail, but since there may be a postage charge, I suggest you call first. Prices and publication availability are subject to change.

Atlanta Chamber of Commerce
P O Box 1740, Atlanta, GA 30301.
Attn: Public Information Dept.
(404) 586-8403

1) Atlanta City Map - $2.00

2) Atlanta's largest employers, Fortune 500 companies with offices in Atlanta, and Atlanta headquartered firms. $10

3) Manufacturing Directory - Lists more than 1500 manufacturing firms in metro Atlanta, including Standard Industrial Classifications. Good source to locating companies in your manufacturing specialty. $25.00

4) "Atlanta Quick Look" - Includes the Newcomers Guide, Employment Services and Larger Employers publications. Good start if you are not local. No charge.

Multi-national Corporations

If you are interested in foreign companies with facilities in Atlanta, order the *Georgia International Facilities* book. This 125-page book includes information on the 34 countries with Georgia operations, plus the consulates, trade offices and chambers of commerce of each country. Currently there is no charge for this major publication! Order from
Georgia Department of Industry and Trade, Research Division
230 Peachtree Street, P O Box 1776, Atlanta, GA 30301.

Atlanta Multicultural Directory

This is a "must-buy" for all foreign nationals living in Atlanta. Published by the Atlanta Council of International Organizations (ACIO), a non-profit community service organization, it includes a tremendous amount of information relevant to living and working in Atlanta.

Send a $12.00 check made payable to ACIO, your name and address, to
ACIO, Directory Order
P O Box 56076
Atlanta, GA 30343.

National Business Employment Weekly

Published by Dow Jones & Company, who also publishes *The Wall Street Journal*, this periodical contains a wealth of information and should be a part of your job search. Within the 50± pages you will find informative articles on many facets of job hunting and alternative strategies written by professional job search counselors. It also contains hundreds of job openings from *The Wall Street Journal*, mostly for upper-level executives, filed by both companies and executive search firms. Finally, under the heading "Calendar of Events," it lists events and services for job seekers that are either free or of nominal cost.

The *NBEW* is sold at most book stores and newsstands for $3.95, or you can subscribe by calling (800) 562-4868 and charge to a major credit card. If you are relocating to Atlanta from another region, be aware that special editions are published for different sections of the country, and order the appropriate edition.

Book of Lists

The *Atlanta Business Chronicle* produces an annual publication called the *Book of Lists*, which includes the 25 or so largest companies in various categories, and information about their sales, number of employees, major clients, etc. It is interesting reading in general, and it could be helpful to you to locate companies within a specific industry or profession. The current edition lists 45+ categories, including accounting firms, architectural/engineering firms, auto dealerships, banks, travel agencies, ad and PR agencies, computer companies, credit unions, HMO's, hospitals, hotels, law firms, printers, telecommunications companies, real estate firms and agents, plus many more. To order, send $11.95 (includes postage and handling) to

Atlanta Business Chronicle
1801 Peachtree St NE, Suite 150
Atlanta, GA 30309.

Physicians' Desk Reference (PDR)

The primary focus of this weighty book is to provide doctors with detailed information on all prescription drugs. In addition, it lists drug manufacturers, complete with the addresses and phone numbers of their corporate headquarters and regional offices, and even includes the names and contact data for their sales and operations managers. If you are seeking a job in some medical field, either sales or management, the PDR will supply you with names to contact and information on the products marketed by each company. The PDR is available at most public libraries, or if you have a friend who is a doctor or who works in a medical facility, you can probably borrow one.

National Trade and Professional Associations of the U. S.

I made reference to this catalogue in "Tool #9: Professional and Trade Associations." It is available at most public libraries, but you may order it if you wish. Send $48.00 (postpaid) to

Columbia Books, Inc., Publishers
1350 New York Ave NW, Suite 207
Washington, DC 20005-3286.

Georgia Association of Personnel Consultants

The local chapter of the National Association of Personnel Services publishes a directory of their 140 members with contact information and classified by their areas of specialty. Remember, however, that not all Atlanta agencies are members of the association. To order, send a stamped, self-addressed envelope and a check for $6 to

GAPS
P O Box 500386
Atlanta, GA 31150-0386.

Georgia Manufacturers Register

Lists 8,500 Georgia manufacturers, with contact data, sales figures, size, primary executives (including personnel, accounting managers, engineering managers, etc.), import status, brand of computer, and more. You can order a copy for $83, but I suggest you reference the free public library instead.

Manufacturers' News, Inc.
1633 Central Street
Evanston, IL 60201-9729
(708) 864-7000 – To order directory on IBM disk

CHAPTER V

STEP FOUR:

INTERVIEWING TECHNIQUES

CHAPTER V

Step Four: Interviewing Techniques

Congratulations!

The fact that you are being given an interview indicates that you obviously have presented yourself well so far and that the interviewer has at least some interest in you to grant you some of his/her time. You have worked hard to get to this point, but don't let up yet.

Preparation

Remember this quotation:

"The successful job-seeker is the one who is willing to do what the unsuccessful will not: Preparation."

Preparation is important in every part of your job search, and it is absolutely essential to a successful interview. Nervous? That could be because you haven't adequately prepared! Being prepared not only settles the stomach, it impresses the interviewer as well.

Research the company, and when possible, research the job and interviewer. Learn as much about the company as timely possible, but don't feel that you must know more than the interviewer. Here is the basic information to digest:

• Most importantly, know the company's products or services. What do they offer, provide, manufacture, or sell?

• What is their annual growth and how profitable are they?

• What can you find out about their industry in general, including competitors?

• What is their ranking within their industry?

• Research the company's history.

• Try to determine their reputation. Are they considered aggressive? What is their personnel turnover rate? How are they regarded by their customers? This information is subjective and may be difficult to obtain, but if you have a reliable source, it is good information to know.

• Every corporation has its individual "culture," a nebulous term to describe a company's philosophy, attitudes, dress codes, and the image it strives to project. Knowing these factors can direct you with your answers and behavior during the interview.

• Find out as much as you can about the interviewer(s), especially background and previous employment, interviewing techniques, hobbies, interests, etc. If your interview was arranged through an intermediary, that person may be able to relay good insight into the whims of the interviewer(s); good personnel agencies always should have this information.

Researching most of the company data is easy, and there are many sources. The simplest method is to call the company and ask for an annual report, information brochure, or recruiting information to be mailed to you. If the company declines, as many privately-held companies will, or if you are short on time, go to your college placement center or the public library. Some good reference books include *Standard and Poor's, Moody's, Million Dollar Directory, American Corporate Families* and *Thomas Register of American Manufacturers*. All these are readily available on the second floor at the Atlanta-Fulton County Library downtown (Take MARTA to Peachtree Center station; exit Ellis

Street and then West Peachtree escalator), as well as the public libraries in the metro counties.

Networking is also a good source. Ask friends or business contacts if they are familiar with the company; however, keep in mind you may be hearing biased information or rumor, and treat this information accordingly. If you know some of the company's clients, you can carefully and discreetly call them for information.

Anticipate certain questions and be ready with your answers. I recently spoke with a Vice President of Human Resources who told me that for his last job search, he wrote down fifty questions an interviewer might ask. Then he wrote down his answers, and put it aside for a few days. Reading them later, he realized how bad some of his answers really were, and he thought them through again. That took a lot of time – but then too, his thoroughness paid off in a big way!

It is impossible to anticipate every question you might be asked, but knowing what your interviewers are seeking with their questions will help you plan your responses. Of course, you must have the technical expertise required for the position. Excluding that, interviewers look for three primary factors:

1) Clear and certain job focus. You know what job you are currently seeking and how it fits into your career plans.

2) Your life patterns – that is, demonstrated patterns of success, accomplishment, over-achievement, etc., and the opposites.

3) Your ability to "sell yourself" – that is, convincing the interviewer you are the one to hire! In my experiences, more applicants are rejected for failing this, than for any other reason.

The following characteristics are ones most often rated by an interviewer. Read these through several times, and think how they may be asked to you and how you will respond to best "sell yourself."

Intelligence: Conceptual ability, breadth of knowledge, verbal expression, organized thoughts, analytical thought process, logical decision-making.

Decisiveness: Non-ambivalence, willingness to commit self when asked, makes definite choices, lets you know where he/she stands on issues, not tentative.

Energy and Enthusiasm: Animated, spontaneous, fast-paced throughout, positive attitude, optimistic outlook.

Results-orientation: Responses revolve around task accomplishment, gets to the point, emphasizes achievements, provides information relevant to interview objectives, able to give specific instances and examples.

Maturity: Acceptance of responsibility for one's actions, poised, self-confident, appropriately dressed, relaxed, ability to reflect on experiences, understands strengths and weaknesses, clear career goals.

Assertiveness: Responds in a forceful manner, does not ramble, speaks in a convincing tone, persuasive, good at selling self and ideas, good communicator.

Sensitivity: Sincere, friendly, tactful, responsive, not aloof, listens as well as speaks, asks relevant questions.

Openness: Discusses short-comings as well as strengths, is not pre-occupied with saying the right thing, consistent responsiveness regardless of content.

Tough-mindedness: Stands up to interviewer when there is disagreement, discusses persons and events critically, does not allow emotions to cloud perceptions.

The "Stress Interview"

I recently read an article stating that the so-called "stress interview" is becoming popular again. It has been around for as many years as I have been in personnel, but had fallen into disfavor because of its basically negative approach. According to the article, however, in today's stressful business environment, companies would like to put you in a stress situation and then judge how well you can perform. Although I doubt you will encounter this style of interviewing often, you should be prepared in the event you do.

In a stress interview, the interviewer will appear to disagree with nearly everything you say, in order to see how you react. His/her comments, questions, and general body language are geared to lead you astray, to offer you opportunities to make mistakes, and to generally make you uncomfortable. Oftentimes, the interviewer will ask a question, and then after you have given your answer, will sit quietly as though expecting you to continue.

If you sense you are in this type of interview, stick to your guns, and above all, do not begin to contradict yourself or start to ramble in a vain attempt to please the interviewer. In particular, once you have answered a question to your own satisfaction, stop and wait for the interviewer to continue; in my practice, I have had many applicants rejected because they didn't know when to stop talking.

Interviewing Tips

Over the years, interview styles and questions have changed. Many years ago, the vogue questions were "What are your strengths?" and conversely, "What are your weaknesses?" Until recently, "Tell me about yourself" was the technique of choice, and it continues to be very popular with many interviewers. Although you will still encounter those questions, the current fad in interviewing now revolves around open-ended questions asking for specific examples or instances: "Give me an example of how you . . . ."

The following are frequently asked questions that you should anticipate and for which you should have planned an answer:

1) How did you choose your college? Why did you choose your major? What did you intend to do with that degree?

2) Why did you leave your past employers?

3) Pick three adjectives to describe yourself.

4) Give me a specific example of a problem you overcame in your job.

5) What are the qualities of a good manager [salesperson, accountant, engineer, etc.]?

THE MOST FREQUENTLY ASKED INTERVIEW QUESTION IS

"Tell me about yourself."

What will you say?

Your answer should be no more than two minutes, and yet it will set the tenor for the remaining part of the interview. Plan your reply well in advance and rehearse it often. If you wait until you're sitting in front of the interviewer to come up with an answer, you have blown the interview!

Here are some guidelines:
- Be concise, and keep your response to a maximum of two minutes.
- Be upbeat, emphasizing accomplishments and achievements.
- Include data you want to discuss further during the interview.

6) How would you rate your success with your job? Why were you successful?

7) What did you like [or dislike] most about your last job? If you could change anything about your last job, what would it be?

8) Rank these in order of preference: salary, location, nature of the job.

9) Where do you expect to be in your career in five years?

10) Tell me about yourself.

11) What do you consider the major accomplishment(s) or achievements(s) in your life and/or career?

12) Give me an example of an unpopular policy you had to implement and how you did it.

13) Why are you considering a job change?

14) Evaluate your present and past supervisors. (Recent grads may be asked to evaluate their instructors.)

15) Why haven't you found a job after so many months?

16) What interests you about this job?

17) What can you contribute to our organization?

18) How well do you communicate with others? Give me an example of a communications problem you encountered and how you solved it.

19) What constructive criticism have former bosses made to you, and what did you do in response?

20) If you were hiring for this position, what would you look for?

21) Are you interviewing with other companies?

There are many "right" answers to those questions, and undoubtedly, there are just as many wrong ones. Before reading further, decide what your answers would be. If you have access to a tape or video recorder, record your answers now, and then review your performance. After you have read my suggested responses and reviewed your answers, repeat this exercise.

Here are some reasons behind the questions and some suggestions for your consideration:

1) *How did you choose your college? Why did you choose your major? What did you intend to do with that degree?*

Even if you attended the University of Saint Playboy-in-the-Caribbean and majored in underwater basket-weaving, you must present a logical reason for doing so. Companies want to feel that you are and have been in control of your life, and that you made your decisions based on a logical career plan.

2) *Why did you leave your past employers?*

Never say anything derogatory about former employers. Rather, you left your previous employment for more responsibility, a greater challenge and a better career opportunity. If your departure was the result of a reduction-in-force, make that clear, and note that your position was not refilled.

3) *Pick three adjectives to describe yourself.*

This must be the oldest and simplest question of all, but it still amazes me how many applicants are stunned when I ask it. There are other ways of phrasing this question, such as "What are your strong points?" or "How would your best friend (or employer) describe you?"

Remember, this is a business interview, so pick adjectives that are business-oriented. Unless you are pursuing a career in the Scouts, do not be "loyal, thrifty, brave, obedient, etc." Here are some good choices: aggressive, ambitious, assertive, self-motivated, goal-oriented, self-disciplined, persistent, good communicator, competitive, team player, etc. Having chosen your adjectives, now think of specific instances illustrating how you have used those qualities, and be prepared to relate them.

4) *Give me a specific example of a problem you overcame in your job.*

The interviewer is essentially asking you what you have accomplished in your job. Choose an achievement that best illustrates your results-orientation.

5) *What are the qualities of a good manager [salesperson, accountant, engineer, etc.]?*

Obviously, you must exemplify the same qualities of a good whatever, so pick adjectives similar to the ones you chose in question #3. Then be prepared with several good illustrations.

6) *How would you rate your success with your job? Why were you successful?*

Always rate yourself highly, but not perfect. Even if you were fired from your last job, you should rate yourself well. On a scale of one to ten, you should pick eight or nine. Why were you successful? Because you possess the qualities of a good whatever that you identified in questions #3 and #5. Again, be prepared with specific examples.

7) *What did you like [or dislike] most about your last job? If you could change anything about your last job, what would it be?*

Since you knew what your job would be, there must have been something about it that you liked, or why else would you have taken it? Thus, you should have many items about your job that you like and only a few that you dislike, although these dislikes obviously outweigh the positive aspects of your job. Above all, do not blame your displeasure on any person, especially your supervisor; the interviewer will question your version of the conflict. Never make any references to location, personality conflicts, or any answer that would allow the interviewer to conclude that you could be the problem.

Let me stress, however, that you should not suppress your feelings about your present employment. If you are seriously considering a job change, then you must have serious misgivings about your job. You should discuss them tactfully, yet frankly and forcefully, showing that you have given this considerable thought and have concluded that your talents would be best used elsewhere. Your thoughts here must be organized and logical, and expressed well enough to convince the interviewer.

8) *Rank these in order of preference: salary, location, nature of the job.*

This is another easy question, but frequently missed. Always have location last, even if you really don't mean it. Should the location of the job – Atlanta or other – be highly desirable to you, don't mention it during your interview. Companies need to think you are more interested in them and their position than you are in where you are located, and thus, nature of the job should be first, except possibly in the case of commissioned salespersons.

9) *Where do you expect to be in your career in five years?*

This can be tough if you don't know the company's normal career path. Certainly you expect to have been promoted, perhaps more than once. I suggest you answer with a question such as, "I expect to have achieved at least one promotion, but I am not familiar with your company's career path for this position. What should I reasonably expect?" Do not give the impression that you expect too much too soon and might become a disgruntled employee. And don't say you expect to be in the interviewer's position; that weak answer went out years ago!

10) *Tell me about yourself.*

Remember the "30-second resume"? Roll it out again, and keep it upbeat and spontaneous. Now you have time to add some more information, especially accomplishments, but keep it to a maximum of two minutes. You know you will encounter this question during nearly every interview, so you should have prepared and rehearsed it well in advance. There is no excuse for not being prepared for this old question.

11) *What do you consider the major accomplishment(s) or achievement(s) in your life and career?*

Surely you must have thought about this many times, but I am always surprised at how often an applicant falls apart when this is asked. Here is your chance to really pat yourself on the back, and don't be shy!

12) *Give me an example of an unpopular policy you had to implement and how you did it.*

This question was recently asked to one of my applicants applying for a personnel management position, and it could also be asked of many other positions. For example, if you are a salesperson, how do you tell your clients about an expected price increase? How do manufacturing managers explain increased productivity goals? Your answer will reveal much about your intelligence, results-orientation, and sensitivity, so be prepared with a thoughtful answer.

13) *Why are you considering a job change?*

Your answer here will be similar to your response in question #2. Now, however, you will add current considerations such as these:

• you are seeking a more dynamic or aggressive company;

• you want to use your knowledge and experience to transfer into a faster-growing industry (avoid saying a more stable industry, which sounds as if you are running away);

• you are seeking a company that will allow you more personal input into daily operations;

• you are seeking a company that gives more personal responsibility for final results;

• you would like to be better compensated for your contribution (especially good for salespersons);

• you would like to be more challenged than you are in your current position.

Note that these answers are positive in tone (versus, "I am *not* being adequately compensated....," etc.) Again, do not denigrate an employer, past or present.

14) *Evaluate your present and past supervisors. (Recent grads may be asked to evaluate their instructors.)*

Here you are displaying your tough-mindedness and objectivity. Using specific examples, mention a few good and bad points about current or former bosses, and how you might have acted differently. Most of your supervisors were probably good, so be certain that your praise is greater than your fault-finding, lest you be considered too negative or possessing a "bad attitude." Also, do not be too derogatory and never personal – you are commenting on performance as a supervisor, not as a "person."

15) *Why haven't you found a job after so many months?*

The standard reply is this: "Finding a job is easy; finding the right job takes a while longer." Quite likely, this will not satisfy the interviewer, and you may be asked for more details regarding your prolonged job search. Since this is essentially a negative discussion, try to end it as soon as possible, without getting defensive. If you have received job offers that you declined, explain why – with good, logical reasons, of course!

16) *What interests you about this job?*

If you don't have a good answer to this question, your interview is over. Your preparation should have given you at least some information about the job, and you must show how your qualities match the nature of this job.

17) *What can you contribute to our organization?*

If you can't sell yourself now, you never will. From your preparation, you should already know how your background and experience will benefit them, so tell them now – be assertive and lay it on thick! Show how their needs mesh closely with your own qualities, and include several examples.

18) *How well do you communicate with others? Give me an example of a communications problem you encountered and how you solved it.*

Over the years, I have reviewed thousands of job requisition forms, and nearly all have listed good communicative skills as a requirement for the job. Spend some time reflecting on how well you communicate your thoughts and ideas, and have several examples ready that demonstrate your ability to overcome problems communicating with others (superiors, subordinates, peers, clients, etc.).

19) *What constructive criticism have former bosses made to you, and what did you do in response?*

In other words, how well do you take criticism? This question is a variation of "What are your weak points?" or "What are your limitations?"

If your answer is that you never have been criticized, then I think you are lying and so will the interviewer! Since we are all imperfect, we all have made mistakes and thus encountered criticism. You must freely and openly admit your shortcomings (but not too many and not too severe!) and give specific examples of what you have done to overcome them.

20) *If you were hiring for this position, what would you look for?*

This is too easy. Describe yourself, using a variation of the adjectives you used in questions #3 and #6.

21) *Are you interviewing with other companies?*

Suppress the urge to answer, "None of your business," even though that indeed is the case. Reply something like this: "Yes, and it is very important that I choose a position that I will both enjoy and find challenging, as well as a company where I feel comfortable and can establish my career. I would like this job search to be my last. I feel that what ABC Company has to offer is exactly what I am seeking, and I would like to be a part of your organization."

Some interviewers may ask for what positions or with what companies you are interviewing, to determine if you have established a solid job focus. Politely decline to reveal the name of any company, but you can reveal other positions for which you are interviewing, being certain that these positions are similar to the one for which you are being interviewed and thereby confirm your job focus.

These 21 questions and answers are only a few of the many you might encounter, and I do recommend that you write down as many questions and your answers as you can. Then rehearse your answers aloud, perhaps to a friend for criticism.

Relocation

In addition to the above questions, you will undoubtedly be asked about your availability for relocation. How you handle the following questions can determine the result of your interview:

- Are you available for immediate relocation?

- Will you be open for relocation at a later date?

- Does your spouse also have a career, and will relocation be a problem for him/her?[1]

- Are there any potential problems that could affect your relocation, now or in the future?

These are definitely some of the most important questions you will encounter during the interview. I know I may get redundant here, but I must emphasize the importance of how you handle this series of questions. It is paramount that the interviewer feel that your major concern is the job – its nature, responsibilities, scope and potential. Be careful that you say nothing that will give the interviewer the impression that location is more important, or even equally so. If you say anything that leads the interviewer to conclude that location will be a primary factor in your career, you likely will not be considered further.

Unless the company with whom you are interviewing has operations in only one location, you may be required to move to another locale, either now or later. Since restricting your geographic availability eliminates an infinite number of jobs for which you could be qualified, I strongly urge you to consider any relocation as just another part of the

---

[1]Yes, this question is legal, although it must be carefully presented so it will not suggest sex discrimination. Usually, it will not be asked so straight-forwardly, but the information somehow will be gleaned.

total package, and evaluate it accordingly. If you are happy with your job, you most likely will be happy regardless of the location. Plus, companies need to think you are promotable, which usually involves a transfer, even if you are then assigned in Atlanta. If you are just starting your career, you may want to consider other Sunbelt locations, planning to request a transfer or promotion to Atlanta when one occurs. In fact, if you really like the company and its career path, that plan is a very viable alternative, especially if your company is Atlanta-headquartered.

On the initial, screening interview, companies sometimes decline to reveal the location of their opening, in order to determine your promotability/transferability. I have even had companies describe the position as requiring a relocation, even though it was for Atlanta! Furthermore, even if (or especially if) you know the position for which you are interviewing is in Atlanta, you should state your availability for relocation, so that the company will feel you are promotable.

Consequently, unless there are absolutely no circumstances under which you will consider relocation, I urge you to state that you are totally open for relocation, now as well as later. Should you receive a job offer in a location unacceptable to you, you can simply say no. But you will never have the opportunity to evaluate the whole offer, if your restrictions stop the interview process at the beginning.

Realistically, however, I realize that you may have a logical reason for your relocation restrictions, or even simply that you prefer to remain in Atlanta; after all, that is probably why you bought *ATLANTA JOBS*, and not Cleveland Jobs! From my own personnel experiences, I know that finding applicants who will relocate is perhaps the single greatest problem in job placement, and I suggest that most corporate recruiters would concur.

So if you don't want to relocate, how do you answer these questions? That depends on your reasons and how well you present them, although any reason will be viewed with suspicion.

A few years ago, I secured employment in Atlanta for an applicant whose child was in extensive therapy at Emory University Hospital, and thus he needed to remain here for the near future. That was an understandable reason, and the company wanted him enough to accept this, at least temporarily.

On the other hand, I also have interviewed hundreds, maybe thousands, of applicants (especially recent grads) who simply liked it here, and would not relocate. From a corporate standpoint, that's not a good reason, and again I urge you to reconsider, or at least come up with a better, more acceptable reason.

In between these two extremes are many valid cases for remaining in Atlanta. For example, dual-career families especially can be a potential problem. In this case, tell the interviewer that relocation would be considered, assuming that your spouse could continue his/her career at that locale. In fact, with the rapid increase of two-career families, many companies now offer all sorts of job placement and assistance to relocated spouses, and it would be proper to ask the interviewer if that company has any such programs.

Financial considerations, such as owning real estate here, may seem like a valid reason to you, but from a company's viewpoint, it is merely another roadblock to promotions and transfers. Wanting to be near aging or ailing parents could be acceptable for a short time, but the interviewer will want to know how you plan to handle this situation in the future. If you have still other reasons for wanting to stay in Atlanta, first try to view them from the company's perspective before you explain them to the interviewer.

In summary, you should be as flexible in your inflexibility as possible. Nevertheless, if there are legitimate reasons for your inability to move, let the interviewer know. Realize, however, that he/she may not agree that your reasons are justified for spurning their career opportunity, and so for the last time, I again suggest you carefully consider your stance on this subject. But whatever you decide, decide it *before* the interview, and be prepared with your answer.

Salary Questions[1]

One of the hardest questions to handle during an interview is "What are your salary requirements?" It is difficult to answer for several reasons:

- You may not know the full scope of the position.

---

[1] For a thorough discussion of salary negotiating, see Chapter VII. For now, we will concern ourselves with the interview questions related to salary.

• You are afraid to over-price yourself and miss out on a good career opportunity.

• If you name a figure too low, that may be interpreted as being under qualified.

• You suspect that your past compensation is higher than they have budgeted for this position and you fear being labeled overqualified.

• You certainly do not want to name a figure that may be less than the salary they are prepared to offer.

In short, if you name a figure too high or too low, you may be eliminated from consideration.

When this question is asked on your first, exploring interview, you have good reason for avoiding an answer, especially if you have not yet determined the full responsibilities and duties of the position. In this case, I suggest you say, "I have researched your company and know that you offer fair and competitive salaries. But since I do not yet know the full scope of the position or its potential, I am hesitant to state a figure now. Can we discuss salary later?" If the interviewer persists, I suggest you give a broad salary range (but not too broad!), adding that you will be able to give a more specific figure when you learn more about the position.

However, if your interview has been arranged through a third party (*e.g.*, a personnel agency or employee of the company), you already should know their salary structure. In this case, omit the run-around and simply say what they want to hear.

After you have had one or more interviews, you should be knowledgeable enough to determine what salary to request. By then, you will know what is expected in the position and you may have been given a hint as to what salary they have in mind. Although you must be prepared to name a salary if pressed, I encourage you to allow the company to state a figure first. If the figure is what you had anticipated, say that the salary is in line with your thoughts too. If the figure is higher than you expected, don't salivate, but simply say that the figure is acceptable.

If the salary stated is less than what you feel the position should command or less than you feel you deserve, then be prepared to negotiate, using the guidelines and principles explained in "Chapter VII: Salary Negotiating."

"Why were you fired?"

Even more difficult to handle are questions concerning your dismissal from a prior job, especially your most recent. Short of an absolute lie, avoid any comment that would reveal that to be the case. Say that you left your position to pursue other opportunities (which is true) and that you have letters of recommendation, should your interviewer wish to see them.[1] However, if you were the victim of a corporate reduction-in-force, state that as the cause and then indicate that your position was not refilled.

Nevertheless, if your interviewer knows you were fired or is perceptive enough to conclude that, be prepared with a counter-attack. Recognize that no excuse will be entirely adequate, but attempt to put your dismissal in the most positive light possible.

The best approach is to be open and honest, and go for empathy. We all make mistakes in life and the important thing is to learn from them. How many times have you heard, "Experience is the best teacher"? Reveal the reason for your termination, and then discuss what you have learned from the experience and what you have done to remedy that situation. Since it is unlikely that you can convince the interviewer that you were fired without cause, you can use your understanding of the firing to show that you have grown professionally, improved your skills, and are now a more valuable employee than before. If possible, have letters of recommendation from previous supervisors that indicate you have performed well in the past.

---

1   Regarding letters of recommendation, you should always ask for one whenever you change jobs. On future job interviews, you may need one but not be able to locate previous supervisors, who may have changed jobs or moved. Thus, whenever you leave a job, even summer jobs or internships, obtain these letters and keep them on file for future need.

Personnel departments will never authorize a letter of recommendation, for legal reasons too involved to discuss here. However, you often can obtain one from a supervisor. If you were fired by your most recent manager, ask a former supervisor. If you cannot get anyone within your company to write one, then try clients or some other person with whom you dealt in your job. If you have documentation, such as sales quotas or other data that indicate your success, then you can use that instead of a recommendation.

Personality conflicts are a frequent cause for firing, but I suggest you not blame that, since there are two sides to every issue and the interviewer has no reason to believe your version. Definitely don't imply that for some reason your boss "was out to get you." Instead, consider saying that you had concluded some time ago that your position was no longer challenging and that you were not growing professionally. You had decided to look elsewhere, and your attitude may have reflected that. Then detail your logic in deciding to change jobs. Again, have letters of recommendation to show your success.

Oftentimes, when your company learns that you are actively seeking other employment, you will be terminated immediately. If that was the case, you have an okay excuse available, but you will need to explain why you had decided to leave your employer.

If there was some other reason for your dismissal and you want to discuss it, be certain you have sufficient documentation to support your case.

If you were terminated for immorality or dishonesty, you are in deep trouble, and no excuse is acceptable. Admit your mistake and explain what you have done to overcome it or compensate for it.

Have questions of your own.

Either during and/or at the end of your interview, you must have several pertinent, well-conceived questions to ask. If you don't, the interviewer will think you disinterested or unintelligent; surely everything was not explained thoroughly!

There are some questions you can plan in advance to ask, but you also need to have some spontaneous questions that show you have listened and comprehended what the interviewer has said. Choose questions that show interest in the job, company and career path. Although it is important to ask questions, it is more important to ask *good* questions! And make them flow logically and spontaneously, and not sound rehearsed or "canned."

Here are some suggestions, and you will want to add more:

1) What are the projections for the growth of your company and its industry?

2) What is a reasonable career path for me to expect?

3) Why is the position open?

4) What characteristics seem to be present in your most successful employees?

5) Why has your company been so successful?

6) What problems has the company encountered in the manufacturing process [or sales, accounting, engineering, etc.]?

7) What do you want done differently by the next person to fill this job?

Unless specifically asked, here are some topics you should not discuss on your first interview:

1) Salary and benefits. Again, you should seem more interested in the job and potential with the company, than you are in immediate compensation.

2) Location, unless you can work it into the conversation without giving the impression that location is of primary importance.

3) How soon to the first promotion or salary review. Although the interviewer undoubtedly will be evaluating your long-term potential, you must not seem overly concerned with the next step. Rather stress how well you can accomplish the job for which you are interviewing.

Preparation is undoubtedly the most important factor in interviewing, but there are other subjects you should consider. Many of these are "givens," but let's go over them anyway.

1) **Proper dress**: Always dress conservatively and traditionally. Pay attention to details such as polished shoes, clean fingernails, limited cologne, etc. Do not wear anything distracting, such as tinted glasses or flashy jewelry. There is no excuse for failing an interview because you were inappropriately attired.

2) **Punctuality**: Always arrive a few minutes early, but never more than ten minutes. If you are not familiar with the area where

INTERVIEW CHECK LIST

Have you . . .

√ Researched the company and the position?

√ Rehearsed probable questions and your answers?

√ Prepared your questions?

√ Checked your attire?

√ Packed your resume, business cards, etc.?

√ Determined the location of the interview?

the interview is to take place, make a practice trip the day or night before. As with proper dress, there is no excuse for failing the interview because you were late.

3) **Body language**: Sit up straight in the chair and do not slouch. Gesticulate some, but don't get carried away. Be appropriately animated and seem genuinely interested. Project a positive, optimistic mien.

4) **First impression**: Strive to make an excellent first impression. From my own perspective and from my discussion with other interviewers, a truism to remember is that 90% of the interview occurs in the first minute! Offer a firm, dry handshake, and do not sit until told to do so. Be poised, and with an air of self-confidence. Thank the interviewer for seeing you, and then wait for the session to begin.

5) **Ending the interview**: When you sense the interview is over, again thank the interviewer for his/her time and consideration, and shake hands as you leave. If you have not already been informed of their selection process, now is the time to ask. How many additional interviews will be required, and with whom? Ask when you can expect to hear from them, should you be selected for the position.

6) **Thank-you note**: As soon after the interview as possible, send the interviewer a short note expressing your interest and again thanking him/her. Refer to "Chapter VIII: Correspondence" for more information on this subject.

And finally, consider these few admonitions:

1) Never chew gum and do not smoke, even if offered. If having a luncheon or dinner interview, do not drink alcohol.

2) Never use profanity. Over the years, I have been amazed at the number of applicants who were rejected because of this. Even the mildest "four-letter word" could be offensive to the interviewer or may be interpreted as a lack of sensitivity on your part.

3) Never "bad-mouth" former employers or teachers. Present a positive attitude and avoid making any negative statements.

4) Don't make excuses for failures or mistakes. Avoid even mentioning them at all, but if you must, present them as positive learning experiences from which you gained much insight and knowledge.

5) Be careful not to make statements that interviewers might view as "red flags." Try to imagine yourself on the other side of the desk, listening to your answers. Are you saying things that seem to disturb the interviewer? For example, I recently spoke with a former school teacher who was telling potential employers that she resigned from teaching on the advice of her psychiatrist! Almost a year later, she couldn't understand why she hadn't found a job.

Evaluate your interview. Immediately after each interview, sit down with pen and paper, and think through the interview and your performance. Record specific questions you were asked and what a better answer from you might have been. List things you might have done better and how. What did you do well? What did you say that the interviewer seemed to like? Dislike? What have you learned from the interview that will be helpful in future interviews? *This critical evaluation is extremely important; don't skip over it!*

Conclusion

Interviewing – and interviewing well – is a job in itself, and the more you do it, the better you will become. I mentioned earlier practicing with a friend, and I suggest it again. Although some interviewers may not appreciate this, I also suggest that you accept one or two interviews in which you have little interest, just for the interviewing experience.

During the past twenty years, I have interviewed thousands of applicants and overseen the interviews of countless others. In addition, I have discussed interviewing techniques with numerous corporate recruiters and compiled their thoughts also. Thus, the information I have relayed here is from personal knowledge and experience. I guarantee that if you follow my suggestions, you will have the best possible interview.

CHAPTER VI

STEP FIVE:

FOLLOW THROUGH

CHAPTER VI

Step Five: Follow Through

Pat yourself on the back; you deserve it! When you reflect on all the work you have done to get to this stage, I'm sure you feel the same.

But don't let up now! There are still a few points to cover, and these are also important in obtaining a job offer.

First of all, a thank-you note is now in order. As soon after the interview as possible, send a short note to express your interest and to thank the interviewer(s) for spending time with you. If you can enclose an item relevant to your discussion, such as a newspaper or magazine article, or can mention some other recent media report, do so. If you are sending more than one note, personalize each with a comment relating to your interview with that person.

Most importantly, keep this note short. You have made a good impression; don't ruin it now with overkill. (See "Chapter VIII: Correspondence" for instructions on writing this note, and to Appendix B for examples.)

If you really want this job and definitely are qualified, then consider this: Are there any individuals (former employers or supervisors, clients, college professors, etc.) who would attest to your abilities? If so, ask one or two of them to call the company and give you a verbal recommendation. Should that person also be regarded highly by your potential employer, this well could be the boost that takes you over the top. Of course, you cannot use this push after every interview or you will wear out your references. Save it for the special ones you truly want.

The Interview Process

Most companies do not extend job offers after the first interview, unless that interview was an all-inclusive interview with several authorities. Generally, companies have a three-interview process, although this can vary widely from company to company. My personal opinion is that any company that can't make a decision within three meetings has a serious decision-making problem! However, there are companies that will drag out the interviewing and hiring process, so don't be upset if you're called for more interviews.

The first interview is a basic screening, usually conducted by a personnel representative, and this sometimes could be simply a phone interview. The second interview is most often with the primary decision-maker(s) or the person to whom the position will report. By the time you are invited back for a third interview, the decision has been made to offer you the job, or almost so. The final interviewer will be a higher authority, perhaps in corporate headquarters or at the location where you will be employed.

Sometimes the second or third interview will be a simulated role playing or a sort of on-the-job situation. For example, sales applicants are frequently sent to conduct sales calls with a company sales representative. This allows the applicant to better understand the nature of the job and the company's salesperson to relay his/her impressions of the applicant to the hiring authorities.

My reason for explaining the standard procedure is this: If you anticipate that you will be called for another interview, you must do additional research on the company before that next interview. The company will expect that if you are sincerely interested in the position, you will have done something more to learn more about them and/or their position. For example, if you are interviewing for a job in college textbook sales, you could call on a few college professors and ask about the company's books and reputation. If you are interviewing for a position as Plant Engineer, you could do research on the product they manufacture and the process involved, and have several relevant statements and questions ready to show for your efforts.

I cannot overstress the importance of this additional preparation. In practice, I have had applicants rejected after the second interview because they had not taken the time to investigate the company and position further, and thus could not display additional knowledge of the company or its products. Do this extra research; it will separate you from other applicants and impress the interviewers.

CHAPTER VII

SALARY NEGOTIATION

CHAPTER VII

Salary Negotiation[1]

How much are you worth?

You have a job offer, or expect one very soon, and you are concerned about the total compensation package – salary and benefits. Is it enough, and what is "enough"? Could you negotiate a better package?

Many job seekers have developed an attitude that salary negotiation is somehow a "dirty business" and they think that companies frown on any suggestion that you may feel that their offer is inadequate or could be enhanced. This simply is not true, and you need to orient yourself to understand that salary negotiation is just another part of the employment process.

Salary negotiation is not a true science, in that there are no hard-and-fast rules that fit every instance. All negotiating, including salary negotiating, involves some "gut feeling." Even acknowledging that some guesswork and being-in-the-right-place-at-the-right-time is involved, however, the key to "naming your salary" is knowledge:

---

[1] How to answer salary-related interview questions, such as "What are your salary requirements?" are discussed in "Chapter V: Interviewing Techniques."

- knowledge of the company's compensation system and its flexibility,

- and knowledge of your ability to perform the job and your value to the company.

Compensation Systems

The first item you need to learn is how the company's compensation plan works. Is it a well-defined system or determined at the whim of the company's owner? During subsequent interviews, but never your first, you can ask questions such as these:

"How is your compensation package determined? Do you have a formal classification system or is it determined on an individual basis?"

"How often do you conduct performance and/or salary reviews?"

Or more to the point, "How are salary, benefits, and promotional opportunities determined with your company?"

Most major corporations, as well as many smaller organizations, utilize a compensation system referred to as a "point-factor system." This means that each job is classified based on several factors, including

1) The requirements needed for the job,

2) The duties and expectations of the job, and

3) The salary range assigned to the position.

These factors will remain constant, regardless of who is in the position. When you are being considered for employment, the interviewer is evaluating you with reference to those three factors, plus one more:

4) How promotable are you? Or, what is your potential with the firm?

Even if the company does not have a formal compensation system, these four factors still will determine your starting compensation, so let's discuss each one.

Requirements: If you have the minimum requirements for the job, you can expect the minimum of the salary range. However, if you have additional talents that could be useful later, you can negotiate.

Duties and expectations: How well can you perform the job now and how much training will you need? If you have previous experience doing the same functions or training related to the position, you have a bargaining tool. If you have experience doing the same functions plus additional duties as well, you have another tool.

Salary range: Note that the salary is a salary *range*, not a specific figure. Companies generally prefer to hire at the middle of the salary range ("mid-range") or lower, and reserve the upper range for salary raises to incumbents. However, if you can demonstrate your ability to perform the full job right away, you may be able to go above mid-range.

Long-range potential: No company is so short-sighted that it plans only for its immediate needs. In fact, I have had many applicants rejected for a position for which they were perfectly qualified, but the company determined that they were "not promotable," *i.e.*, they lacked potential for growth within the company. On the positive side, if the company views you as having the ability to thrive in their culture, they may be willing to pay more now.

Now you must answer the question I posed earlier, "How much are you worth"? Several publications list the salaries of many job classifications, and if you are unsure of the salaries being paid to other workers at your level, you can research the information. The libraries in Atlanta and surrounding counties have these:

- *Occupational Outlook Handbook*
  (Mostly entry level positions)
  Published by US Government Office, Washington, DC

- *The American Almanac of Jobs and Salaries*
  by John W. Wright
  Avon Books, NYC

The US Department of Labor also publishes salary information that is updated every few years. To order by phone and charge to a major credit card, call the Publications Office here in Atlanta at (404) 347-1900 and request the booklet "White Collar Pay - Private Goods Producing Industries."

Since salaries often vary by geographic location, these national figures do not always reflect salaries in the Atlanta area. The Atlanta chapter of the Society for Human Resource Management commissioned a study of local salaries in 1989, which is available to their membership only. However, if you know a personnel manager or even are willing to make a cold-call to one, you can probably obtain the information you need. Other professional associations frequently conduct salary studies for their specific membership, and if you are a member of an association, you can obtain the information from the headquarters office.

In addition, you can network for the basic information. Call someone in a similar position and ask what the usual salary range is for that position. Ask the personnel agency recruiter with whom you are working. College professors in your field are likely to know the current wage.

Learning about comparable salaries for the position is useful, but you still haven't determined *your* value for this specific situation. By the time you receive the offer, you should know all the duties of the job, as well as your potential with the company. Be as objective as possible, and determine what salary you should expect. You should conduct this self-evaluation before your final interview, if possible, so you will be in the position of knowing whether or not to accept the offer. If you are satisfied that the offer is fair, accept it, and confirm a starting date.

But if you feel you are worth more, then let's negotiate!

Your first effort should be simply to get the salary increased. Tactfully, say that you appreciate the offer and are enthusiastic at the prospects of joining their firm. However, you feel you are worth more than their offer and then explain your reasons. For example, describe the success in your previous employment, stressing your accomplishments and achievements. Or point out that you need no additional training for the position and can be a productive employee immediately.

If the company states flatly that the salary is not negotiable, consider some other possibilities:

Creating a new job classification: One method of negotiating a higher compensation is to create a new position, tailor-made for your background and thus not yet firmly classified. For example, if your previous experience included all the duties for which you are being hired, plus you have some additional experience you also can perform now, you can create a new position above the one for which you are being hired.

Indirect compensation: Another area for negotiation is in "indirect compensation," *i.e.*, benefits and other non-salary considerations. For example, the company may offer to pay for additional education and training courses or they may pay for association dues or you may be able to get another week's paid vacation. An increase in expense allowances or offering the use of a company car are other examples.

Sign-on bonus or executive bonus: These bonuses are one-time cash payments, generally paid when you begin employment. They are not included in your annual salary and do not affect future compensation. Their primary use is in overcoming "internal equity," *i.e.*, paying you more than other employees in the same job classification, but they also can be used simply as an inducement to have you accept the position. This form of additional compensation is becoming more popular, but it is generally reserved for upper level positions.

Performance review: During your interviewing, you should have asked how often the company conducts "performance reviews," a critique of your performance and success in the job. These reviews are generally tied to salary increases, and if the company agrees to review you earlier than usual, you can have your salary increased sooner.

If their offer is not negotiable in any way, then you must decide if you feel the job satisfaction, potential, or some other factors are worth the lesser salary. Continue to be polite and upbeat, and leave on a positive note. Thank the interviewer for the offer and then say that you want to discuss it with your spouse or other family member or friend. State that you will give them a decision by the end of the week or some other specific date; don't say "in a few days or so." Having said that you will call by a certain date with your decision, definitely do so.

Conclusion

We have dealt with the question "What are you worth?" Now I want to make a distinction between that question and "What can you get?"

If you are a consummate negotiator, you might be able to receive an offer that exceeds your worth. Don't do it. You must realize that if you somehow are able to negotiate a compensation higher than what you are worth, you are heading for trouble. When the company realizes your limitations, your career there will be dead. If the offer is fair, don't tamper with it. Save your negotiating skills for a later time when you really need them.

Also, to avoid later misunderstanding, request a letter from your new employer outlining your full compensation agreement (including salary, incentive program, expenses, or any other monetary considerations), starting date, and job title or function. This is a reasonable and accepted request, and I require all of my placements to have this letter prior to beginning employment. Most large corporations provide such a letter as a matter of course, but if it has not been mentioned, you should ask for one. Certainly, never resign your current position without it.

CHAPTER VIII

CORRESPONDENCE

**Cover Letter
Broadcast Letter
Thank-You Note
Salary History**

CHAPTER VIII

Correspondence

COVER LETTER

Think back to our discussion of resume preparation. Remember that the purpose of a resume is to get you an interview and that it must be perfect since it is to be the first impression that the company will have of you. The same is true of cover letters, and more:

- It will be read before your resume, and thus it establishes an even earlier impression of you than does your resume.

- Companies realize that you may have had your resume professionally prepared, and thus the cover letter could be a more accurate reflection of you than your resume.

- It serves as an introduction to your resume, an enticement to the reader to peruse your resume.

- It includes information not on your resume, but requested by the company, such as salary history, restrictions, and availability.

- It can zero in on specific experience you have that fits the needs of the company.

- It allows you to emphasize the accomplishments and achievements that illustrate your general qualifications.

It can also highlight information contained in your resume that is important and germane to the job for which you are applying. However, the purpose of the cover letter is *not* to repeat the same information in your resume. That is not necessary, since your cover letter will always be accompanied by your resume. Rather, you should emphasize factors you feel will be important to the reader and will encourage him/her to read your resume and invite you for an interview. Appendix B contains many examples.

Even still, that is a lot of information to include in one document! Unfortunately, the temptation to expound on every facet of your background can sometimes be overwhelming, and I have received cover letters that were even longer than the accompanying resume!

Thus, **Rule #1** in writing a cover letter is this: Keep it brief and to the point. In my discussions with other personnel managers, I find total agreement in that a short, concise cover letter is more effective than a long, detailed one. Recruiters often feel that a long, wordy letter indicates an excessively verbose person. Don't trap yourself by trying to include too much information.

Rule #2: Strive to make your cover letter appear to be a personal, original response. Your resume is somewhat generic in nature, and the cover letter is your opportunity to make it seem relevant to the company and their needs. Thus, do not adopt an obvious form letter, and never use a fill-in-the-blanks form. If you are sending out a large number of resumes and cover letters, using a word processor can be helpful in personalizing a basic form letter.

Another strong suggestion is to find out the name of the individual with whom you are corresponding, and include it on the envelope and in your letter's salutation. I realize that this is not always possible, but personnel managers really notice which applicants took the extra time to learn their name. It may seem like a minor detail to you, but some recruiters feel it is an indication of thoroughness and attention to detail.

On this subject of originality, let me stress the importance of not copying verbatim a cover letter you have read somewhere, not even the ones illustrated here. I assure you that companies will receive many other copies of it, and your chance to appear original and personal will be lost. To illustrate, there is a popular cover letter now circulating around Atlanta (its origin unknown to me), which starts with some mumbo-jumbo about being able to set meaningful goals and objectives. I receive at least ten copies of it each week from applicants, each of whom must think that he/she is the only one using it! I recognize it from the first sentence and don't bother to read the rest of it. Not only did it fail miserably to achieve its objective, but it also created somewhat of a negative first impression.

Type your cover letter on the same paper as your resume, and proof-read it carefully for accuracy and neatness. This is the company's initial impression of you, so make it good.

Format

All cover letters have the same basic format, with some variations to suit a specific purpose. The three sections of a cover letter are Purpose, Qualifications, and Closing. Usually these sections are incorporated into three paragraphs, each representing a section. Refer to Appendix B for examples.

1) *Purpose*: The Purpose section explains why you are contacting the company and for what position(s) you would like to be considered. For example, you are responding to a classified ad, you were referred by someone, or you are making a direct inquiry. One or two sentences should be enough for this.

2) *Qualifications*: Although the Qualifications section will be the longest section, it should highlight only the best of your qualifications, not explain in detail. Stress your accomplishments and achievements, and the specific experience or background that qualifies you for your job objective. This section may be one or two paragraphs, depending on your layout, but it should never be more than eight or ten sentences, preferably less. You are trying to make a strong first impression by emphasizing a few hard-hitting facts. If you dilute this with a lengthy description, you will lose the impact.

3) *Closing*: End your cover letter with a standard closing paragraph of two or three sentences. First, thank the reader for his/her

time and consideration. Then state your availability for an interview and indicate that you plan to call in a few days. Do not say you will call to arrange an interview. Although you want your cover letter to be aggressive and upbeat, that is too aggressive and presumptuous, and some recruiters find it offensive.

Now let's address some specific situations:

Responding to Classified Advertising

In this case, your opening Purpose sentence is simply, "I am enclosing my resume in response to your __(date)__ classified ad for a _____."

Since you have read the ad, you have some knowledge of what the company is seeking. Thus, the objective of your Qualifications section is to show how closely you fit that job description. Refer to the ad, and using your highlighting pen, mark the key factors sought by the company. Then tailor your letter to fit those requirements, using specific references to that ad. You may even use the same words from the ad. One very effective method is to use three or four "bullet sentences" or phrases to emphasize your qualifications that closely match their description.

In addition to the standard information in your closing paragraph, include data not in your resume but requested by the company, such as compensation or availability.

Making a Direct Contact

In the above example, you were responding to a specific opening you knew existed. In making a Direct Contact, you do not have that information, and thus your cover letter will be more open and general.

The Purpose paragraph states that you are writing to inquire about opportunities in your field or job objective. Mention why you chose to contact them (*e.g.*, you read a magazine article about them or you know of their reputation), which makes your letter seem more personal.

The Qualifications section will emphasize a few of your career honors and/or accomplishments. Since you don't know what their needs might be, use this section to show your general patterns of achievement, and don't get too specific.

186

Close your letter with a standard Closing paragraph.

Referral Letters

In between the response to an ad and a blind Direct Contact letter is this situation. Here, a source you developed through networking has referred you to the company.

In your opening paragraph, mention the person or organization that referred you, and for what position(s). This assumes, of course, that you have permission to use that name and that it will be known to the reader.

The content of the Qualifications section will be dictated by the quantity and quality of information you were given, using a variation of the above two formats. For example, if you were told of a specific opening, use the former; if all you know is that there might be some position, use the latter.

Again, use a standard Closing paragraph.

BROADCAST LETTER

Broadcast letters were discussed in Chapter IV as "Tool #1: Mass Mailings." This correspondence is a one-page information letter, combining the best of the cover letter and resume, and is used in place of a resume with cover letter when you are trying to blanket a large number of companies. Examples are in Appendix A.

Your purpose is to present a few hard-hitting facts about your background that will encourage the reader to call you for more information or a complete resume. Thus, you will include only the most important and positive data, emphasizing what you can contribute to the company's "bottom line."

The most important part of your broadcast letter is the first paragraph, which states your most significant achievement, preferable in only one sentence. This strong opening sentence will gain the reader's attention and serve as an enticement to read further.

Remembering that all companies are very "bottom-line" oriented, you want to direct your appeal to what you can offer the reader and the company. What have you accomplished with your previous employers that contributed ultimately to increased profitability? For example, if you have been in manufacturing management did you increase productivity or decrease rejects? If your background is in human resources, did you find new ways to contain benefit costs or reduce employee turnover? Salespersons should emphasize sales increases or new clients. Select a few of these and include them in your second paragraph.

Next, if you have an advanced degree, special training, and/or other outstanding skills, mention them in a short, separate paragraph. If you don't have advanced education, omit this paragraph. Remember, you are trying to impress the reader with your accomplishments and abilities, not your academics.

Conclude your letter with a vigorous statement such as, "Should you be looking for someone who can bring this expertise to your organization, please call me," or "Should your company be in need of a results-oriented, bottom-line manager, please call me."

In writing your broadcast letter, also follow these guidelines:

- Do not include dates, unless these events happened in the past year.

- Do not specify company names, unless they are recognized as industry leaders.

- Bullet statements are more emphatic than ordinary sentences, but don't overuse them or they will lose their effectiveness.

- This letter must never be more than one page and do not include so much information that the reader loses interest.

THANK-YOU NOTE

You may wonder if this correspondence is really necessary. Frankly, I have spoken with many interviewers who said that they attach little or no significance to these notes, and that the notes will not affect their decision. On the other hand, I have spoken with others who feel that this extra detail is indicative of a more thorough person, one who is willing to do more than may be required in order to assure success.

Even those former interviewers usually admit that it could be the feather that tips the scales, when two applicants are so identically qualified. Since you have nothing to lose and much to gain by sending a short note, I recommend you do so. Several examples are included in Appendix B.

Your reasons for sending a thank-you note are

1) to thank the interviewer for time and consideration,

2) to express your interest in the position, and

3) to reinforce the positive impression you created during your interview.

Remember this is a note, not a letter. It should be only a very few sentences, so do not go into details. Assuming you had a good interview, don't ruin it now with verbosity and overkill. If your interview did not convince the interviewer that you are a likely candidate for the position, now is too late. You should, however, re-emphasize in one or two sentences why you fit the position. For an additional, personal touch, you can make reference to a topic you discussed during the interview. If you recently read (or heard) a news article you think might be of interest to the interviewer, you can mention it, or better yet, enclose it in your thank-you note.

Thank-you notes can be handwritten for expediency, although typewritten is best. As always, proofread carefully for accuracy and neatness. As with cover letters, companies may feel this note is a more accurate reflection of you than your resume.

SALARY HISTORY

I recently surveyed *The Atlanta Journal-Constitution* Sunday want ads, and observed that at least 90% of the professional-level, company-sponsored ads requested either a salary history, current salary, or salary required. In addition, numerous search firms also have begun asking that information. Some companies even stated that those resumes accompanied by salary histories would be considered first, or that resumes without a salary history would not be considered at all!

For many reasons, you often would rather not reveal your salary information prior to the interview. If your salary or salary requirements are too high or too low, you may be excluded from a job for which you are qualified and that you really want. Perhaps you are willing to accept a salary cut in order to remain in Atlanta, to gain valuable experience, to associate with a more dynamic company or industry, or to change career directions. But for whatever reason, you would like not to include this requested information – but you must. How?

If you are being asked only for current salary or salary required, you can include that in your cover letter, either in the final paragraph or in a separate paragraph. If salary is not your main motivation, you can add that you are more interested in other factors than compensation. Here are some examples, and others are included in Appendix B.

Thank you for your time and consideration, and I will call you next week to confirm that you have received my resume. My current salary is $45,000, and although I am seeking a comparable salary, I am more interested in long-range potential and opportunity with your company.

As I am seeking to make a career change from sales into manufacturing management, I do not expect to maintain my current salary of $45,000. Rather, I am more interested in developing my new career, using my product knowledge and experience, and thus the career opportunity with your company is my priority.

However, if salary is a primary consideration, make that clear:

Thank you for your time and consideration, and I will call you in a few days to confirm that you have received my resume. My current salary is $55,000, and I am seeking compensation in the $60,000 range.

Salary histories can be handled in one of two ways. If you have been employed for only a few years with the same company and have had no major promotions or salary increases, a simple addition to your cover letter is sufficient:

During my five-year employment with ABC Corporation, I have progressed from a trainee salary of $23,000 to my current base salary of $36,000. In addition, I receive a quarterly incentive

190

bonus, up to 10% of base salary, and a car and expense account are furnished.

If you have had more than one employer or have received several promotions, you may wish to include a separate "Salary History" page. Examples are given in Appendix B.

Whether you include this information in your cover letter or on a separate sheet, keep in mind why companies want this information. The most obvious reason is to ascertain if your salary requirements are within the salary range they are offering, but there are other, more subtle reasons as well.

You may remember in our interviewing discussion that interviewers evaluate your life patterns – that is, demonstrated patterns of success, accomplishment, over-achievement, etc., and the opposites. If your salary history reflects a steady increase in salary, it suggests success with your company(s). If your salary has been decreasing or vacillating, that suggests problems. Also, if your salary is far below your peer group, it will be viewed negatively. Consequently, if you have some oddity in your salary history, you should explain it in one or two positively-worded sentences.

Conclusion

You may have noticed a recurrent theme running throughout this chapter – and for that matter, throughout the entire book. That theme is to keep all of your correspondence concise, to the point, and relevant to your objective. Trust me on this one: company interviewers and other readers really respect the applicant who can sift out the chaff from the wheat. I am not suggesting that you exclude important information in the name of brevity, but that you learn to discern the important from the unimportant, and the most important from the less important. You need only to include the information necessary for the reader to get an accurate, positive assessment of your skills and abilities. Beyond that, you are wasting your words and the reader's time.

CHAPTER IX

"WHAT AM I DOING WRONG?"

CHAPTER IX

"What am I doing wrong?"

If you are following my suggestions so far, you should have all the interviews you can handle. Take care not to tire yourself by planning too many interviews in a short period. Interviews can be stressful, and you should plan to have no more than two on one day. Plus, you need time to research each company before the interview.

In today's slow economy, many applicants are finding their job search has stretched into many months, often through no fault of their own. Keeping a positive attitude in light of mounting bills is difficult, and casting blame on the economy, yourself, or some other factor is not helping either.

If you think you are following my plan but still not finding enough interviews, then you need to conduct some serious evaluations of your job search techniques. Conducting an objective evaluation of yourself may be difficult, and you may need to ask others for help. What you see in the mirror could be entirely different from what someone else may see.

Evaluate your organization. Are your materials organized so that you can refer to them quickly? Are you spending enough time on your job search and is your time well planned? Are you keeping complete records of your activities and are you following through on all you have learned?

Evaluate your resume. Have you discussed your resume with any-one, especially a corporate recruiter? Does your resume emphasize accomplishments and achievements? Would a topical resume format be more effective?

From my experiences, the most common resume mistake is having a resume that is too long or detailed. A two-page resume is the most you need, and one page is definitely preferable. If you have reduced the margins or the size of the type to squeeze your information onto two pages, then you have too much.

Lately I have spoken with a number of job seekers who blamed their resume for a lack of interviews. In some cases they were at least partially correct, but generally speaking, the problem was more in their marketing approach than with the resume. Don't waste time nit-picking your resume, when that time would be better spent on your marketing efforts.

Evaluate your marketing approach. First, reread Chapter IV, and I'll bet you have overlooked some of the tools I have described. Are you attending job network groups; Atlanta is fortunate to have at least a dozen of these, and I highly recommend you attend several? Have you used the free services described in the Public Agencies section? Have you sought out privately funded organizations that offer job assistance to specific constituencies (*e.g.*, blacks, women, Hispanics, Jews, older employees, etc.); I have included many of these services in Chapter IV? Are you attending professional association meetings? Have you conducted "information interviews"? How effective is your "30-second resume"? You may even need to read this text a third or fourth time, in order to catch every suggestion mentioned.

Are you spending enough time cultivating a job network? Recognizing that more job seekers find employment through some form of job networking than all other methods combined, constantly strive to add new contacts to your networking resources.

Evaluate your interviewing techniques. Have you practiced your in-terview with a friend? Have you listed potential questions and your an-swers, and discussed them with someone who will know how to in-terview correctly? Do you objectively evaluate your interview after each one? Have you asked the recruiter at a personnel agency where you are registered to critique your interview? Have you recontacted a company with whom you interviewed to ask their human resources representative for a critique of your interview there? When asking for opinions, stress that you really need an honest, objective answer, and don't become defensive to what you hear.

Videotaping a mock interview could be very helpful in graphically revealing your mistakes, but if that is not possible, you should at least audio-tape your interview for evaluation. Have a friend conduct the interview and test you with questions that you are not expecting.

Evaluate your personal appearance. Individuals often have difficulty judging their own appearance, and family and friends may find this too personal to discuss objectively. I encourage you to ask a non-interested acquaintance or business associate for an unbiased, blunt critique of your over-all appearance, not just your attire. If you have the time and money, there are several listings in the Yellow Pages for "image consultants," but for free advice, you can ask your personnel agent or out-placement counselor. Believe me, companies are very aware of the image you would project as their employee!

Evaluate your product - yourself: Back in Chapter IV, I made the analogy that you are now in a sales/marketing position, with yourself as the product. Just as every company periodically evaluates its product line, you too must objectively appraise your career potential to include the future trends in your industry and your ability to remain competitive in it. In today's rapidly changing world, your industry or specialty may be going the way of the dinosaurs. For example, is your industry growing? Do you have the advanced training or education needed to keep ahead of your peers? Now could be the time to consider a career change or to study the advancements in your field. Also, in choosing which companies to target, lean toward the ones considered to be industry leaders, not the "has-beens."

Evaluate your attitude. I recently read an article suggesting that half of your job search success depends on your attitude and behavior. Are you really trying or have you decided, "What's the use?" Are you projecting an air of desperation? Has your prolonged job search tinged your interviews with bitterness or sarcasm? Keep your interviews upbeat and strive to maintain your self-confidence, even in the face of repeated disappointment.

When your job search has begun to run out of steam, don't panic. Calmly sit down and assess what you have done so far: What has worked best? What has been less successful? Don't be afraid to try new approaches and ideas, especially various forms of job networking.

Energizing Your Marketing Approach

I am often asked what is the most common mistake made by job seekers. Although there are many, probably the worst is a poor marketing approach. Too many applicants conduct a "passive" job search when they should be more "active." Let me illustrate.

Applicants frequently tell me that this is the first time they have had to look for a job themselves, that in the past they received unsolicited calls from companies offering them a job. The implication here is that a job search is somehow beneath them and that they are afraid to get their hands dirty looking for one. I personally don't care if this is their first or tenth job search, but they are embarrassed and uncomfortable with their relative position. This psychological discomfort encourages and allows them to take the easy way out and attempt a "passive job search":

- They call personnel agencies, hoping that these firms will do all the work for them;

- They buy a book with hundreds or thousands of company names and addresses, and then blindly send out as many resumes as they have stamps; or

- They read the want ads and respond to every one that sounds even vaguely close to their background.

And then they sit at home, waiting for the phone to ring with their next glorious job offer. Or they go play tennis, occasionally checking for messages on their answering machine.

True, personnel agencies do find jobs for their applicants; your "resume blizzard" occasionally might locate an opening; and companies obviously will hire from their classified advertising. Nevertheless, remember that fewer than 25% of all job seekers will find their jobs through the total of these three sources combined. If you passively sit waiting by the phone, you still may be sitting there long after your unemployment benefits have expired!

My sarcasm is not meant to further irritate sensitive nerves, but to point out the folly of the "passive job search." You need to be

198

conducting an "active job search," using as many approaches as possible and remaining in control over all the segments in your search:

• Instead of calling all the personnel agencies listed in the Yellow Pages, research which ones will be most helpful to you, using the criteria described in Chapter IV. Then establish a strong working relationship with those few agencies.

• Prudently select the companies to which you send your resume, contacting only those you have reason to think will have recurring needs for your background. I have included in Appendix C the 300+ most active hiring companies in Atlanta and the types of individuals they generally seek. You may need to do additional research as well. Limiting your resume blizzard to those companies will save time and money by not sending your resume to companies who will have no interest. Plus, you will receive fewer rejection letters!

• In responding to classified ads, follow the procedure outlined in Chapter IV, phoning the companies first when possible and then following up on your resume.

Those steps will cover your bases with the "visible job market," but if you stop there you will be eliminating the other 75% of available job openings. Now you should add these to your job search:

• Remembering that more job seekers find employment through some form of job networking than through all other sources combined, establish a job networking campaign. Use professional associations, job network groups, "information interviews," and other sources that you develop. These tools are discussed fully in "Chapter IV: Get That Interview!"

• Volunteer your time to help at associations, not just your professional group, but other non-profit or charity organizations. Volunteering will allow you to display your abilities to a new set of contacts, many of whom may be executives with useful connections. In addition, you will keep your skills current and have a positive outlet for your frustrations.

• Search out your college alumni association, speak with the president, and plan to attend their meetings. You likely will find alumni with backgrounds and degrees similar to yours, and their experiences can be very helpful in your job search. Also, many alumni associations have a job search coordinator to help members and some conduct annual job fairs.

• Use public agencies to locate government jobs, as well as some private sector jobs. List with public job banks, newsletters, and free computer job matching systems.

• Locate privately funded organizations that offer employment assistance for specific minority groups, as well as other special-need groups. Many of these organizations are mentioned in Chapter IV, and you may find others as well.

• Add helpful publications to your data base, to be used for your marketing campaign and for interview preparation. Visit your public library and review the many publications in their career help section.

• Use personnel agencies for more than just company contacts. A knowledgeable personnel recruiter can make valuable suggestions regarding your resume, interviewing techniques, appearance, and more.

No company can exist for long if it passively relies on the whims of others. On the contrary, companies are actively reviewing their marketing techniques at all times and using as many approaches as possible. You too must aggressively market your product – yourself – as much and in as many ways as possible.

Interviewing Faux Pas

During the past twenty years, I have interviewed thousands of applicants and overseen many of their interviews with companies. Here are the major interviewing mistakes I have observed.

• *Failure to prepare.* You must never attempt an interview without prior research and preparation. If you're nervous before an interview, that could be a sign you are not adequately prepared. Being prepared not only settles the stomach, it impresses the interviewer as well!

Your preparation will include three factors:

1) Research the company (and when possible, the interviewer). Call the company and request an annual report, information brochure, or recruiting information to be mailed to you. Visit your local library or the placement department of a local college and review their company

information. Network, by asking friends and business associates what they know of the company.

2) Anticipate certain questions from the interviewer. Write down in advance as many probable questions as you can and decide your answers. Start with the most popular interview question of all, "Tell me about yourself."

3) Plan questions of your own. There are some questions you can plan in advance to ask, but you also need to have some spontaneous questions that show you have listened and comprehended what the interviewer has said. Choose questions that show interest in the job, company, and career path.

• _Lack of focus._ This is especially true of recent grads, but older applicants suffer from this also. If I had a dime for every applicant who has expressed a desire for "personnel" or "public relations," I could retire tomorrow! When I then ask why they want a career in personnel, they all answer, "Because I like people." Believe me, simply "liking people" is no logic for pursuing a career in personnel – which incidentally in now called Human Resources anyway – and no interviewer will accept that answer. Worse still is the reply, "I enjoy entertaining," as a reason for a career in public relations.[1]

If you really do want a career in Human Resources, your answer should be more like this: "I have spoken with a number of human resources professionals to learn more about the field. I think that the skills I possess closely match those that seem to be necessary for success in human resources, and I especially feel that my ability to listen carefully and then analyze what I have heard could be developed as a recruiter. In addition, I am interested in learning more about government regulations concerning compensation and benefit programs, and I have recently attended a seminar sponsored by the International Foundation of Employee Benefit Plans." That answer shows a seriousness and commitment, not just a frivolous afterthought, and your interviewer will be impressed.

In short, your reasons for pursuing a specific career objective must be well-defined and expressed with a clear knowledge of why you

---

[1] In all fairness, I must confess that when I decided to leave teaching and moved to Atlanta to seek a new career, I listed my two career objectives as "personnel" and "public relations." I have learned a lot since then!

expect to be successful in that capacity. In other words, you must show job focus.

• *Unwillingness to relocate.* Unless you are interviewing with a company that has only one location, you must accept the possibility of relocating to another city at some time in your career with them. In fact, unless you say otherwise, companies will expect you to be available for transfers, especially for a promotion. And if you do indicate your unwillingness to relocate, your interview will be dead at that moment!

I strongly urge you to say that you are open for relocation, even if you would rather not, in order to continue the interviewing process. The offer may be so tempting that you will forget your reluctance to move, or the initial assignment could be just where you want to be. Even if the offer is not what you want, you will never have the chance to evaluate it if you cut off the possibility of an offer early in the interviewing process by saying "no" to relocation.

• *Verbosity.* This is my own personal "pet peeve," and I have seen many applicants flunk an interview because they didn't know when to stop talking. If this is a well-developed character trait of yours, there may be little you can do to curb it now. Try objectively to listen to yourself, and if you are taking more than three or four minutes to answer a simple question, you probably are talking too much. Interviewers are much more impressed with a concise answer than a long, detailed one.

• *Profanity.* I am constantly amazed at the number of applicants who use profanity during an interview, and I have had dozens of applicants rejected for this reason. Even the mildest four-letter expletive may be offensive to your interviewer, and it will be viewed as insensitive and immature.

• *Blaming others for your problems at work, especially a supervisor.* Why should the interviewer accept your version of the situation? Never denigrate an employer or supervisor, or complain that you were mistreated. When asked why you are changing jobs, the best answer is that you are seeking a greater challenge and more opportunity for career advancement.

If you were fired, acknowledge your mistake and explain what you have done to overcome the problem. If your termination was the result of a reduction-in-force, stress that your position has not been refilled.

• _Too much emphasis on salary and benefits._ Never bring up the subject of compensation on your first interview with a company, unless you have firmly established your ability to perform the job and have shown strong interest in the company and position. Generally speaking, wait for the interviewer to broach the subject first.

• _Being overly concerned with promotions_, especially the first promotion. Similar to the problem above, don't give the impression that you are more concerned with your first promotion and/or salary review than you are in performing the position for which you are interviewing. This will be interpreted as a concern that you may become bored with the initial assignment or that you feel over-qualified for the job.

The company indeed will be evaluating you as a career employee, including promotions, and that will be a major factor in their decision to hire you or not. Nevertheless, you want to impress on them your ability to perform the job at hand. During the interviewing process, you may ask what their career path usually entails, but avoid asking directly, "How long to the first promotion?"

• _Not showing enthusiasm for the job._ Always appear enthusiastic about the job and the company, until you have decided the position is not right for you. Unless you demonstrate your enthusiasm, the interviewer will assume you are not interested and may offer the position to some other candidate. And if you do want the job, don't hesitate to say so, clearly and emphatically!

• _"Applicants say and do the dumbest things."_ This catch-all category includes blunders such as these:

> • The school teacher who told the company interviewer she was changing careers on the advice of her psychiatrist;

> • The young man who freely acknowledged that he was fired for having an affair with his boss's wife (in fact, he seemed pleased!);

> • The applicant who supplied a potential employer with personal references who gave him terrible recommendations;

> • The recent grad who told interviewers he wanted a job for a year or two, until he decided to begin graduate school.

203

Every personnel recruiter has a list of these jewels, and we often enjoy sitting around and exchanging laughs over them. Maybe one day I will write a book about them, and also include some of the funniest resumes I have received. You wouldn't believe some of the resumes job applicants send out – ah, but that must wait for another day!

You too may be saying something absurd without realizing it. When evaluating your interviewing techniques, try to imagine yourself on the other side of the desk, listening to your answers. In your analysis of each interview, observe which answers seemed to disturb the interviewer.

Conclusion

This covers most of the mistakes you may be committing, but now it is up to you to make corrections. In your planning, allot time for frequent evaluations and analyses of your job search methods, and how you can improve on them. Use as many approaches as you can, and be open to suggestions for still more.

You probably have heard the truism, "Finding a job is a job in itself." Now you understand what that means.

CHAPTER   X

CONCLUSION

CHAPTER X

CONCLUSION

I am often asked for a final word of advice to job seekers, and I generally reply _persistence_. Persistence takes many forms:

• If you have decided that after much thought and logical reasoning, you want a specific job or a specific company and you think you are qualified, don't take "no" for a final answer. Keep trying, using as many techniques as you can for gaining an interview and evaluation, and you may have your wish. I have witnessed many surprises over the years, so be persistent!

• Probably the hardest part of conducting a job search is keeping your spirits up, especially when you have just received a mail box full of rejection letters. Remember "Persistence," say it aloud several times, put the letters away, and then immediately start back to work on your job search.

• As I have said many, many times, networking may be the most time consuming marketing tool, but it also yields the best results. Even though you may be tired of all the networking meetings, continue to attend them. When you would rather do anything than speak with another potential source, call anyway. You never know when the next encounter may be **the** one.

Accepting New Employment

YES! All the organization, preparation, and work has paid off! But before accepting a job offer, evaluate it thoroughly.

If you already have decided to accept or reject the offer, you certainly can say so when the offer is extended. If you have not, however, don't feel pressured into making a decision on the spot. Rather, you should thank the person for the offer, express how highly you value the company and position, and then state that you will give them your decision on a specific date, usually less than a week. Do not say "in a few days," but specify exactly when.

Don't be frightened into accepting the first offer you receive, but don't reject it just because it is the first offer and you wonder what else is available. Sit down with pen and paper and objectively decide if it is best for you. Draw a line down the center of the paper and label one side "pro's" and the other, "con's." Here are some factors to consider, and you may have other priorities as well:
• Salary (Review "Chapter VII: Salary Negotiation," if necessary.)
• Location
• Job responsibilities
• Potential with the company
• Experience to be gained
• Company reputation
• Most importantly, how does this position fit in with your career plans, immediate and long-term? How will it look on your next resume?

Dealing with rejection

Life indeed would be nice if you received an interview from every company you contact and a job offer from every interview. Unfortunately, that is just not reality.

In my discussions with job seekers, I have found that dealing with rejection is a very common problem. Although I am not a psychologist, I do have some observations on the matter, and I can offer some suggestions on coping with it, and even using it to your advantage.

Let's say that you contacted 25 companies, got 23 "no interests," and two interviews. (Actually that's really good. Don't be surprised if it takes 100 calls!) The first interview was so-so, but you felt that the second interview went extremely well, and thus you excitedly are planning to do more research. Then you receive a rejection letter in the mail. Or worse yet, you never hear from them again, and they refuse to return your phone calls. How do you handle it?

All those personalized cover letters, all those phone calls, all that research – none of it paid off! But did it?

Well, for one thing, there are 25 fewer companies for you to contact! Your research taught you where to find company information, and you gained knowledge on an industry.

Better still, there is one more item you may be overlooking: feedback from the interviewer. Once you know you didn't get the job, call the interviewer and very politely inquire why. Were you not qualified or did you present yourself poorly? Does he/she have any suggestions for you? If the interviewer will be honest with you, this information alone is worth all of your efforts.

Occasionally applicants call me back and want to know why I will not refer them to a certain job opening or why they were turned down for a position for which they had interviewed. When I try to explain, they become defensive and argumentative, and so instead of giving them good feedback and advice, I just shut down and try to end the conversation as quickly as possible.

Those applicants missed out on some excellent constructive criticism that could have been very helpful in future interviews. Thus, when asking for this constructive criticism, do not be argumentative, but leave with a positive impression. Stress your need for good critiques and advice. Also, there may be another job opening later that you will fit.

Nevertheless, you must accept the fact that you will hear "No" far more often than you will "Yes." That's life, and we simply learn to expect it and deal with it. During your career search, you will speak with many people – companies, agencies, network sources, *et al.* – but unfortunately, only a few will be able to assist you. Surely they would if they could, and they harbor no personal ill will toward you.

Anticipate the problems and rejections you will undoubtedly encounter, and learn to face them with a positive attitude. When needed, call on your emotional support system for a lift. In addition, allot time to work on developing and maintaining your self-confidence and a strong self-image. Then begin each day with the enthusiasm needed to start over at Step One, if necessary. After all, tomorrow is another day!

Beyond rejection

If you have correctly followed the steps in the CAREER SEARCH SYSTEM, you should be receiving interviews and offers. If you are not, then I suggest that you may not have assessed realistically your wants or abilities, and you are interviewing for positions that are not available or that are beyond your grasp.

Perhaps you should consult an industrial psychologist or career counselor to gain insight into your capabilities. Consider taking courses or re-training for one of the "hot" fields of the '90's, such as the environment, health care, or computer science.

The System works! I know it does, because I have seen it in action countless times. Follow it through and you will have a most successful job search.

Best wishes!

FINAL SUGGESTION

After you have accepted new employment, send a thank-you letter to all the people who helped you or even tried to help, letting them know of your new assignment and new responsibilities. You may need their help again in the future, plus they may alert you to other opportunities later.

APPENDIX

APPENDIX A:

SAMPLE RESUMES, REFERENCE PAGES, and BUSINESS CARDS

The following resumes all conform to the CAREER SEARCH SYSTEM principles of the "Power Resume":
- All emphasize accomplishments and achievements when possible.
- They are all very positive in tone and include no negative factors.
- They are neat, accurate and to the point.
- Most are one page, or two pages maximum.
- All were typed with at least an electronic typewriter and letter-quality printer. Most were formatted using a word processor and printed with a laser printer.

I have included examples of several different backgrounds (accountant, engineer, sales rep, etc.), formats (functional/chronological and topical) and various lay-outs. There are also resumes for a career change (named "Tanner" and "Lindsey"), re-entering the workforce ("Rose"), and one illustrating combining jobs ("Smith"). In addition, you will find good examples of the use of "Objective" and/or "Summary" (or sometimes "Qualifications"), the inclusion and omission of "Personal," and various methods of describing your education.

The sample business cards are neat, informative and uncluttered. They do not attempt to be a condensed resume.

LLANA S. FRANCO

Temporary address:
348 Bulldog Drive
Athens, GA 30601
(404) 353-7621

Permanent Address:
1234 Azalea Road NW
Atlanta, GA 30327
(404) 262-7890

Summary

Recent college graduate majoring in **International Business and Spanish**. Career objective is employment with a multi-national corporation, preferably with operations in Latin America. Areas of interest include marketing, international banking and finance, and import/export operations.

Education

UNIVERSITY OF GEORGIA, Bachelor of Business Administration, graduation planned for June, 1990. Relevant curriculum has included the following:

- Macro and Micro Economics
- Principles of Accounting I & II
- International Marketing
- Statistics
- Commercial Spanish
- Business Law I & II

Employment

IBM Corporation (Summer Internship, 1989):
Diverse duties giving exposure to the operations of a major multi-national corporation. Worked in both Marketing and Personnel departments, under minimal supervision. Operated IBM 5520 Word Processor.

Elson's Gift Shops, Atlanta International Airport (Summers 1986 - 1988):
Sales Clerk, serving international passengers and using Spanish and Portuguese languages daily.

U S Army Hospital, Fort Benning, GA (Summer 1985):
Medical Clerk, working with wounded Salvadoran military personnel.

Personal

Born January 23, 1968 . . . . . Single, excellent health . . . . . Open for travel and relocation, including international . . . . . Fluent in Spanish and Portuguese . . . . . Interests include international events, reading and art.

References available on request.

EDMOND R. SMITH

1200 Franklin Road, Apt. F-1
Charlotte, NC 28754
(704) 847-1234

Summary

College graduate with double major in Accounting and English, and with more than fifteen years financial experience. Consistently promoted as a result of dependable performance culminating in accurate accomplishments. Seeking position as **Internal Auditor** or **Financial Control Supervisor**. Open for travel and relocation.

Experience

AUDITING:

Western Union Telegraph Co. (12/84 - present)
As *Senior Internal Auditor* and *Supervisor Financial Control*, conducted autonomous audits of all accounting and money order processing functions. Detected and corrected error in audit procedure, resulting in a revenue increase of $272,000 per year. As *Internal Audit Supervisor*, reviewed work papers, prepared audit reports and supervised up to eight staff auditors in performance of all internal audit assignments.

PRIVATE
ACCOUNTING:

Convenient Systems, Inc. and E. L. Lowie & Co. (9/79 - 11/84)
As *Assistant Controller*, supervised eight accountants in the preparation and adjustment of monthly financial statements. Designed and implemented new profit and loss statement format for retail and manufacturing locations. As *Accounting Manager*, supervised accounting staff of six, and insured proper and accurate recording of all daily accounting transactions.

PUBLIC
ACCOUNTING:

A. M. Pullen & Co. (6/76 - 9/79)
As *Senior Accountant,* planned and conducted audit engagements; drafted audit programs; prepared time budgets, financial statements and accountants' reports; and filed federal, state and city tax returns.

Education

University of North Carolina at Greensboro
Accounting major, 1976
Maintained GPA 3.0/4.0

University of North Carolina at Chapel Hill
Bachelor of Arts in English Education, 1973
Financed education through summer employment, student loans and part-time employment during school year.

SUSAN B. SWIFT

3829 Helen Lane
Durham, NC 27702
(919) 282-4837

PROFESSIONAL EXPERIENCE

Professional background has been selling food products to the grocery industry, including twelve years experience as a food manufacturer's representative. Worked with two national manufacturers calling on grocery chains, wholesalers and drug chain accounts, covering the states of Georgia and Florida. Extensive experience with food brokers, headquarters presentations, new item introductions, business reviews, and SAMI and Nelson data.

EMPLOYMENT HISTORY
1987 to present

Wyeth-Ayerst Laboratories, Philadelphia, PA
Sales Manager, Atlanta District
Manage sales, promotions, pricing and plan-o-grams. Full sales responsibility for grocery chains, wholesalers and drug accounts for the sales of infant formula in Georgia and Florida. Sell and coordinate distribution with 51 major accounts with total sales of $6.7M in 1987. Performed under an MBO system for bonuses and pay raises.
Accomplishments:
• 45% sales increase (1989 over 1988)
• 42 new item placements in 1989
• Manage Eckerd Drug Company account
• Manage major food brokerage companies in Georgia and Florida

1985 - 1987

Common Communications, Atlanta, GA
Sales Representative
Calling on large and small business owners, sold communications equipment and systems. Developed clientele through referrals and cold calling.

1977 - 1985

Sunshine Biscuit Company, Atlanta, GA
Account Manager
Supervised and coordinated activities of two major retail chain accounts. Full sales responsibilities, including promotions, business reviews, credits and new item presentations. Also maintained 55 other retail accounts.
Accomplishments:
• 30% sales increase per year for three consecutive years with Kroger account
• 1981 received Salesman of the Year Award for highest division sales

EDUCATION

B. B. A., Georgia State University, Atlanta, GA, 1979.
Self-financed all personal and tuition expenses.

FRANK N. CHRISTOPHER
398 Colony Court
Smyrna, GA 30020
(404) 435-0876

OBJECTIVE	Marketing and sales position with a product- or service-oriented firm, where experience and qualifications can be effectively used. Seeking career opportunity conducive to personal and professional growth.
QUALIFICATIONS	**Background and Scope of Development:** Currently employed as Marketing Representative with Xerox Corporation. Prior experience with IBM Corporation and First Atlanta Bank. Master's Degree and Bachelor's Degree in Business Administration. **Capabilities:** Three years of corporate sales experience has involved such areas as cold calling, prospecting, territory management and extensive sales training.
EXPERIENCE	**XEROX CORPORATION** June 1986 - present *Marketing Representative* • Market entire office product line of computers, typewriters, copiers, facsimile and systems. Activities include developing new accounts and managing established accounts. <u>Accomplishments</u>: Consistently surpass sales quotas and performance goals. **IBM CORPORATION** February 1985 - May 1986 *Marketing Support Intern* • Responsibilities included cold calls, sales and training of IBM equipment for the general sales force. <u>Accomplishments</u>: Achieved highest sales ranking of the year during internship. **FIRST ATLANTA BANK** September 1982 - January 1985 *Financial and Budget Analyst* • Prepared detailed financial data including the assets and liabilities of First Atlanta Bank and holding companies, and presented monthly to senior management.
EDUCATION	Samford University, Birmingham, AL **MASTER OF BUSINESS ADMINISTRATION,** June 1985 **BACHELOR OF SCIENCE** in Marketing, June 1982 <u>Activities</u>: Served as President of Alpha Kappa Psi, business fraternity; Vice-President, Pi Kappa Phi, social fraternity; President, Intrafraternal Council.

LOUIS C. CARTWELL

1234 Apple Lane NW
Columbia, SC 29202
(803) 250-0215

Summary

MBA graduate with five years management experience in United States Army as commissioned officer. Seeking Management Development Program with a major corporation, utilizing well-developed supervisory skills.

Experience

UNITED STATES ARMY
(June 1984 - present)

CAPTAIN, eligible for promotion. Available for employment October 1990. Summary of duties and responsibilities follows:

Maintenance Management: As Company Maintenance Officer, coordinated all scheduled and unscheduled maintenance for organic vehicles, engineer and support equipment from 1985 to date. Managed training of all maintenance personnel and equipment operators to insure cost effective utilization of manpower and material.

General Management: Managed safety program for the 8th Aviation Company in 1986 - 1987. As Safety Officer, identified areas of high accident potential, suggested corrective actions and educated unit personnel in accident proofing techniques. Managed Unit Postal Facility serving eighty men. While Platoon Leader in an aviation unit, motivated and trained up to 25 men in the accomplishment of a wide variety of activities. Served six months as Financial Custodian over funds for 1,000 dependent children.

Aviation: Received private pilot's license in 1984. Completed Army Aviation helicopter training with honors in 1985 and received FAA commercial helicopter certification. Have flown 850 accident-free hours to date flying VIP missions in support of the Division Commanding General and his staff.

Education

MASTER OF SCIENCE in Business Administration with honors, Boston University, 1987. Completed program while working full-time in the Army.

BACHELOR OF BUSINESS ADMINISTRATION in Management, North Georgia College, 1984. Served as President, Student Government Association. Active in Sigma Nu fraternity, distinguished Military Graduate.

Personal

Born November 27, 1963. . . . . 6'0", 170 lb., excellent health. . . . . Married, one child. . . . . Open for travel and relocation. . . . . . Interests include historical reading, tennis, racquetball and physical fitness. . . . . References available on request.

CHARLES G. PULLER

244 Mecklenburg Avenue
Greensboro, NC 28664
(919) 954-1042

Objective

To secure a position in Manufacturing Management, either in production, operations or administration, where education, abilities and experience can be best utilized.

Experience

JOHN H. HARLAND COMPANY, printer of bank stationery and other commercial printing. (1981 - Present)
PRODUCTION MANAGER, Greensboro, NC (1986 - present):
Have profit center responsibility for subsidiary involved in technical printing (forms, stationery, cards and mail order checks) and related direct mail operations. Direct the activities of four Supervisors managing a staff of 40 persons. Oversee inventory/quality control, efficiency, personnel, audit preparation and purchasing. Extensive involvement in overall company efficiency planning.
> *Accomplishments*: Reduced labor costs by 5% per month. Boosted profit margin by 4% (from minus 2% to plus 2% level). Won "Best Quality Division" awards (1987 and 1988). Reduced turnover from over 50% to under 20%.

ASSISTANT PLANT MANAGER, Orlando, FL (1983 - 1986):
Supervised staff of 15 administrative employees in a check printing facility. Directed all daily operations in such areas as personnel management, accounting, safety, audit preparation, billing, customer service, purchasing, security, attitude surveys, customer relations and P&L statements. Served as Sales/Plant Coordinator for 13 Sales Representatives in Colorado, Wyoming, Utah and Montana.
> *Accomplishments*: Heavily involved in planning and implementation of move into new printing facility. Received three "A's" on periodic plant audits. Developed new Employee Training Manual later utilized in three plants. Established procedure that reduced weekly billing errors by over 40%.

PLANT SUPERINTENDENT, Orlando, FL (1981 - 1983):
Directed activities of 50 production employees and five supervisors in a check printing facility. Managed production planning, scheduling, maintenance, quality control, inventory control and cost containment.
> *Accomplishments*: Increased operational efficiency by 12% per year. Improved delivery time from 79% to 93%. Established quality standards for employees, reducing rerun rate from 3.4% to 2.6%.

Education

MASTER OF BUSINESS ADMINISTRATION, concentration in accounting, University of Florida, 1989. GPA 3.8/4.0.

BACHELOR OF SCIENCE in Industrial Management, North Carolina State University, 1980. GPA 3.7/4.0.

References available on request.

SUSAN W. LINDSEY
5849 Bacchus Way
Richmond, Virginia 23226
(804) 355-0912

A results-oriented manager, with more than seven years of achievement in training, development and administration. Proficient in German and French. Available for travel and relocation.

OBJECTIVE
A management position in training and development or product support.

EDUCATION
BOSTON COLLEGE, Chestnut Hill, Massachusetts, 1980
BACHELOR OF ARTS in Education, *magna cum laude*
Dean's List, all semesters
Most Valuable Player, Water Polo, Fall 1976. Varsity Letter in Swimming.

PROFESSIONAL ABILITIES

TRAINING:
- Received special recognition for superior technical training of co-workers in specialized instructional strategies.
- Trained and supervised more than 150 workers in basic skills competence, providing effective corrective and positive feedback.
- Documented detailed policies and procedures to enhance delivery of organizational objectives.
- Effectively analyzed causes of worker performance problems; recommended, implemented and monitored the alternatives.
- Conducted ongoing performance appraisals at regular intervals.
- Motivated and coached workers to improve productivity and to achieve successful performance.

PROGRAM DESIGN:
- Organized, developed, implemented courseware and systems for work management, basics instruction and training development.
- Analyzed job tasks, established measurable objectives, tracked performance and successful completion of assignments.
- Created successful performance feedback systems and established system to monitor and record results.
- Planned and produced audio-visual courseware.
- Organized, planned and conducted educational tours, related to increasing job knowledge and performance.

COMMUNICATION SKILLS:
- Developed and delivered presentations to groups of up to 100 people.
- Counseled, interviewed and negotiated with co-workers, management, public officials and the general public to enhance inter-communication and working relationships.
- Edited reports, researched, composed and distributed written information and materials.

EMPLOYMENT HISTORY

1985 - 1990	Educator, Stuttgart, West Germany Department of Defense Dependent Schools
1980 - 1985	Educator, Richmond City Public School System

BARBARA B. ROSE
1899 Flagstone Road
Providence, RI 02906
(401) 874-7892

CAREER OBJECTIVE

A corporate position utilizing proven skills in organization and management.

SUMMARY OF QUALIFICATIONS

Strengths: More than ten years experience in planning, financing and administering business activities and fund raising events for several non-profit organizations. Have well-developed skills in
- organizing and streamlining projects,
- managing personnel and delegating responsibility, and
- working within budgets and resources.

Education: University of Florida, Gainesville, FL
Bachelor of Arts in English, 1973
Graduated *cum laude,* GPA 3.63/4.0
Active in student government, sorority (Rush Chairperson and Treasurer) and volunteer civic projects.

EXPERIENCE HISTORY

ATLANTA HUMANE SOCIETY AUXILIARY
Elected as Board Member (1979 - 1989), Assistant Treasurer (1980) and Director (1986 - 1988). Organized and chaired three highly successful fund raisers.
- Originated and implemented new fund raiser ("County Fair") which has become an annual event.
- Was first chairperson to successfully operate Gift Shop at a profit.
- Operated "Casino Party" fund raiser within budget restrictions and exceeded all previous years in gross profits.

ATLANTA CHILDREN'S THEATRE GUILD
Served as Board Member (1978 - 1981), Events chairperson (1978) and Vice-President and Fund Raising Chairperson (1985).
- Investigated and negotiated sites for meetings and luncheons, and was responsible for artwork, printing and mailing invitations.
- Supervised five committees and thirty persons, who were responsible for catering, administration, decorations, transportation and gift shop for Christmas House Fund Raiser. Achieved highest profit to date.
- Established policies and procedures for gift shop, resulting in 50% increase in profit.

FIRST PRESBYTERIAN CHURCH
As Chairman of Christmas Pageant (1990), recruited volunteers, organized and directed participants, and initiated inclusion of other church classes.

REFERENCES AVAILABLE ON REQUEST.

MARGARET H. MARSHALL
77 Smom Court
Kansas City, MO 64198
(816) 395-3790

Objective   Senior manufacturing/engineering management position

Summary   Seven years senior management experience in manufacturing extending from factory operations to multi-facility responsibilities. Achievement in factory modernizations, tightly timed new product introductions and significant capacity increases. Expertise in cost reduction, quality improvement, materials, control, employee relations and strategic planning. Results oriented. MBA from the University of Chicago.

Experience   **SCHWINN BICYCLE COMPANY**, Chicago, Illinois, since 1986

Director of Manufacturing

Responsible for all domestic manufacturing for this leading bicycle manufacturer with plants in Wisconsin and Mississippi. Management responsibilities include materials requirements planning (MRP), capacity planning, staffing and industrial relations, quality assurance (QA), facility maintenance, automation planning, and cost management. Manage a staff of 200 through four direct reports and a budget of approximately $19 million. Report to the Chief Financial Officer.

Results:

• Assessed existing staff, reorganized where necessary and upgraded the professional factory staff.

• Upgraded the manufacturing process, virtually eliminating frame alignment defects, saving $228,000 annually.

• Doubled on-time delivery performance while increasing production volume by 45%.

• Developed a program to use temporary labor to offset cyclical market demands, saving the company $150,000 in labor costs.

• Managed the successful implementation of the manufacturing process for an all new state-of-the-art aluminum bike, the first entirely new (non-steel) bike in Schwinn's history.

• Installed cost control system enabling the organization to better measure factory expenses.

WILSON SPORTING GOODS COMPANY, River Grove, Illinois, 1980 - 1986

Director of Engineering Services

Managed a staff of 28 through four direct reports. Responsible for process automation, facilities engineering, industrial engineering, and operations planning in 13 domestic and foreign factories and four distribution centers. Reported to Senior Vice President, Operations.

Results:

• Established a manufacturing cost reduction program which saved more than $21 million during a five-year period (approximately 3% of the annual manufacturing costs).

• Accomplished a critical $3.7 million tennis ball capacity expansion in concert with the introduction of a blow molded tennis ball "can" and a new specialty product.

• Built a composite tennis racket factory in Kingstown, St. Vincent, and transferred the manufacturing equipment from the US in time to meet demanding production requirements.

• Responsible for $1.7 million of new process equipment and facilities which produced two new golf ball products against a tightly timed introductory schedule.

PROCTER & GAMBLE COMPANY, Cincinnati, Ohio and Jackson, Tennessee, 1971 - 1980

Engineering Manager, Jackson facility, 1978 - 1980

Results:
• Provided design services for automated cookie mix production.

• Accomplished energy conservation projects which reduced utility costs by 11%.

Operations Manager, Jackson facility, 1975 - 1977
Packaging Department Manager, Cincinnati, 1973 - 1975
Deodorizer Department Manager, Cincinnati, 1971 - 1973

Education   MBA, Executive Program, University of Chicago, 1985
BSIE, Georgia Institute of Technology, 1970

Honors: Tau Beta Pi - Engineering Honor Society
Alpha Pi Mu - Industrial Engineering Honor Society

WILLIAM D. BAXTER

231 South Street
Greenwood, SC 29661
(803) 684-2716

EXPERIENCE

ELMHURST CHEMICALS, Spartanburg, SC

Process Engineer (January 1986 - present):
Responsible for directing and controlling a number of distinct chemical processes, including blends and specialty chemicals for the plastics, automotive, and textile industries.

Achievements:
- Implemented a quality program that allows the middle 30% of a product's specifications to be obtained consistently.
- Implemented a statistical process control program on 25 products that has improved quality 15%.
- Aided in research and development of five new fiber finish products.
- Assisted in the design and start-up of a $400,000 capacity expansion for a polyolefin clarifier.
- Implemented a cost reduction program which cut total variable conversion costs by 9.6% for an annual savings of $75,000, with zero capital investment.
- Have completed 400 hours of continuing education in such areas as public speaking; computer training in Autocad, Lotus, and Wordperfect; statistics; Managerial Grid; Organic Chemistry; and CPR.

DEPENDABLE ENVIRONMENTAL SERVICES, INC., Atlanta, GA

Field Analytical Technician (Summers of 1984 and 1985):
Responsible for observation, documentation, and all sampling techniques on asbestos abatement projects, including project leader on major asbestos abatement projects in Memphis, TN and Charleston, SC.

EDUCATION

Bachelor of Science, Chemical Engineering, December, 1985
Georgia Institute of Technology, Atlanta, GA
Earned 75% of education expenses.

Honor Graduate, Secondary School, June 1981
St. Boniface Academy, Scarsdale, NY

Activities and honors:
- American Institute of Chemical Engineers, 1983 - 85
- Elected Board Member of Student Center, 1982 - 85
- Alpha Sigma Delta Phi Honor Society, 1981 - 82

REFERENCES AVAILABLE ON REQUEST.

226

MARK W. TANNER
5547 Roswell Road NE, Apt S-5
Atlanta, GA 30342
(404) 843-5678

Objective

To apply experience gained in management, physical therapy, and training to a corporate environment. Open for travel and relocation.

Experience

MANAGEMENT: More than seven years supervisory experience of up to ten employees. Interview and hire office and support staff. Handle accounting and bookkeeping functions, client liaison and sales/marketing strategies.

TRAINING: Train all clerical and administrative employees. Write and develop training programs for individual and client needs. Conduct lectures, seminars and platform training classes for up to fifty persons, including managers and other trainers. Highly skilled in one-on-one patient care and education.

GENERAL: Past employment has all involved extensive public contact and has required exceptional communicative skills, oral and written, on a variety of levels. Have developed excellent research skills.

Employment

Operations Manager, Goodhealth Fitness Center, Inc. (1987 - present): Hire, train, and supervise office and professional staff for Physical Therapy facility, which combines the benefits of medical expertise with an exercise center. Responsible for clinical aspects of patient care, education, class development, and progress evaluation. Also handle communications with physicians and other consulting professionals.

Prior employment has been as ***Physical Therapist*** for two major health centers, Dekalb General Hospital and Sinecure Health Center, conducting both in-patient and out-patient treatment.

Education

BACHELOR OF SCIENCE in Biology, University of South Carolina, 1980
Graduated *Phi Beta Kappa*

Certificate in Physical Therapy, University of Oklahoma, 1979.

Additional graduate-level courses taken at Georgia State University and Southern Technical Institute in Physical Therapy and Technical Writing.

227

Shaun H. McDonough

3580 Northside Drive NW
Atlanta, GA 30305
(404) 231-0988

Objective

Seeking career in Insurance and Risk Management. Long range career plans include training in several facets of the insurance industry, including Underwriting, Claims Adjusting, Loss Prevention, Risk Management, and other related fields. Immediate employment objective is a trainee position with a major insurance company.

Education

BACHELOR OF BUSINESS ADMINISTRATION in Risk Management and Insurance, University of Georgia, graduation planned for December, 1992.

Will graduate in the top 10% of the Business School.

Honors/activities: Dean's List several times, GPA 3.4/4.0, elected to membership in Beta Gamma Sigma (business honor society), recipient of academic scholarship for excellence in insurance curriculum, member of Collegiate Insurance Society.

Experience

Several years of *retail sales* in family-owned clothing store during high school and college. Employed full-time during first year of college and during summers. Also assisted with formal *bookkeeping* functions, including general ledger entries, accounts payable and receivable, payroll, and financial statements.

Most recently have been employed part-time at local distribution warehouse, in a shipping and receiving position.

Personal

Born November 17, 1970 . . . . . Married, no children . . . . . 5'10", 165 lb., excellent health . . . . . Open for travel and relocation . . . . . Interests and hobbies include physical fitness, reading, and personal investments.

References available on request.

(Sample references page)

SUSAN B. SWIFT
3829 Helen Lane
Durham, NC   27702
(919) 282-4837

REFERENCES

HENRY C. ROBIN (client)
Purchasing Manager
North Carolina Food and Drug Distributors, Inc.
2173 Coventry Lane
Charlotte, NC   28760
(704) 822-9273

HAROLD T. HILL (former employer)
Southeast Region Sales Manager
Sunshine Foods, Inc.
7893 Chattahoochee Avenue SW
Atlanta, GA   30325
(404) 522-9754

BETTY W. REICHTER, CPA (personal)
Eastland, Wright and Morris, CPA's
8384 Holcombe Bridge Road
Chapel Hill, NC   28876
(919) 777-1829 - office
(919) 929-9293 - home

LLANA S. FRANCO

Temporary address:
348 Bulldog Drive
Athens, GA 30601
(404) 353-7621

Permanent Address:
1234 Azalea Road NW
Atlanta, GA 30327
(404) 262-7890

REFERENCES

Steve R. Smithe (summer internship supervisor)
Director of Marketing
IBM Corporation
1 Atlantic Center, Suite 3890
Atlanta, GA 30309
(404) 888-6255

Dr. Nancy M. Ethyl
Associate Professor of Business
University of Georgia
Athens, GA 30601
(404) 567-8238

Nancy T. Chapman (personal)
Director of Human Resources
ABC Corporation
872 Fourth Street
Atlanta, GA 30308
(404) 876-7725 - office
(404) 252-9872 - home

SAMPLE BUSINESS CARDS

GEOFFREY   WILLIAMS
BBA, University of Georgia, 1991
Marketing major, 3.4 GPA
Dean's List, Intramural Sports, Fraternity President
Sales experience

3445 Piedmont Road NE, #R-3
Atlanta, GA 30342
(404) 278-7873

Human   Resources   Generalist

LINDA   B.   ANALTO
Recruiting • Benefits • Employee Relations
12   years   experience

3890 Little Tongue Road, San Antonio, TX   78204
(512)   898-5241

BS/MS, Mechanical Engineering
Seven years manufacturing experience

JAMES P. NELSON
Pepsico   (1989 - 1992)
Proctor & Gamble   (1985 - 1989)

248 Main Street, Milwaukee, WI   78906
(888)   111-1111

SUZANNE HOYETTE, C.P.A.
Accounting and Financial Management
10 years experience
Seeking position as Corporate Controller

231 E. Atlantic Street, South Hill, VA 23970
(804) 447-8746

Communications Specialist
Spanish Bilingual

JOY K. BAER
345 Cloverhill Lane
Decatur, GA 30303
(404) 377-0987

B.A. Journalism, 1981
M.A. Communications, 1985

MARY W. SMILEY
B.B.A., Management, 1987
First Lieutenant, US Army, 1987 - 1991
Materials Management

8943 Roswell Road NE, Roswell, GA 30076
(404) 789-3333

APPENDIX B: CORRESPONDENCE

All job-related correspondence should conform to these two rules:

(1) Keep it brief, relevant, and to the point.

(2) Make it as personal as possible.

The following cover letters and thank-you notes illustrate those principles. In addition, observe that they are very positive in tone, with an emphasis on achievements and accomplishments.

Finally, remember your purpose in writing these correspondences:

- Including a cover letter with your resume is to create a good, strong first impression and thus get your resume read.

- If you include a separate salary history page, your purpose is not only to relay information requested, but also to continue on the positive track created through your cover letter and resume.

- A thank-you note should express your interest in the position and reinforce the positive impression you made during your interview.

Keeping those objectives in mind will help you compose your documents.

(Cover Letter Sample 1)

1234 Pineland Drive NW
Atlanta, GA 30327
September 28, 1989

Procter & Gamble Distributing Company
7890 Tide Road
Butler, GA 30345

Dear Sirs:

In response to your recent advertisement for a distribution management position, I am enclosing my resume. As you will see from my experiences, I am an over-achiever with a demonstrated pattern of success.

In addition to my B.B.A. in Operations Management, which I entirely self-financed, I have five years of distribution-related experience in the areas that you specified in your ad. As a First Lieutenant in the US Army, I supervised more than forty persons in the operation of a large distribution center, including shipping/receiving, warehousing, inventory control and material management. I received outstanding evaluations and Officer Efficiency Reports.

Thank you for your time and consideration, and I look forward to hearing from you soon. I am available for interviews immediately.

Sincerely yours,

Joseph B. Caan
(404) 255-3456

(Cover Letter Sample 2)

876 Sprayberry Lane
Charlotte, NC 28241
November 17, 1989

Mr. Dick Brookson
Human Resources Manager
Union Camp Corporation
4341 Paper Bag Lane
Savannah, GA 31404

Dear Mr. Brookson:

I am enclosing my resume and salary history in response to your recent advertisement for a Marketing Development Manager. I am additionally familiar with Union Camp through Bill Smith, one of your Sales Managers in Savannah, and a former business associate. We worked together on a quality control problem at our company's Miami facility, and he has offered to be one of my references.

I have eight years of highly successful sales and promotion experience in the wood products industry. I have exceeded my weekly sales quotas by 40%, resulting in a total sales increase of 18%. I attribute this success to my strong problem-solving and interpersonal skills, and my ability to develop a close and creditable relationship with my customers.

Thank you for your time and consideration, and I will call you in a few days to confirm that you have received my resume. As your advertisement requested, I have enclosed my salary history. I am available for an interview at your convenience.

Sincerely yours,

Steve Jarvis
(704) 237-8724

(Cover Letter Sample 3)

ANNA K. DEHOFF

1594 Arden Rd NW
Atlanta, GA 30327
(404) 264-8631

February 23, 1991

Ms. Deborah Beagle
ABC Software Development Company
100 Peachtree St NE
Suite 2104
Asheville, NC 28255

Dear Ms. Beagle:

I am a college graduate in Computer Management and have two years programming experience. I am writing to you to inquire if you have present or projected needs in my field, and I have enclosed my resume for your perusal.

During my two years with XYZ Corporation, I have been rated a "5," which is the highest evaluation possible.

Thank you for your time and consideration. I would appreciate the opportunity to meet with you at your earliest convenience and look forward to hearing from you soon.

Sincerely,

Anna K. DeHoff

(Cover Letter Sample 4)

879 Ridge Point Drive
Smyrna, GA 30339
April 7, 1989

Mr. John Thompson, Director of Personnel
Chicken Little Company
456 Corn Street
College Park, GA 30365

Dear Mr. Thompson:

Thank you for your time on the phone today and for the information regarding your current need for an Industrial Engineer. As you requested, I am enclosing my resume for your review.

During my three years with ABC Textiles, I have been responsible for implementing and managing projects very similar to the ones you described to me. A few of my recent assignments include these:
-- Organized and conducted a study to determine and document causes of dye department downtime.
-- Designed, estimated cost and proposed layout for relocation of maintenance shop, resulting in a 20% increase in efficiency.
-- Assisted Safety Department in training employees on the proper use of new machinery, resulting in a decrease of 25% in time lost due to accidents.

Thank you again, and I look forward to hearing from you soon. My current salary is $37,000 annually, and I am available for relocation.

Sincerely yours,

Lynn K. Parsons
(404) 433-4898

(Cover Letter Sample 5)

4011 Roswell Rd NE, #F-6
Atlanta, GA 30342
November 18, 1989

Cartwell Chemical Company
7890 Riviera Parkway
Jacksonville, FL 32306

Dear Sirs:

Under my direction, production planning has been optimized at multiple facilities, including contract manufacturers and overseas facilities.

As you are advertising for an experienced Department Manager, you may be interested in my qualifications:
    -- As Inventory Control Manager, I reduced inventories from $50M to $42M, while improving product availability.
    -- I designed and implemented a material recovery program that saved more than $175,000 annually.
    -- Working with the MIS Department, I installed a new computerized database and operating program, substantially reducing inventory loss.

In addition, I have a Master's degree in management and a Bachelor's degree in chemistry.

Thank you for your time and consideration, and I will call you soon to confirm that you have received my resume. My enclosed salary history reflects consistent salary promotions in all positions held. I am available for interviews at your convenience.

Sincerely yours,

Celia Mosier
(404) 250-1234

(Cover Letter Sample 6)

4488 Springdale Lane
Charlottesville, VA   23932
January 22, 1992

Ms. Shiela DelRag, Region Sales Manager
ABC Laboratories, Inc.
3333 Interstate Parkway
Marietta, GA   30367

Dear Ms DelRag:

I am contacting you at the suggestion of Mike Douglas, the ABC Laboratories Sales Representative who handles our account. I am seeking to make a career change, out of purchasing and into a medical sales position. My resume is enclosed for your perusal.

My five years of experience as a hospital purchasing agent has given me valuable insight into the problems encountered by both your sales force and their clients, and I believe that knowledge will be most helpful in my new career. In addition, I have recently received my Bachelor's degree in marketing, while employed full-time at Carolinas' Medical Center.

I realize that my current salary of $32,000 may be higher than the salary generally offered to entry-level sales representatives, and thus I am flexible in my compensation requirements. My primary concern now is to establish a career in medical sales.

I trust my experience and initiative will be desirable attributes for ABC Laboratories, and I will call you next week to answer any questions you may have. I am available for an interview at your convenience.

Sincerely yours,

John G. Taylor
(704) 896-3748

(Salary History Sample 1)

LAURIE T. ST. JOHN

3345 Peachtree Road NE
Atlanta, GA 30326
(404) 262-7331

SALARY HISTORY

Bruce D. Morgan & Associates, Importers (1981 - Present):

National Sales Manager (1986 - present)
$57,500 salary + commission + bonus

Region Sales Manager (1983 - 1986)
$35,000 salary + commission

Sales Representative (1981 - 1983)
$18,000 salary + commission

All positions included company car and expense account.

Seeking initial total compensation of $75,000. Long range advancement and income incentives are paramount. Will consider lower salary/draw with high commission potential.

Edmond   R.   Smith

1200 Franklin Road NE, Apt. F-1
Charlotte, NC 28754
(404) 847-1234

Salary History

Western Union Telegraph Company (December 1984 - present)

Senior Internal Auditor (4/89 - present)	$ 41,150
Supervisor Financial Control (4/87 - 4/89)	39,600
Regional Staff Manager (11/85 - 4/87)	37,150
Internal Audit Supervisor (12/84 - 11/85)	32,300

E. L. Lowie & Company (December 1981 - November 1984)

Assistant Controller	$26,500

Convenient Systems, Inc. (October 1979 - November 1981)

Divisional Controller (8/77 - 11/78)	$21,000
Accounting Manager (9/76 - 8/77)	15,600

A. M. Pullen & Company (June 1976 - September 1979) $13,500

LURLINE C. HARRIS

231 E. Rock Springs Rd NE
Atlanta, GA 30324
(404) 876-2388

SALARY HISTORY

Synergism Systems (March 1987 - present)

Director of Compensation and Benefits $55,000

Citizens and Southern National Bank (May 1984 - March 1987)
Senior Compensation Analyst $47,000
Compensation Analyst   42,000
Exempt Recruiter   35,000

(Note: Income reduction accepted in order to enter
corporate Human Resources.)

Blinders Personnel Service (July 1981 - May 1984)

Accounting Division Manager $49,000
Senior Recruiter   40,000
Staff Recruiter   18,000

242

(Thank-you Note Sample 1)

231 E. Rock Springs Rd NE
Atlanta, GA 30324
November 18, 1989

Mr. Thomas C. Browder
Hillside Energy and Automation
235 Peachtree St NE
Suite 2330
Atlanta, GA 30303

Dear Mr. Browder,

Thank you and your staff for the time you spent with me today. I very much enjoyed learning more about Hillside Energy and Automation and the new compensation program you are developing. With my five years of compensation and benefits experience, I am certain I can give excellent direction to your program and would greatly enjoy the challenge.

I am enclosing an article from the recent edition of <u>Compensation Today</u>, which describes a compensation program similar to the one we discussed. I thought it might be of interest to you.

Thank you again, and I look forward to hearing from you soon.

Sincerely yours,

Lurline C. Harris
(404) 876-2388

(Thank-you Note Sample 2)

LLANA S. FRANCO

Temporary address:
348 Bulldog Drive
Athens, GA 30601
(404) 353-7621

Permanent Address:
1234 Azalea Road NW
Atlanta, GA 30327
(404) 262-7890

April 21, 1990

Mr. Wynn Patterholm
Wachovia Bank of Georgia
191Peachtree St NE
Suite 1234
Atlanta, GA 30303

Dear Mr. Patterholm,

As a recent college graduate, I realize that although my business experience is indeed limited, my potential is vast! My achievements and accomplishments to date illustrate the pattern of success I am certain I will continue.

Thank you for your interview time today at the University of Georgia's Career Day. I am very interested in Wachovia's Management Development Program, and I feel that I have much to contribute. I look forward to hearing from you soon. After graduation on May 21, I can be contacted at the permanent address above.

Sincerely yours,

Wendy C. Bloom

(Thank-you Note Sample 3)

789 Park Drive NW
Snellville, GA 30098
September 8, 1989

Mr. Charles J. Lamb
Mobil Chemical Company
P O Box 78
Covington, GA 30302

Dear Mr. Lamb,

Thank you for your time and information yesterday, and especially for the tour of your facility. With your state-of-the-art equipment, I can easily understand why Mobil Chemical has been so successful, and I would like the opportunity to contribute to that success.

As I stated during our interview, I have been the top sales representative in my district with Scott Paper Company for the past three years. That achievement illustrates the abilities I also could bring to Mobil.

Thank you for your consideration. I am available for further interviews at your convenience.

Sincerely yours,

Jan Cotton
(404) 928-5673

APPENDIX C:

Detailed Profiles of Selected Companies

The following employers are among the largest hiring companies in Atlanta. These companies were selected primarily based on the large number of salaried (versus hourly) and professional-level employees hired annually, but also for diversity and variety. In developing a direct contact marketing strategy, these are the ones you should contact on your own. Smaller companies that hire only a few employees each year are not a good source to direct contact, unless you have specific experience in their industry. The Career Search System includes other sources to reach those smaller companies.

I believe that I have included here every Atlanta company that hires 25+ professional-level employees each year, but if you encounter one that I omitted, please let me know. One exception to this, however, is that there are certain industries (*e.g.*, fast foods) and specialties (*e.g.*, health care) for which there are nearly infinite needs. I have not tried to include all of those hiring companies, but rather a few of the largest.

The hiring projections included here are for a "normal" year. Atlanta, like the rest of the nation, has been in recession and thus has experienced a slowdown in employment, although our unemployment rate has continued to remain well below the national average. Some of the companies listed are in a hiring freeze as of this writing, but expect hiring to return to normal as the recession subsides.

EXPLANATION OF TERMINOLOGY

This book is primarily for career-oriented, "white-collar" employees, most often with a college degree (although not always or necessarily), and thus the positions I am describing are of that level. I have frequently made use of the terms **"exempt"** and **"non-exempt"** in describing positions, and unless you have worked in a personnel department, you may not be familiar with their meaning. These terms relate to the federal wage and salary laws, and to avoid boring you with a lengthy explanation of a complex system, just remember that generally speaking, most on-going career positions with executive potential are called "exempt" (that is, they are exempt from the federal wage and salary laws), although there are numerous exceptions. For example, banks frequently hire individuals into non-exempt Teller positions, and then promote into exempt positions when one occurs. Other companies like to hire recent college grads in non-exempt positions, in order to learn their business "from the bottom up."

This explanation may seem irrelevant to you now, but since it does affect your time and income, I have noted it in my company descriptions. Also knowing the number of exempt employees at a specific company will give you a general idea of the career potential there.

Another term you may not understand is **"MIS,"** the abbreviation for Management Information Systems, and which has become a generally accepted acronym for data processing and computer positions.

DISCLAIMER

The information contained herein was obtained from company officials and/or published sources, and is believed to be accurate. However, the author and publisher assume no liability for errors or the consequences thereof. Employment figures are generally approximate and can fluctuate. As noted earlier, the current recession has caused hiring projections to vary. I would greatly appreciate information regarding any errors or omissions, and comments about any companies contained here. Send any information to P O Box 52291, Atlanta, GA 30355.

SELECTED COMPANIES

Note: See preceding page for explanation of terms used.

A. BROWN-OLMSTEAD ASSOCIATES

Profile: One of Atlanta's five largest Public Relations firms. Employs 11, 10 exempt. Has few needs annually, but offers 25 internships (8/quarter) for journalism and PR majors and recent grads; these 3-month internships are unsalaried, but offer excellent experience that can lead to an entry-level PR position.

Procedure: Send resume to Office Manager,
127 Peachtree St, Suite 200, Atlanta, GA 30303.
(404) 659-0919

A.D.A.M. SOFTWARE

Profile: Atlanta-based healthcare software systems developer. Employs 80 here with 65 exempt, and expecting an increase. Most hires are for programmers, illustrators, and sales reps, trainee and experienced. Uses Macintosh computers.

Procedure: Send resume to Human Resources Manager,
1899 Powers Ferry Road SE, Marietta, GA 30067.
(404) 980-0888

A & P SUPERMARKETS

Profile: With the recent acquisition of the Georgia unit of Big Star Supermarkets, A&P is now the second largest food chain in Atlanta, with 61 stores here. No formal training for recent grads, and almost all hiring here is for experienced store managers. Accounting and MIS at headquarters in NJ.

Procedure: Send resume to Director of Personnel,
1200 Whitehall St SW, Atlanta, GA 30310.
(404) 758-4544

A T & T COMPANY

Profile: Southern Area Headquarters for long distance services, covering a 18-state territory. All exempt hiring is handled through this office, and they have needs for both recent grads and experienced personnel in sales; engineering (mostly EE, some others); MIS; and MBA. Fewer needs for liberal arts majors than other more specific degrees. Offers a variety of student employment programs for Inroads, co-ops, and interns, mostly in engineering, marketing, and computer science.

Procedure: Send resume to Management Employment,
1200 Peachtree St NE, Promenade Two, Third Floor, Atlanta, GA 30309.
(404) 810-7001; 810-7010 – info line

A T & T NETWORK CABLE SYSTEMS

Profile: Manufacturing facility producing communications cable — wire, copper and fiber optics. Employs 3000, including 1000+ exempt. Hires recent grads in accounting/finance, engineering (all types, especially EE, ME and ChE) and MIS, and experienced personnel in sales only. Offers internships in engineering.

Procedure: Accounting/finance and sales, send resume to Personnel; engineering and MIS, send resume to Technical and Professional Dept.,
2000 Northeast Expressway, Norcross, 30071.
(404) 798-2600

A T & T NETWORK SYSTEMS

Profile: Southern Region Headquarters location, with more than 2300 employees here, with 1500 management-level. Hires many Engineering Technical Associates, who are primarily two-year engineering grads. Four year grads hired are mostly EE and sales representatives.

Procedure: Send resume to Personnel Department,
6701 Roswell Road NE, Atlanta, GA 30328.
(404) 573-4000

A T & T TRIDOM

Profile: High-tech firm that designs, manufactures and monitors VSAT equipment used to provide digital data services via satellite. Employs 260 with 200 exempt. Seldom hires recent grads without VSAT-related experience. Seeks experienced accounting/finance and MIS, plus sales and hardware and software engineers with datacomm and/or circuit design experience.

Procedure: Send resume to Human Resources,
840 Franklin Court, Marietta, 30067.
(404) 426-4261; job line 514-3411

AARON RENTS

Profile: Atlanta-based, largest furniture rental and sales company in US. Corporate office numbers 100±, plus store managers and staff. Seeks recent grads for manager trainees and experienced personnel for corporate offices.

Procedure: Has no central personnel office. Trainees are hired at region office; send resume to District Manager, 1335 Capital Circle, Marietta, GA 30067

(phone: 956-7164). Each headquarters department hires for own needs; send resume to [specify department or function],
3001 North Fulton Drive NE, Atlanta, GA 30305.
(404) 231-0011

ACADEMY LIFE INSURANCE CO.
Profile: Atlanta-based insurance firm that sells life and personal lines to military personnel, employing 150 with 50 exempt. Hires recent grads and experienced exempt into customer service and underwriting. Uses mostly PC's and seeks systems analysts.
Procedure: Send resume to Human Resources Coordinator,
6600 Peachtree-Dunwoody Rd, 600 Embassy Row, Atlanta, GA 30328.
(404) 698-7000

AETNA
Profile: Major full lines insurance provider. Established new claims center in early 1993, employing 240. Most hires will be for experienced claims adjusters.
Procedure: Send resume to Human Resources,
3587 Parkway Lane, Royal Peachtree Corners, Bldg 4
Norcross, GA 30092.
(404) 242-8787

AGENCY FOR TOXIC SUBSTANCES AND DISEASE REGISTRY (ATSDR)
Profile: Employing 350 here, ATSDR is an Atlanta-headquartered public health service agency that works closely with both the Environmental Protection Agency (EPA) and with state and local health officials to ensure public safety from hazardous materials. Hires MIS and scientific specialists including toxicologists, environmental health scientists and engineers, etc.
Procedure: Currently, their hiring is handled by the Centers for Disease Control, and thus the procedure is the same. Call the Job Line and apply as instructed, or call the CDC Employment Information Service and request a copy of announced positions and an application form.,
1600 Clifton Rd NE, Atlanta, GA 30333.
(404) 639-3616; 332-4577 Job Line

AKZO COATINGS, INC.
Profile: Manufacturer and distributor of technical paint and coatings for auto aftermarket. Employs 250 in Atlanta, 175 exempt. Does not hire recent grads, but seeks experienced exempt in accounting/finance, auto aftermarket sales, manufacturing and distribution, engineering (ChE), and MIS (AS 400; netware/pansophic).
Procedure: Send resume to Human Resources,

5555 Spalding Drive, Norcross, GA 30092.
(404) 662-8464

ALLMERICA FINANCIAL
Profile: Atlanta sales and customer service operations, currently employs 250 in Atlanta and expects to expand work force by 200 during the next year as it consolidates and expands. Hires recent finance and insurance grads, and experienced exempt in insurance specialties, finance, and mutual funds.
Procedure: Send resume to personnel,
1455 Lincoln Parkway, Suite 800, Atlanta, GA 30346.
(404) 353-6000

ALLSTATE INSURANCE
Profile: Provides support for the sales staff of this property and casualty insurance company. This office now employs 125, with 70% exempt, and oversees the hiring for two other Atlanta offices employing 200 more. Currently downsizing. Previous hires include these: recent grads with majors in accounting/finance (including MBA's), economics, and other business degrees. Likes liberal arts majors for claims trainees. Also hires sales trainees and underwriting trainees. Hires few experienced exempt, as most positions are filled by promotions.
Procedure: Send resume to Human Resources,
7000 Central Parkway, Suite 700, Atlanta, GA 30328.
(404) 551-0686; 804-4253 HR Dept

ALPHA PRODUCTS
Profile: Atlanta-based manufacturer of plastic cups and other drink containers, employing 250 with 130 exempt. Moved into new facility1/94. Hires recent grads in accounting/finance and management, then promotes up; few needs for experienced exempt. Seeks entry and experienced MIS (Novell).
Procedure: Send resume to personnel,
500 Interstate West Parkway, Lithia Springs, GA 30057.
(404) 351-3003 (will change with move)

ALUMAX, INC.
Profile: Atlanta-based, world's fifth-largest aluminum producer, employing 120 in Atlanta. Hires entry-level accounting and experienced auditors and MIS (IBM).
Procedure: Send resume to personnel,
5655 Peachtree Pkwy, Norcross, GA 30092.
(404) 246-6600

AMERICA'S FAVORITE CHICKEN COMPANY

Profile: Parent company of Church's and Popeye's fried chicken chains, with 1,900 restaurants nationwide, including 50 in Atlanta. Relocated headquarters and test kitchens to Atlanta in 1993, and employs 190 on corporate staff, 180 exempt. Headquarters seldom hires recent grads, and most experienced exempt needs are in marketing, human resources, training, and operations. Accounting and MIS departments in Texas, not Atlanta.

Procedure: For corporate positions, send resume to personnel,
6 Concourse Pkwy, Suite 1700, Atlanta, GA 30328.
(404) 391-9500

AMERICAN CANCER SOCIETY

Profile: National home office of the largest non-profit health organization in the US; also has state and local offices in Atlanta. Employs 325 at home office (150 exempt), plus state and local offices not hired at this office. Rarely hires recent grads, but recruits experienced personnel in accounting/finance, health education, fund raising, information systems, communications (marketing, public relations, creative services) and scientific and medical fields.

Procedure: Send resume to Human Resources,
1599 Clifton Rd NE, Atlanta, 30329.
(404) 320-3333

AMERICAN RED CROSS

Profile: Non-profit emergency assistance and blood bank, employing 780 in Atlanta, including 200 exempt. Seeks recent grads for accounting/finance, nurses, medical technologists and lab technicians. Also seeks about 20 marketing/sales grads each year for community relations positions in donor resources. Experienced exempt are needed in the same areas, plus MIS (HP 3000 and AS 400).

Procedure: Send resume to Director of Human Resources,
1955 Monroe Drive NE, Atlanta, GA 30324.
(404) 881-9800

AMERICAN SECURITY GROUP

Profile: Dutch-owned credit insurance company, US headquarters in Atlanta, employing 735 here with 175 exempt. Hires recent grads and experienced exempt in all areas, including accounting/finance, sales, management, MIS and insurance specialties.

Procedure: Send resume to Human Resources, Employment Specialist,
P O Box 50355, Atlanta, GA 30302.
(404) 261-9000

AMERICAN SOCIETY OF HEATING, REFRIGERATING, AND AIR CONDITIONING ENGINEERS, INC. (ASHRAE)

Profile: Atlanta-based trade association, employing 100 in headquarters, 65 exempt. Most exempt are in communications (e.g., writing and editing), and they hire only experienced. This support office does not hire engineers (see listing in Appendix E: Trade Associations for engineering assistance).

Procedure: Send resume to personnel,
                1791 Tullie Circle NE, Atlanta, GA 30329.
                (404) 636-8400

AMERICAN SOFTWARE USA, INC.

Profile: Atlanta-based corporation that develops, manufactures and markets software for business applications. Employs 650 in Atlanta, 625 exempt, and they continue to increase. Very rarely hires recent grads, but will hire 100+ experienced exempt, nearly all in MIS, including programmer analysts and systems analysts, or sales-related. MIS applicants must have 2+ years experience in software development using IBM hardware; sales applicants should have 5+ years software sales experience.

Procedure: Send resume to Manager of Corporate Recruiting,
                470 East Paces Ferry Rd NE, Atlanta, GA 30305.
                (404) 264-5599; fax 264-5232

AMOCO FABRICS & FIBERS — R & D CENTER

Profile: Research and development center and information services center for manufacturer of high tech fabrics, fibers and yarns used in industrial, commercial and residential applications. Employs 120 total , 60+% exempt. Hires recent grads and experienced engineers (ChE and textiles mostly) and chemists — BS, MS and PhD level — plus MIS (IBM). Offers internships in chemistry, ChE and Textile Engineering.

Procedure: Send resume to Human Resources Department,
                P O Box 43288, Atlanta, GA 30336.
                (404) 941-1711

AMOCO FOAM – TECHNOLOGY CENTER

Profile: R & D center employing 75 with 45 exempt. All hires are for engineers (ChE, ME, IE, and EE), both recent grads and experienced.

Procedure: Send resume to Human Resources,
                2907 Log Cabin Drive, Smyrna, GA 30080.
                (404) 351-5151

AMOCO PERFORMANCE PRODUCTS

Profile: Corporate headquarters for company that produces and markets high temperature polymers, carbon fibers, advanced composites and high performance parts. Applications range from medical and food service equipment to aerospace and automotive needs to sporting goods.

Employs 400 with 300 exempt. Hires recent grads in accounting/finance and engineering (ChE and ME). Seeks experienced exempt in marketing, sales, engineering, analytical chemistry, polymers, and other research personnel.

Procedure: Send resume to Director, Human Resources,
4500 McGinnis Ferry Rd, Alpharetta, GA 30202.
(404) 772-8200

AMREP, INC

Profile: Atlanta-based manufacturer of specialty chemicals, lubricants, and grease products, employing 150 with 25 exempt. Seeks technical personnel (ChE, IE, and chemistry, aerosol experience good) and experienced sales.

Procedure: Send resume to Director of Human Resources,
990 Industrial Park Drive, Marietta, GA 30062.
(404) 422-2071

ANHEUSER-BUSCH

Profile: Brewery employing 400+, 100+ exempt. Hires mostly experienced exempt in accounting and production management or for specialty backgrounds. Has several coop positions.

Procedure: Does not maintain a resume file, so sending a resume may not be productive. Advertises all exempt openings in the Sunday classifieds of The Atlanta Journal and Constitution.,
P O Box 200248, Cartersville, GA 30120.
(404) 386-2000; 387-3765 non-exempt job info line

ARTHRITIS FOUNDATION

Profile: Corporate headquarters for this non-profit organization, providing education and fundraising activities relative to arthritis disease. Employs 125 with 50+% exempt. Hires no recent grads, but experienced exempt positions may become available in accounting, MIS (DEC VAX), fundraising, program coordination, writing and other editorial staff.

Procedure: Send resume to Employment Compensation Specialist,
1314 Spring Street NW, Atlanta, GA 30309.
(404) 872-7100

ARTHUR ANDERSEN & CO./ANDERSEN CONSULTING

Profile: Big Six Certified Public Accounting firm, and largest CPA firm in Atlanta. Has three divisions (audit, tax, and business advisory services) and employs 1300+ total, 70% exempt. Hires 200+ recent grads each year for the three divisions, and seeks accounting/finance, computer science majors and MBA or MAcc degrees. Hires very few experienced accountants, and they must enter the same training program as recent grads. Hires interns during the summer and winter quarters

Procedure: Send resume to Director of Recruiting.,

255

133 Peachtree St NE, 25th Floor, Atlanta, GA 30303.
(404) 658-1776

ATHLETE'S FOOT, THE

Profile: Corporate headquarters for this specialty retailer in athletic footwear. Has 625 stores worldwide, including 275 company-owned (others franchised). Employs 250 at headquarters with 100 exempt. Most grads hired are for Retail Management or occasionally in accounting. Hires 30+ experienced personnel annually in accounting/finance, MIS (AS 400 and PC's), retail operations, buyers and franchise coordinators.

Procedure: Send resume to Human Resources,
1950 Vaughn Road, Kennesaw, GA 30144.
(404) 514-4500

ATLANTA GAS LIGHT COMPANY

Profile: Public gas utility headquartered in Atlanta. Employs 2,000 with 775 exempt (3800 companywide). Hires mostly recent grads in engineering (ME, CE, IE), MIS and accounting. Has co-ops in engineering and computer science.

Procedure: Send resume to Personnel Manager,
P O Box 4569, Atlanta, GA 30302.
(404) 584-4164

ATLANTA JOURNAL-CONSTITUTION

Profile: Largest newspaper in the Southeast, employing 5500 (many of whom are part-time) with 625 exempt. Recent grads are hired in accounting, customer service, and advertising as Account Executives or Sales Support; recent journalism grads need some work experience with a smaller newspaper or internship. Will also seek experienced exempt, in all areas including journalism. In addition, they offer 30 internships, mostly in news journalism.

Procedure: Journalists, reporters, and interns in newsroom, send resume to Managing Editor. For other positions, do not send resume, as Human Resources Dept. no longer accepts unsolicited resumes or walk-in applicants. All available positions are advertised in the Sunday edition of the A J-C and you must respond to a specific opening then.,
72 Marietta St NW, Atlanta, GA 30303.
(404) 526-5151; Job Information Line 526-5092

ATLANTA LIFE INSURANCE CO.

Profile: Corporate headquarters for the largest black stock-owned insurance company in the US, founded in 1905. Markets group health and life insurance in 15 states. Employs 300 in Atlanta, including 165 at headquarters with 55 exempt. Hires only a few recent grads on an as-needed basis in accounting/finance, MIS and actuarial. Hires experienced exempt in accounting/finance, sales and MIS.

Procedure: Send resume to Assistant VP, Director of Personnel,
100 Auburn Ave NE, P O Box 897, Atlanta, GA 30301.
(404) 659-2100

ATLANTIC SOUTHEAST AIRLINES

Profile: Atlanta-based feeder airline for Delta Airlines, employing 1800 nationwide and growing. Like Delta's career policy, all employees pass through the same entry-level training program, and there are openings for all types--accounting/finance, sales, management, MIS, etc, plus flight attendants.

Procedure: They receive thousands of resumes and applications, and thus do not respond to all. If in Atlanta, you can complete an application form at their offices on Wednesday from 8-5 pm; out of Atlanta, call for application. They will notify you if you are being considered for an opening. Do not mail your resume.,
100 Hartsfield Centre Pkwy, Suite 800 (old Atlanta airport), Atlanta, GA 30354.
(404) 766-1400

ATLANTIC STEEL

Profile: Steel producer employing 825 with 150 exempt. Hires some recent grads, and seeks experienced exempt in all areas. Has IBM mainframe and PC compatibles.

Procedure: Send resume to Manager of Personnel,
P O Box 1714, Atlanta, GA 30301.
(404) 897-4500

B B D O SOUTH

Profile: Largest advertising agency in the Southeast, headquartered in NYC. Employs 175 in Atlanta with approximately 140 exempt. Hires a few recent grads, mostly for entry-level, non-exempt positions, but with good opportunity for advancement. Hires experienced advertising personnel and accountants.

Procedure: Send resume to Director of Human Resources,
3414 Peachtree Rd NE, Suite 1600, Atlanta, GA 30326.
(404) 231-1700

BANK SOUTH

Profile: Corporate headquarters for one of Atlanta's largest banks with 140 branches (including 45 in Kroger Supermarkets) and employing 3000 total in Atlanta, 900 exempt. Recent grads are hired in accounting and auditing, or for Management Associate Program (hired throughout the year). Experienced exempt needs are banking professionals, accounting/finance, and MIS (IBM 38). Will hire up to 200 new employees each year in all functions.

Procedure: Send resume to Human Resources Division,
Mail Code 8, PO Box 5092, Atlanta, GA 30302.
(404) 529-4111; non-exempt Job Line: 529-4285

BARCO CHROMATICS, INC.

Profile: Atlanta-based manufacturer of high performance color graphic work stations, employing 500+ with one-half exempt. Most needs are for engineers (EE generally), entry and experienced. Seldom has openings for MIS or accounting.

Procedure: Send resume to Director of Personnel,
2558 Mountain Industrial Blvd, Tucker, GA 30084.
(404) 493-7000

BARD, C. R. INC. — UROLOGICAL DIVISION

Profile: Division headquarters facility that manufactures and markets urinary medical supplies. Employs 500+ with 165 exempt. Seeks both recent grads and experienced exempt for accounting/finance, engineering (ME mostly, especially with plastics background), bioscience, sales, and materials management.

Procedure: Send resume to Division Personnel Manager,
8195 Industrial Park Blvd, Covington, GA 30209.
(404) 784-6100 or (800) 526-4455 x6749

BEL TRONICS

Profile: US headquarters for manufacturer of consumer electronics (primarily radar detectors) and telecommunications hardware. Employs 180 with 20 exempt. Hires entry-level accounting/finance and electronic technicians, and experienced engineers (EE).

Procedure: Send resume to personnel,
8100 Sagl Parkway, Covington, GA 30209.
(404) 787-6500

BELL NORTHERN RESEARCH (BNR)

Profile: Northern Telecom subsidiary conducting research and development for telecommunications equipment and systems. Employs 300 with 90% exempt. Nearly all hiring is computer-related, either electrical engineering, computer engineering or computer science, both recent grads and experienced exempt. Has 15 co-ops.

Procedure: Send resume to Staffing Dept.,
1 Ravinia Drive, Atlanta, GA 30346.
(404) 246-2000; 840-5501 job info line

BELLSOUTH CORPORATION

BellSouth is the largest corporation headquartered in Atlanta and the Southeast. With 100,000+ employees in nine southeastern states, and with 15,000+ of those located here, it is also one of Atlanta's largest corporate employers.

All BellSouth subsidiaries fall into two categories, "regulated" (i.e., regulated by various statutes) and "non-regulated." The regulated companies, including southern Bell, employ most of the total here, and have consolidated their employment recruiting into two offices:

(1) BellSouth Management Employment Center, which handles exempt employment
(2) Southern Bell General Employment Office, which hires mostly non-exempt.

Each non-regulated BellSouth company conducts its own hiring, and I have included here the most active of those.

BELLSOUTH ADVERTISING AND PUBLISHING CORP.

Profile: Responsible for sales and information included in BellSouth Yellow Pages. Employs approximately 1100, with 50% exempt. Hires recent grads and experienced personnel in sales (40+) annually and graphic arts.

Procedure: Send resume to Employment Manager,
2295 Park Lake Dr, Suite 490, Atlanta, GA 30345.
(404) 491-1900; Job Information Line: 491-1747

BELLSOUTH CELLULAR CORP./BELLSOUTH MOBILITY

Profile: Headquarters for wire-line provider of cellular communications service in 26 SE cities. Employs 500 in Atlanta (1/2 exempt), and will have an increase, mostly in other SE cities. Hires 10 recent grads and 100 experienced exempt each year in accounting/finance, sales, engineering (EE and radio engineering) and MIS (IBM with MSA software). Has needs for MBA's in finance and marketing, and has marketing/product development section.

Procedure: Send resume to Director of Personnel,
1100 Abernathy Rd, 500 North Park Town Center, Atlanta, GA 30328.
(404) 604-6100

BELLSOUTH ENTERPRISES

Profile: Holding company for non-regulated BellSouth subsidiaries. They conduct hiring for smaller subsidiaries, as well as their own corporate staff. Most needs are for accounting/finance backgrounds--some recent grads, but mostly experienced, and certification is highly desirable.

Procedure: Send resume to Employment Manager,,
1100 Peachtree St NE, Room 5 A 07, Atlanta, GA 30309.
(404) 249-4000

BELLSOUTH INTERNATIONAL

Profile: Develops marketing and business opportunities for telecommunications services in Europe, the Pacific Rim, and Latin America. Seeks backgrounds in accounting, finance, marketing, and technical specialties (telecomm-related, e.g., cellular engineering, radio frequency engineering, etc.), mostly experienced, but some recent grads. Also seeks recent grads and experienced international MBA's in marketing.

Procedure: Send resume to Employment Manager,,
1100 Peachtree St NE, Room 5 A 07, Atlanta, GA 30309.
(404) 249-4000

BELLSOUTH MANAGEMENT EMPLOYMENT CENTER

Profile: Hires all exempt employees for BellSouth's regulated companies and for BellSouth's non-regulated Corporate Headquarters. Hires recent grads and experienced specialists, as well as numerous college students for summer internships and co-op positions. Primary needs currently are for computer science and engineering. [Note: Sales/marketing personnel are hired by BellSouth Communications in Birmingham, AL; (205) 985-6585 or (800) 368-3395 job line]

Procedure: Send resume and cover letter to address below, and it will be circulated to the appropriate recruiter.,
1760 Century Circle NE, Suite 6, Atlanta, 30345.
(404) 249-2000; 329-9455 Job Line

BELLSOUTH — SOUTHERN BELL GENERAL EMP. OFFICE

Profile: Hires non-exempt employment for Southern Bell/Georgia's regulated companies, approximately 12,000 total employees. Most needs are for marketing graduates to be in customer service/telemarketing (hired 150 in 1993) and for two- and four-year technical graduates to be technicians (hired 100 in 1993). Hiring will continue in 1994, although some reduction-in-force is anticipated.

Procedure: Send resume to
193-100 Perimeter Center Place, Atlanta, GA 30346.
(404) 391-2300, but first call job info line @ 391-3294

BIG STAR SUPERMARKETS

Profile: Big Star parent Grand Union sold all Atlanta stores in 1993 to A&P.
Procedure: See A&P listing.,

BLOCKBUSTER VIDEO

Profile: Nation's largest retailer of video rentals and supplies, with 60+ stores in Atlanta. Most store managers are hired as either Ass't Store Managers or as entry-level hourly positions, then promoted up. Promotes heavily from within.

Procedure: Send resume to Recruiter,
2900 S. Cobb Drive, Smyrna, GA 30080.
(404) 431-0132

BLUE CROSS/BLUE SHIELD OF GEORGIA

Profile: BC/BS is the nation's largest health care insurer, although each member company operates autonomously. This office employs 650 with 225 exempt. Recent grads with no related experience are usually hired into non-exempt positions, then promoted when an exempt position occurs; many are hired annually into accounting and insurance specialties. Experienced exempt are needed in accounting/finance, sales, management and insurance specialties (risk management, underwriting, etc.) No engineering needs and few MIS (IBM with Cobol, LAN, WAN). Hired 150 in 1992, reflecting both internal promotions and new hires.

Procedure: Send resume to Employment Representative,
3350 Peachtree Rd NE, Atlanta, GA 30326.
(404) 842-8001; 842-8460 job line

BOYS & GIRLS CLUBS OF AMERICA

Profile: Moving corporate headquarters from NYC to Atlanta in February, 1994. At this writing, hiring projections are undetermined.

Procedure: Send resume to personnel,
1230 West Peachtree St. NW, Atlanta, GA 30309.
(404) 892-3317 (region office)

BUTLER GROUP, INC. (D/B/A BUTLER SHOES)

Profile: Atlanta-based specialty retail chain, with 230 stores nationwide. Headquarters employs 100 with 60 exempt. Recent grads hired are mostly for store management, and they promote heavily from within; there are occasional needs for accounting and MIS.

Procedure: Send resume to personnel,
1600 Terrell Mill Road, Marietta, GA 30067.
(404) 955-6400

BUYPASS THE SYSTEM

Profile: Atlanta-based point-of-sale check and debit card processor, employing 300 here. Hires recent grads for accounting/finance and customer support, and experienced exempt in technical, management, and sales positions.

Procedure: Send resume to personnel,
360 Interstate Parkway, Suite 400, Atlanta, GA 30339.
(404) 953-2664

BYERS ENGINEERING CO.

Profile: Atlanta-based consulting firm that provides engineering and computer graphic services for major utilities; employs 900+. Two divisions, each conducting their own recruitment: Information Systems hires only experienced MIS (DEC VAX); engineering division requires telephony experience.

Procedure: Send resume to Human Resources Manager at the appropriate division; both located at,

261

6285 Barfield Rd, Atlanta, GA 30328.
(404) 843-1000 x 320 for MIS; x 402 for engineering

CANADA LIFE ASSURANCE COMPANY

Profile: North American corporate headquarters for international life insurance company. Employs 230 here, 100 exempt. Hires recent grads for underwriter trainees and seek experienced pension and actuarial specialists.

Procedure: Send resume to personnel,
6201 Powers Ferry Road NE, Atlanta, GA 30339.
(404) 953-1959

CARAUSTAR INDUSTRIES

Profile: Atlanta-based manufacturer and converter of paperboard products, employing 550 in Atlanta. Hires mostly technical and engineering backgrounds, including pulp and paper, both recent grads and experienced exempt. Good source for Junior Military Officers, especially USN.

Procedure: Send resume to Human Resources,
3100 Washington St, Austell, GA 30001.
(404) 948-3100

CARE

Profile: World's largest private international relief and development organization. Moved headquarters from NYC to Atlanta in 1993, and employs 225 here with 120 exempt. Hires recent grads and experienced exempt in all areas as needed.

Procedure: Send resume with cover letter expressing areas of expertise to Human Resources,
151 Ellis Street, Atlanta, GA 30303.
(404) 681-2552

CENTERS FOR DISEASE CONTROL AND PREVENTION

Profile: Atlanta-based federal agency that provides national leadership for public health efforts to prevent disease and disability and to promote health. Employs 3500 in Atlanta, and hires several hundred scientific and medical research specialists annually, both recent grads and experienced, including advanced degree and experienced epidemiologists, statisticians, mathematical statisticians, health scientists, medical officers, microbiologists, toxicologists, etc. Seeks MIS experience in LAN and IBM mainframe; knowledge of C language, SPSS, SAS.

Procedure: Maintains a recorded list of vacancies. Printed copies of an announced position and application forms may be obtained by contacting CDC Employment Information Service at ,
1600 Clifton Rd NE, Atlanta, GA 30333.
(404) 639-3616; 332-4577 Job Information Line

CH2M HILL

Profile: Environmental, consulting engineering firm with 140 employees in Atlanta, 120 exempt. Hires both recent grads and experienced engineers (environmental-related, ChE, CE), preferably at the Master's level. No needs for accounting or MIS here.

Procedure: Send resume to Region Human Resources Administrator, 115 Perimeter Center Place NE, Suite 700, Atlanta, GA 30346. (404) 604-9095

CHECKERS DRIVE-IN RESTAURANTS OF N. A.

Profile: Region office for rapidly growing fast food chain, currently with 300± units. This office hires management (trainee and experienced) for nine states, probably 200+ annually. Occasional need for real estate site selectors.

Procedure: Send resume to Regional Human Resources Manager, P O Box 80391, Atlanta, GA 30366. (404) 986-9799

CHICK-FIL-A

Profile: Corporate headquarters for 470-unit fast food chain. Chick-fil-A does not own or franchise units; rather, each unit is individually owned and operated, and thus they do not hire restaurant managers. Headquarters staff numbers 195 with 115 exempt. There will be openings for entry-level and experienced accountants and for experienced exempt in marketing, and operations management assistance. Has internship in marketing.

Procedure: Send resume to Personnel Administrator, 5200 Buffington Road, Atlanta, GA 30349. (404) 765-8127

CIBA VISION CORPORATION

Profile: Division headquarters for Ciba-Geigy unit that manufactures, distributes and conducts research/development of soft contact lens and eye care products. Total employment in Atlanta is 2600, with 700 exempt. Currently hires few recent grads. Seeks experienced exempt in numerous specialties, including manufacturing managers, product managers, accountants, sales reps, R&D scientists (polymers, micro-biologists, etc.) and MIS (AS 400).

Procedure: Send resume to Staffing Specialist, 11460 Johns Creek Pkwy, Duluth, GA 30136-1518. (404) 448-1200

CLUETT, PEABODY & CO., INC.

Profile: Manufactures Arrow-brand clothing, and employs 275 total in Atlanta. Seeks recent grads, mostly for production management, engineering (IE,

IET mostly) and MIS (IBM). Experienced needs in same areas, plus accounting.

Procedure: Send resume to Human Resources Manager,
4150 Boulder Ridge Drive SW, Atlanta, GA 30336.
(404) 346-5300

COCA-COLA BOTTLING COMPANY OF ATLANTA

Profile: Also functions as Atlanta Region of Coca-Cola Enterprises. Bottles and distributes Coca-Cola brands of soft drinks, and a division of Coca-Cola Enterprises. Employs 1800+, including 300 exempt. Hires both experienced personnel and recent grads into sales, accounting, engineering (all types), chemists, and manufacturing operations.

Procedure: Send resume to Personnel,
100 Galleria Pkwy, Suite 700, Atlanta, GA 30339.
(404) 852-7000; job line 852-7144

COCA-COLA COMPANY/COCA-COLA USA

Profile: Second largest Fortune 500 corporation headquartered in Atlanta. With 3500± employees in Atlanta, The Coca-Cola Company and Coca-Cola USA hire experienced exempt personnel in a number of functional areas, such as accounting/finance, MIS, marketing, and R&D (chemists and engineers--all types). The Coca-Cola Company provides staff support for Coca-Cola subsidiaries world-wide; Coca-Cola USA is the flagship operating unit for sales and distribution of Coca-Cola and allied brands.

Procedure: The Coca-Cola Company maintains an applicant database that both the Corporate division and Coca-Cola USA can access. Thus a resume sent to The Coca-Cola Company can be reviewed by all staffing departments.
Send resume to Staffing Department,
P O Drawer 1734, Atlanta, GA 30301 .
(404) 676-2662 - recording; 676-2665 for information and resume status

COCA-COLA ENTERPRISES

Profile: CCE is the third largest Fortune 500 company headquartered in Atlanta, and is the world's largest bottler of Coca-Cola brands of soft drinks. This office is the headquarters support and employs 175+, mostly exempt. Hires a few recent grads, but mostly experienced personnel, in accounting/finance and MIS, plus occasionally in legal, marketing, and purchasing. Each bottling company operates autonomously (see listing for Coca-Cola Bottling Co. of Atlanta).

Procedure: Send resume to Human Resources,
P O Box 1778, Atlanta, GA 30301.
(404) 676-2100

COHN & WOLFE/ATLANTA

Profile: Corporate headquarters for the largest Public Relations firm in the Southeast and the 13th largest in US. Most personnel hired are experienced PR professionals. Only recent grads hired are those with internship experience or extensive writing experience, especially with campus news publications. Offers internships during spring and summer quarters for PR majors in their junior and senior years in college.

Procedure: Send resume to General Manager,
225 Peachtree St NE, Suite 2300, Atlanta, GA 30303.
(404) 688-5900

COLONIAL PIPELINE

Profile: Atlanta-based, nation's largest petroleum pipeline company. Employs 225 in Atlanta, 160 exempt. Nearly all exempt hires are recent grads in accounting/finance and engineering (CE, EE, ME), and then promoted up; seldom needs experienced exempt.

Procedure: Send resume to Human Resources,
P O Box 18855   (945 E. Paces Ferry Rd, 27th Floor), Atlanta, GA 30326.
(404) 841-2306

COMMUNICATION CHANNELS

Profile: Atlanta-based publisher of 50 trade magazines, plus trade shows and direct mail operations. Employs 250 in Atlanta, 100+ exempt. Most hires are entry-level journalists and a few accountants.

Procedure: Semd resume to personnel,
6151 Powers Ferry Road NW, Atlanta, GA 30339.
(404) 955-2500

COMPASS MANAGEMENT AND LEASING

Profile: Subsidiary of Equitable Real Estate Investment Management, headquartered in Atlanta. Employs 350 with 100 exempt. Seldom hires recent grads, but has needs for experienced exempt in accounting/finance, and for property management and commercial real estate backgrounds.

Procedure: Send resume to Human Resources Manager,
3414 Peachtree Road NE, Suite 850, Atlanta, GA 30326.
(404) 240-2121

CONFEDERATION LIFE INSURANCE COMPANY

Profile: Canadian life and health insurance company, US headquarters in Atlanta, employing 900 here, including 225 exempt. Hires recent grads in math, economics, and general business, and especially risk management. Seeks experienced exempt with insurance backgrounds, and some accounting/finance and MIS (IBM 3090 with Cobol, CICS, and IMS software). Hires 150 exempt and non-exempt annually.

Procedure: Send resume to Human Resources,

P O Box 105103, Atlanta, GA 30348.
(404) 953-5100

CONSTAR INTERNATIONAL

Profile: (Formerly Sewell Plastics.) Division of Crown Cork & Seal that manufactures plastics, especially packaging and bottles. Employs 500 here, 115 exempt. Seldom hires recent grads. Experienced exempt are needed for accounting/finance, manufacturing management, and engineering (various types); sales reps must have packaging experience. No MIS needs.

Procedure: Send resume to Human Resources,
5375 Drake Drive SW, Atlanta, GA 30336.
(404) 691-4256

CONTEL CELLULAR

Profile: Atlanta-based marketer of cellular telephones, employing 1100 with 650 exempt. Hires no recent grads, but seeks experience exempt in engineering (software, radio and microwave backgrounds), sales, customer service, and marketing.

Procedure: Send resume to Director of Human Resources,
245 Perimeter Center Pkwy, Atlanta, GA 30346.
(404) 804-3400

COOPERS & LYBRAND

Profile: Big 6 CPA firm employing 375 here and expecting an increase. Hires mostly recent accounting/finance grads for audit position and promotes up.

Procedure: Send resume to personnel,
1155 Peachtree St, Suite 1100, Atlanta, GA 30309.
(404) 870-1100

COTTON STATES INSURANCE GROUP

Profile: Atlanta-based property and casualty, and life and health insurance company. Employs 500 total, 200 exempt. Has been down-sizing in the last year, and thus will probably need only experienced personnel, mostly in property and casualty claims and MIS (IBM ES 9000 NIVS/XA).

Procedure: Send resume to Employment Manager,
P O Box 105303, Atlanta, GA 30348.
(404) 391-8600

COUSINS PROPERTIES

Profile: Atlanta-based real estate developer and manager, employing 100 with 65 exempt. Hires recent accounting grads.

Procedure: Send resume to Personnel,
2500 Windy Ridge Parkway, Marietta, GA 30067.

(404) 955-2200

COVIA
Profile: Customer support center for United Airline division that markets software systems to travel agencies, hotels and airlines; this office is only involved in trouble shooting for system users. Employs 475 with 25 exempt. Hires experienced computer reservations systems individuals, then promotes into higher positions; thus, seldom needs experienced exempt.
Procedure: Send resume to Human Resources Dept.,
54 Perimeter Center East, Atlanta, GA 30346.
(404) 393-7911

CRAWFORD AND COMPANY
Profile: Provides insurance industry and risk management industry with full spectrum of services, primarily claims-related. Corporate headquarters in Atlanta employs 900 (400 exempt), and they have branches throughout the US. Hires 100+ recent grads each year, mostly in casualty claims adjusting (BBA best, but others ok). Has summer internship program in Risk Management. Experienced personnel are hired for accounting/finance, MIS, risk control, and health and rehabilitation.
Procedure: For claims adjustors (including trainees); risk control; and health and rehabilitation personnel, send resume to Personnel Manager, SE Region Office
5780 Peachtree Dunwoody Rd, Atlanta, GA 30342. Accountants and MIS personnel, send resume to Employment Manager at headquarters,
P O Box 5047, Atlanta, GA 30302.
(404) 256-0830 - SE Region Office; (404) 847-4080 - headquarters

CREDITOR RESOURCES, INC.
Profile: Atlanta-based credit life and disability insurance administrator, employing 250 with 80 exempt. Hires recent grads (all types) and experienced exempt with insurance or credit banking experience.
Procedure: Send resume to Personnel Assistant,
1100 Johnson Ferry Road, Suite 300, Atlanta, GA 30342.
(404) 257-8200; 257-8301 job info line

CURTIS 1000
Profile: Subsidiary of Atlanta-based American Business Products, employing 1800 nationwide and 280 in Atlanta, 50 exempt. Prints all types of commercial stationery and business forms. Seeks recent grads for management training program and then promotes up; thus, occasionally needs experienced exempt and sales representatives.
Procedure: Send resume to Vice President of Human Resources,
P O Box 105683, Atlanta, GA 30348.

(404) 951-1000

D & B SOFTWARE
Profile: Subsidiary of Dun and Bradstreet that designs and manufactures business software systems in finance, human resources, and manufacturing. Employs 1000 in Atlanta with 750 exempt. Expects to hire up to 300 exempt (not all for Atlanta) in accounting/finance, MIS (IBM) and sales (no trainees).
Procedure: Send resume to Director of Recruiting,
             3445 Peachtree Rd NE, Atlanta, GA 30326.
             (404) 239-2000

DATA GENERAL CORPORATION
Profile: Southeast Area Office and Worldwide Customer Support Center for Fortune 300 company that manufactures and sells computers and work stations. Employs 300 here (600 in SE), with 240 exempt. Hires no recent grads, but seeks experienced sales and systems professionals with open systems experience, plus sales support, technical support, and marketing personnel. No accounting/finance in Atlanta. Has 3 co-ops in systems engineering.
Procedure: Send resume to Human Resources,
             4170 Ashford-Dunwoody Rd, Suite 300, Atlanta, GA 30319.
             (404) 705-2500; fax 705-2620

DELOITTE AND TOUCHE MANAGEMENT CONSULTING GROUP
Profile: Southeast headquarters for D&T's consulting division, employing 135 here, all exempt. Seeks recent MBA's with specific industry experience (e.g., finance, government, health care, retail, utilities, information systems, et al.), and will hire 20 annually.
Procedure: Send resume to Recruiting Manager,
             285 Peachtree Center Ave, Suite 2000, Atlanta, GA 30303-1234.
             (404) 220-1000

DELOITTE & TOUCHE
Profile: Third largest CPA firm in Atlanta, one of the Big 6 international CPA firms. Employs 450 in Atlanta, 375 exempt. Has four divisions: accounting, audit, tax services, and management consulting services. Hires mostly recent accounting/finance grads and will hire 50+ each year.
Procedure: Send resume to Recruiting Director,
             100 Peachtree St NE, Suite 1700, Atlanta, GA 30303-1943.
             (404) 220-1500

DELTA AIRLINES
Profile: Headquartered in Atlanta and the largest airline serving Atlanta, Delta employs 27,000 here and is Atlanta's largest corporate employer. Only

experienced personnel hired are pilots, flight attendants, and reservation agents. Otherwise, a career path with Delta means starting in an hourly position, such as baggage handler, mechanic, or clerk, and working up.

Procedure: Obtain an application form, complete it, and return that plus your resume to Employment Office, listed below. Application forms are available by calling their office, but the easiest method is to go by any Delta ticket office, including the airport, and request one.,
P O Box 20530, Hartsfield International Airport, Atlanta, GA 30320.
(404) 765-2501

DEPARTMENT OF THE ARMY CIVILIAN PERSONNEL OFFICE

Profile: This office handles all recruiting for civilian positions at Atlanta's Fort McPherson and Fort Gillem, plus Fort Buchanan in Puerto Rico; and for all southeastern Army Technicians, who are weekday civilians and weekend Army Reservists. Most civilian positions require that you already be in the government merit system, although there are exceptions, especially for medical personnel and engineers. Prior civil service is not required for Army Technicians, but you must join the Reserves upon employment. There are usually 100 current openings, approximately one-half professional level (GS 9 and above).

Procedure: Use either of these two procedures: (1) call or write them and request a copy of their list of current vacancies, which is updated and published the 1st and 15th of every month. (2) Call the Job Hot Lines and if you are interested in a specific opening on the recording, leave your name and address at the end of the recording; they will then send you an application form and information regarding the specific position in which you are interested. The Job Hot Lines are updated every Friday. The address is Directorate of Civilian Personnel, Attn: J. I. C. (stands for Job Information Center), Building 246, Fort McPherson, GA 30330-5000.
(404) 752-2906; Job Info Lines: 752-2737 or 752-3521

DIGITAL COMMUNICATIONS ASSOCIATES

Profile: Corporate headquarters for this designer, manufacturer, and marketer of DOS, Macintosh, OS/2 and Windows micro to mainframe connectivity software products. Employs 550 in Atlanta with 375 exempt. They project annual hiring needs of a few recent grads and 30 experienced personnel, mostly electrical engineers and computer science majors. Experience with PC's, LAN's, Gateways, and communications protocols is preferred.

Procedure: Call DCA Jobline, available 24 hours/day from any Touch-Tone telephone and follow verbal instructions. ONLY resumes with specific position number included will be considered.,
1000 Alderman Drive, Alpharetta, GA 30201.
(404) 442-4000; 442-4010 - Job line

DIGITAL EQUIPMENT CORPORATION

Profile: World's second largest manufacturer of computer systems, with 1375 employees in Atlanta, including 1100 exempt. Hires liberal arts and technical recent grads, as well as experienced personnel, into all disciplines--sales, engineering, MIS, accounting/finance, marketing analysis, management, etc.

Procedure: Send resume to Employment,
                5555 Windward Pkwy West, Alpharetta, GA 30201-7407.
                (404) 772-2070

DITTLER BROTHERS, INC.

Profile: Atlanta-based printer that produces promotional games, lotteries, direct mail, directories, airline timetables, ticket jackets, pop-ups and specialty finishing. Employs 175+ with 75+ exempt in Atlanta, plus this office staffs the Oakwood, GA facility which employs 500+ with 110+ exempt. Hires a few recent grads in management and engineering (EE, ME, et al.), but most needs are for experienced exempt in all functions. Uses AS 400, IBM PC's, and IBM 4341 mainframe.

Procedure: Send resume to Director of Human Resources,
                1375 Seaboard Industrial Blvd, Atlanta, GA 30318.
                (404) 355-3423

DOBBS INTERNATIONAL SERVICES

Profile: Provides airline catering service at Atlanta airport. Employs 1300 in Atlanta, 20% exempt. Will hire 25+ entry-level, mostly for production management and customer service assistants, who assist drivers in their 85-truck fleet.

Procedure: Send resume to Personnel Services Manager,
                P O Box 45485, Atlanta, GA 30320.
                (404) 530-6300

EATON CORPORATION – INDUSTRIAL CONTROLS DIVISION

Profile: Assembly plant for electric and electronic control systems (Cutler Hammer products). Employs 200 with 50 exempt. Seeks recent engineering (EE) grads, and experienced exempt in accounting/finance, sales, management, and engineering. No MIS.

Procedure: Send resume to Human Resources Manager,
                3001 McCall Drive, Doraville, GA 30340.
                (404) 451-2331

ECC INTERNATIONAL

Profile: British-owned company producing and marketing kaolin and clay, employing 180 in Atlanta headquarters (100+ exempt), plus manufacturing facility near Augusta, GA. Seeks experienced exempt in accounting/finance, sales, marketing, chemistry, and MIS (IBM).

Procedure: Send resume to Human Resources Manager,

5775 Peachtree Dunwoody Road NE, Suite 200G, Atlanta, GA 30342.
(404) 843-1551

ECKERD DRUGS

Profile: Operates 120 retail stores in Atlanta, employing 1500 total with 380 exempt. This office hires almost entirely for store management and will hire 100 recent grads as manager trainees and 50 experienced retail managers for Atlanta positions.

Procedure: Send resume to Human Resources Manager — Atlanta Region,
36 Herring Road, Newnan, GA 30265.
(404) 254-4400

ELECTROLUX CORPORATION

Profile: Corporate headquarters for international manufacturer and distributor of vacuum cleaners and other home cleaning products and services. Employs 210 at headquarters, with 100 exempt. Hires some recent grads, but prefers experience, for accounting/finance, administration and MIS (IBM). Sales reps are hired by local sales offices.

Procedure: Send resume to Human Resources Representative,
2300 Windy Ridge Pkwy, Suite 900 South, Marietta, GA 30067.
(404) 933-1000

ELECTROMAGNETIC SCIENCES

Profile: Atlanta-based company that designs, manufactures and sells microwave components, microwave sub-systems and radio-link terminals. This office also handles staffing for their LXE subsidiary, which manufactures radio-link data terminal products. Employment for both is 750 with 300 exempt. Hires a few recent grads in engineering (mostly ME and EE) and hires 25+ experienced personnel in sales and engineering. Has six co-ops in engineering.

Procedure: Send resume to Human Resources Manager,
P O Box 7700, Norcross, GA 30091.
(404) 448-5770

EMORY UNIVERSITY/EMORY UNIVERSITY HOSPITAL

Profile: Private, Methodist-affiliated university with 9000 students. Employs 3775 non-faculty university personnel and 2800 hospital personnel. Only recent grads hired would be in scientific research or for non-exempt positions, awaiting an exempt opening, as some experience is preferred for most positions. Hires experienced personnel in accounting/finance, administration, MIS (IBM) and research; prior academic experience is not required for most positions. Hospital has 600+ beds and is also a teaching and research insititute. Hospital hires recent grads in medical specialties, such as nursing, pharmacology, respiratory/physical therapy, etc.

Procedure: For hospital and university positions, apply in person Monday - Thursday 9:00 - 4:00, if possible. Otherwise, send resume to Emory University Human Resources Department,
1762 Clifton Road NE, Atlanta, GA 30322.
(404) 727-7611

ENCORE SYSTEMS
Profile: Atlanta-based developer and marketer of computerized Property Management Systems to hotels and cruise lines, employing 140. Seeks experienced exempt with hotel operations experience, plus programmers (UNIX C) and other MIS.
Procedure: Send resume to Personnel,
900 Circle 75 Parkway, Suite 1700, Atlanta, GA 30339.
(404) 612-3500

EQUIFAX, INC.
Profile: Headquartered in Atlanta, Equifax is the nation's largest computer-based information gathering company, with offices throughout the US and Europe. Employs 3000 in Atlanta, 600 exempt. Seeks recent grads in accounting/finance, operations management, and MIS (IBM and DEC VAX); liberal arts grads often hired for customer service, and marketing grads for research and analysis positions. Experienced exempt are hired for the same areas and insurance background is helpful. Also seeks recent MBA grads in accounting/finance and experienced MBA's in marketing.
Procedure: Send resume to Human Resources,
1600 Peachtree Street, Atlanta, GA 30309.
(404) 885-8000; 885-8550 job hot line

EQUIFAX INFORMATION SERVICES CENTER
Profile: Credit reporting office, employing 700. Most needs will be for entry-level and experienced credit or customer service personnel (most work is done by phone), plus some accounting.
Procedure: Send resume to Human Resources Manager,
3200 Windy Hill Road, Suite 500, Marietta, GA 30067.
(404) 612-3000; 612-2558 job information line

EQUIFAX —TECHNOLOGY CENTER
Profile: One of the largest data centers in Atlanta, employing 800 with 480 exempt. At least 90% of their hiring is for MIS personnel, recent grads and experienced, and they have IBM, PC's, Amdahl, and DEC VAX hardware, UNIX, VMS environments; uses Cobol, Assembler, C and Natural.
Procedure: Send resume to Human Resources, JL,
P O Box 740006, Atlanta, GA 30374-0006.
(404) 885-8000; job line 740-4635

EQUITABLE REAL ESTATE INVESTMENT MANAGEMENT

Profile: National headquarters in Atlanta, one of 70 subsidiaries of the Equitable Insurance Company, and one of the most profitable. Manages $38 billion in real estate assets throughout the US and Japan. Employs 330 total at headquarters, most of whom are exempt. Only recent grads hired are for accounting/finance, probably 5+ per year.

Procedure: Send resume to Director of Human Resources,
            3414 Peachtree Road NE, Atlanta, GA 30326-1162.
            (404) 239-5000

ERNST & YOUNG

Profile: World's largest CPA and consulting firm, employing 730 in Atlanta with 625 exempt. Atlanta office for Tax, Audit, and Entrepreneurial Services divisions of E&Y, each with their own recruiter. Hires mostly recent accounting/finance grads and MBA's, plus a limited number of experienced exempt for Health Care Consulting; Management Consulting; Special Services Group; Acturial, Benefits and Compensations Group.

Procedure: Send resume to Director of Recruiting—[specify division],
            600 Peachtree St NE, Atlanta, GA 30308.
            (404) 874-8300

FEDERAL HOME LOAN BANK OF ATLANTA

Profile: The Federal Home Loan Bank of Atlanta, one of 12 districts Banks in the Federal Home Loan Bank System, is an $18B reserve credit bank that provides low-cost financing and other banking services to its nearly 600 member financial institutions that offer housing finance to consumers in seven SE states and DC. Employs 280 here with 165 exempt. Backgrounds in finance, accounting, and banking are given most consideration.

Procedure: Send resume to Manager of Employment,
            1475 Peachtree St NE, Atlanta, GA 30309.
            (404) 888-8000

FEDERAL HOME LOAN MORTGAGE CORPORATION

Profile: SE region office for government sponsored enterprise. Employs 50 with 45 exempt. Hires no recent grads and experienced exempt must have previous mortgage experience.

Procedure: Call the Job Info Line at (703) 903-2970 and apply as directed. Or send resume to Human Resources,
            2839 Paces Ferry Road NW, Atlanta, GA 30339.
            (404) 438-3800

FEDERAL NATIONAL MORTGAGE ASSOC. (FANNIE MAE)

Profile: Secondary mortgage company, employing 230 in Atlanta, 150 exempt. Hires a few recent grads and prefers backgrounds in mortgage lending and real estate sales. Uses IBM PC's.

Procedure: Prefers that you first call the job info line and then respond to a specific opening. Send resume to Human Resources,
950 East Paces Ferry Rd, Suite 1900, Atlanta, GA 30326-1161.
(404) 365-6000; 398-6242 job info line

FEDERAL RESERVE BANK OF ATLANTA

Profile: Head office for the Sixth District of the Federal Reserve System, employing 1000 here with 425 exempt. Regulates commercial banks, conducts economic research used to impact monetary policy made by the Federal Reserve Board in DC, and provides financial services such as check clearing services, cash distribution, ACH, electronic payments and wire transfers. Will hire up to 15 recent grads in accounting/finance/business, including MBA's. Will hire 60 experienced personnel in accounting/finance, operations management, audit, regulation, data-base analysis and MIS (IBM mainframe, AS 400 & Unisys; programmers in C and OS/2 PM, CASE tools and DB2, Cobol and CL). Commercial banking experience preferred.

Procedure: Send resume to Employment Specialist,
104 Marietta Street NW, Atlanta, GA 30303-2713.
(404) 521-8500; 521-8767 job information line

FIRST FINANCIAL MANAGEMENT CORPORATION

Profile: Atlanta-based information services holding company for several subsidiaries, all of which conduct their own recruiting. Corporate office employs 110 with 90 exempt, and seeks experienced accounting/finance and MIS (Unisys).

Procedure: Send resume to Manager of Personnel and Employee Relations,
3 Corporate Square, Suite 700, Atlanta, GA 30329.
(404) 321-0120

FIRST NORTH AMERICAN NATIONAL BANK

Profile: Operates as the credit card bank for Richmond, VA-based Circuit City, a national retailer of electronics and home appliances. Employs 100, 20 exempt. Nearly all exempt hiring is for recent accounting/finance grads to enter credit training program. Also needs part-time in their Credit Extension Department.

Procedure: Send resume to Personnel,
1800 Parkway Place, Suite 500, Atlanta, GA 30067.
(404) 423-7900

FIRST UNION NATIONAL BANK OF GEORGIA

Profile: Second largest bank in Georgia, and subsidiary of Charlotte, NC-based First Union Bank, one of the largest bank holding companies in the Southeast. Operates 93 branches in the Atlanta area, employing 1700, including 270 exempt. Conducts campus recruiting with corporate human resources department, and will hire 20 recent grads for management training classes beginning in January, May and September. Will also seek 40± experienced personnel, including accountants and banking professionals.

Procedure: Send resume to VP and Manager of Personnel,
P O Box 740074, Personnel Mail Code 9048 (Located at 999 Peachtree St NE, Suite 1050, but use the P O box for mail.), Atlanta, GA 30374.
(404) 827-7119 HR Dept.; 827-7150 job info line

FISERV, INC.

Profile: (Formerly Basis Information Technologies, division of First Financial Management Company.) Provides data processing services to financial institutions. Employs 300 with 75 exempt. Purchased in 1993 and is currently reorganizing; thus, employment needs are uncertain at this writing. Formerly sought experienced exempt in accounting/finance, management (banking and loan application backgrounds ideal), and MIS (IBM) – programmers, operators, and especially with Hogan background.

Procedure: Send resume to Human Resources,
3 Corporate Square, Suite 500, Atlanta, GA 30329.
(404) 321-0120; 321-2292 - HR Dept.

FLEXEL, INC.

Profile: Atlanta-based, privately-held manufacturer of flexible materials and specialty films. Corporate staff numbers 70, 30 exempt. Most hires are experienced accountants, MIS (IBM 38), sales reps, and corporate administration.

Procedure: Send resume to Human Resources Department,
115 Perimeter Center Place, Suite 1100, Atlanta, GA 30346.
(404) 393-0696

FORD MOTOR COMPANY—ATLANTA ASSEMBLY PLANT 340

Profile: This facility assembles Ford Taurus and Mercury Sable cars, employing 2450 hourly and 250 salaried exempt. Most exempt hiring here is for electrical engineers (trainee and experienced) in manufacturing management, plus some needs in industrial relations (MBA best). Accounting/finance is centralized in Detroit.

Procedure: Send resume to Salaried Personnel Office,
340 Henry Ford II Avenue, Hapeville, GA 30354.
(404) 669-1546

G E C MARCONI AVIONICS

Profile: Corporate headquarters for the US subsidiary of GEC Ltd of the UK. Electronics manufacturer, whose major products include Heads-Up display for fighter aircraft. Employs 275 with 150 exempt. No entry-level positions, and most experienced exempt hires are in MIS (DEC VAX) and accounting, some EE.

Procedure: Send resume to Personnel Dept,
            P O Box 81999, Atlanta, GA 30366.
            (404) 448-1947

G E CAPITAL SERVICES CORP.

Profile: Computer support organization of GE Capital, relocating from Conn. and consolidating metro offices. Currently employs 110, mostly exempt, and continues to transfer staff here from Conn. Hires recent computer science grads for Help Desk (customer service) and experienced software programmers (IBM systems).

Procedure: Send resume to Human Resources Representative,
            1001 Windward Concourse, Alpharetta, GA 30202.
            (404) 422-6112

G T E TELECOMMUNICATIONS PRODUCTS AND SERVICES

Profile: Atlanta-based parent of GTE MobilNet and Contel Cellular, employing 1000 with 250 exempt and expecting an increase. Provides support functions for subsidiaries. Hires few recent grads, and but seeks experienced exempt in marketing (including international), accounting, finance, engineers (mostly EE with RF concentration, cellular technology, and network operations), and MIS (DEC VAX, IBM PC's, and Macintosh). Conducts most management-level hiring for subsidiaries.

Procedure: Send resume to Staffing,
            245 Perimeter Center Parkway, Atlanta, GA 30346.
            (404) 391-8000

GAY & TAYLOR, INC.

Profile: Atlanta-based insurance services firm, offering insurance adjusting and risk services management. Employs 186 in Atlanta, mostly at local branches. Corporate staff numbers 85, 45 exempt, and seeks experienced staff, including accounting/finance and MIS (AS 400 and Paradox PAL). Claims adjusters are hired at the local branches, degree not always necessary.

Procedure: For corporate positions, send resume to Human Resources,
            6 Concourse Pkwy, Suite 2000, Atlanta, GA 30328.
            (404) 395-1000

GENERAL ELECTRIC COMPUTER SERVICES

Profile: National headquarters for GE subsidiary that does maintenance, rental and repair of industrial, electrical and test instruments, and computer equipment. Employs 600 with 300 exempt. Most recent grads hired are in engineering and MIS (DEC and Prime) or for technician positions (two- and four-year degrees). Hires experienced personnel in accounting/finance, sales and MIS.

Procedure: Send resume to Staffing Consultant,
6875 Jimmy Carter Blvd, Suite 3200, Norcross, GA 30071.
(404) 246-6200

GENERAL MOTORS

Profile: GM continues to downsize in Atlanta. The Doraville facility remains on a one shift basis and will have no exempt needs.

Procedure: If you wish to contact them, their address is,
3900 Motors Industrial Way, Doraville, GA 30360.
(404) 455-5100 - recording

GENUINE PARTS CO.

Profile: Atlanta-based automotive parts distributor/wholesaler, employing 175 at headquarters, 90 exempt. (See also NAPA Auto Parts.) Hires mostly exempt personnel for management trainee positions which will involve assignments throughout the US. Promotes heavily from within and thus seldom needs experienced personnel.

Procedure: Send resume to Human Resources,
2999 Circle 75 Parkway, Atlanta, GA 30339.
(404) 953-1700

GEORGIA FEDERAL BANK

Profile: Purchased by First Union National Bank of Georgia.

Procedure: See listing for First Union National Bank of Georgia.,

GEORGIA INSTITUTE OF TECHNOLOGY

Profile: Third largest university in Georgia and second largest in Atlanta, with 12,000+ students. Has 4000 employees (including faculty), with approximately 1000 exempt. Technical and engineering employees are hired through the Georgia Tech Research Institute (see listing). Thus, this office hires mostly accounting and general management, plus positions in public relations, public administration, marketing and finance. Experience in higher education desirable. Hires approximately 15 recent grads and 60 experienced exempt annually.

Procedure: Do not send open resume, since they do not have a computerized applicant filing system. Call the Job Information Line, and if you wish to apply for one of those positions, either apply in person or call for instructions. Personnel department is located at,
955 Fowler St NW, Atlanta, GA 30332.

(404) 894-3245 for instructions and general information; 894-4592 for Job Information Line

GEORGIA LOTTERY CORPORATION

Profile: Administers the Georgia lottery, employing 230. Seeks recent grads and experienced exempt in accounting/finance, sales/marketing, and MIS operations (DEC VAX, LAN environment).

Procedure: Send resume to human resources`,
250 Williams St, Suite 3000, Atlanta, GA 30303-1071.
(404) 215-5000;

GEORGIA MARBLE

Profile: Atlanta-based corporation involved in mining and quarrying of marble, which is then crushed or sawed into smaller sizes for end-user needs. Employs 55 at headquarters, one-half exempt. Hires a few recent grads each year in production management and engineering (IE and ME). Hires experienced exempt in accounting/finance, sales, production management, engineering and MIS (IBM 38). Also seeks occasional geologist, trainee or experienced.

Procedure: Send resume to Human Resources Manager,
1201 Roberts Blvd, Bldg 100, Kennesaw, GA 30144-3619.
(404) 421-6500

GEORGIA POWER COMPANY

Profile: Largest electric utility in Georgia and a subsidiary of Atlanta-based Southern Company (see listing). Employs 5000+ in Atlanta, with 2000 exempt. Most recent grads hired are engineers or other technical degree; non-technical positions (accounting/finance, marketing and management) require business major. Also seeks experienced exempt, mostly with technical backgrounds. Has 200 engineering co-ops, which are hired through college placement departments, not through this office, and these co-ops often fill the entry positions. Rarely needs MIS. (See Southern Company Services.)

Procedure: Send resume to Professional Employment,
P O Box 4545, Atlanta, GA 30302.
(404) 526-7665

GEORGIA STATE UNIVERSITY

Profile: Georgia's second largest and Atlanta's largest university, with more than 20,000 students, graduate and undergraduates. Employs 1500 non-faculty personnel, 400± exempt, 900 faculty. Most recent grads hired are for student services (counseling, financial aid, etc.). Will need many experienced personnel, especially in general administration (office managers), MIS (Amdahl and Unisys), Advisors (student services) and trainers. Also seeks biology, chemistry and other science majors (including social science) for research positions. Experience in an academic setting is a definite plus.

Procedure: Best method is to call their Job Information Line and apply for a specific opening, since they receive many resumes and an open resume may not receive much attention; they do not maintain a resume file. If you are in Atlanta, you can apply in person; otherwise, mail your resume with a cover letter indicating for which opening you are applying.,
Employment Office, University Plaza, 1 Park Place South, Atlanta, GA 30303.
(404) 651-3330 for general information; 651-4270 for Job Info Line

GEORGIA TECH RESEARCH INSTITUTE

Profile: Operates 8 research laboratories: one each in environmental-related, materials science (including polymers and super-conductors), and economics (acts as consultant to Georgia industries); and 7 in electronics and computer science, some for industry, but mostly for defense applications. Employs 900 including 550 engineers and scientists. Hires 10 recent grads and 25 experienced exempt annually, mostly with technical backgrounds, especially EE and computer science, but also in ME, physics, chemistry, metallurgy, IE and environmental. Economics lab hires mostly MBA's with industrial experience. Hires no office staff types, such as accountants, which are hired through the University (see listing.).

Procedure: Accepts applications Monday - Wednesday, 8-5 pm, or send resume to Office of Human Resources,
955 Fowler Street, Atlanta, GA 30332-0435.
(404) 894-9412

GEORGIA-PACIFIC CORPORATION

Profile: Atlanta-based Fortune 50 forest products company and Atlanta's largest Fortune 500 firm. Headquarters employs 2650 with 1500 exempt. Entry-level accountants and sales reps are hired mostly through campus recruiting, and experienced personnel in accounting/finance, sales, engineering (mostly environmental, ChE, ME, EE), logistics, transportation, MIS (several systems) and other corporate staff types are hired throughout the year. Up to 250 exempt employees are hired annually.

Procedure: Send resume to Manager of Corporate Staffing,
133 Peachtree Street NW, Atlanta, GA 30303.
(404) 652-4000; 521-5211 job line

GOLDER ASSOCIATES

Profile: Environmental consulting firm, employing 95 here with 70 exempt. Seeks recent grads and experienced exempt with environmental-related degrees and backgrounds, mostly engineers or geologists, and occasionally an experienced accountant.

Procedure: Send resume to Human Resources,
3730 Chamblee Tucker Road, Atlanta, GA 30341.
(404) 496-1893 (Phone calls are discouraged.)

GRADY HEALTH SYSTEM (FULTON-DEKALB HOSP. AUTH.)
Profile: Atlanta's largest hospital, employing 6,500 total, including part-time,
900+ exempt. Hires 200+ exempt annually, recent grads and experienced,
in accounting/finance, department management and MIS (IBM). Also
seeks many health care specialists, especially RN, LPN, OT and PT.
Seldom needs engineers.
Procedure: Send resume to Supervisor, Employment. If there is a current need for
your background, they will send you an application form.,
80 Butler Street SE, Atlanta, GA 30335.
(404) 616-1900; Job line 616-5627

GTE CUSTOMER NETWORKS
Profile: National headquarters location for GTE subsidiary that sells, installs and
services telecommunications equipment. Employs 85 here (60 exempt),
plus this office handles staffing needs nationwide. Seldom hires recent
grads, but seeks experienced exempt in accounting, purchasing, human
resources and other central office support types. No MIS.
Procedure: Send resume to Manager, Human Resources,
1117 Perimeter Center West, Suite W-200, Atlanta, GA 30338.
(404) 698-5800

H B O & COMPANY
Profile: Atlanta-based supplier of hospital information systems, second largest in
US. Employs 1000 in Atlanta, 850 exempt. Most entry-level hires have
technical program or healthcare backgrounds, plus an occasional
accountant. Any experience in healthcare, especially from a hospital
environment, is highly desirable, and experienced exempt are sought in
accounting/finance, sales, customer service, technical support and MIS
(IBM, HP 3000, DG, UNIX). No engineering function here.
Procedure: Send resume to Human Resources,
301 Perimeter Center North, Atlanta, GA 30346.
(404) 393-6000; 393-6015 job info line

HARLAND, JOHN H. COMPANY
Profile: Corporate headquarters for the second largest bank stationery (mostly
checks) company in the US. Employs 425 (200 exempt) in headquarters,
plus 650 in manufacturing locally. Hires recent grads as sales trainees,
but few remain in Atlanta after training. Experienced personnel are hired
in accounting/finance, sales, production management, and MIS. Good
source for Junior Military Officers.
Procedure: Send resume to Employment Manager,

P O Box 105250, Department D M, Atlanta, GA 30348.
(404) 981-9460

HAVERTY FURNITURE COMPANY

Profile: Corporate headquarters for retail furniture chain, operating 13 stores in Atlanta and 80+ in the SE and SW. Employs 350 in Atlanta (120 at Hq) with 100 exempt. Prefers to hire recent BBA's in management and marketing for management and administrative positions, including store management trainees, and then promote from within. Also seeks recent MIS grads and promotes up, but will need a few experienced MIS personnel (AS 400). Hires entry-level and experienced accounting/finance.

Procedure: Send resume to Personnel Director,
866 West Peachtree St NW, Atlanta, GA 30308.
(404) 881-1911

HEALTHDYNE, INC.

Profile: Atlanta-based national corporation that provides home health care services and manufactures medical equipment. Headquarters staff numbers 200, 140exempt, and there are only a few needs there. Hires mostly registered nurses and pharmacists. Nurses must have 3+ years of recent experience in labor and delivery or 3+ years of recent experience in infusion therapy. Openings are located throughout the continental US.

Procedure: Send resume to Human Resources,
1850 Parkway Place, Marietta, GA 30067.
(404) 423-4500

HEALTHDYNE TECHNOLOGIES

Profile: Home care subsidiary of Atlanta-based Healthdyne, Inc. Employs 375 here with 80 exempt. Hires recent grads and experienced accounting/finance, and experienced manufacturing managers (mostly with engineering degrees) and staff engineers (design, ME, EE and electronic). No MIS here.

Procedure: Send resume to Professional Recruiter,
1255 Kennestone Circle NW, Marietta, GA 30066.
(404) 499-1212

HEERY INTERNATIONAL

Profile: Atlanta-based architectural, engineering, and construction management firm, specializing in commercial, institutional, industrial, and recreational facilities, including the 1996 Olympic stadium. Employs 300 in Atlanta with 100 exempt. Most hiring (both recent grads and experienced) is for construction-related engineers (CE, ME, construction management, architecture and interior design) and MIS (Microstation and Intergraph CADD specialists).

Procedure: Send resume to Corporate Recruiter,
999 Peachtree Street NE, Atlanta, GA 30367.
(404) 881-9880

HEWLETT-PACKARD COMPANY

Profile: Southern Sales Region and Business Center Offices, covering 12 states and Puerto Rico, for the second largest computer manufacturer. Employs 1800 in Atlanta, with 1100 exempt, and most are currently in sales or sales support. Hires a few recent grads, mostly electrical engineering and computer science grads, for sales and systems support training, including UNIX backgrounds. HP will transfer an additional 200 employees into the new Atlanta Business Center during 1993; this center has accounting/finance operations and Information Technology and may need personnel later.

Procedure: Send resume to Personnel Department,
2015 South Park Place, Atlanta, GA 30339.
(404) 955-1500

HILTON HOTELS (ATLANTA HILTON AND TOWERS)

Profile: With 1250 rooms and 750 employees (110 exempt), this downtown hotel is Atlanta's third largest. Most hiring is for rooms and food/beverage divisions, and some experience is generally required. Will hire a few accountants annually, recent grads and experienced.

Procedure: If in Atlanta, the Hilton prefers that you apply in person, Monday and Wednesday mornings from 9:00 am to noon. Otherwise, send resume to Employment Manager,
255 Courtland Street, Atlanta, GA 30303.
(404) 659-2000; 222-6807 Job Hotline

HITACHI HOME ELECTRONICS

Profile: Corporate headquarters support and sales office for Hitachi subsidiary that manufactures and sells TV's, VCR's, etc. Employs 140 with 60 exempt. Hires recent grads and experienced exempt in accounting/finance, sales, and MIS (Hitachi). No manufacturing or engineering here.

Procedure: Send resume to Human Resources,
3890 Steve Reynolds Blvd, Norcross, GA 30093.
(404) 279-5600

HITACHI TELECOM (USA)

Profile: US corporate headquarters for Tokyo-based Hitachi, employing 70 with 40 exempt. Manufactures telephone switching equipment (PBX's). Recently downsized and expects few needs. May seek recent software engineering grads, and experienced electrical engineers and telephony personnel.

Procedure: Send resume to Personnel and Administration,

2990 Gateway Drive, Norcross, GA 30071.
(404) 446-8820

HOLIDAY INN WORLDWIDE

Profile: World's largest single-brand hotel chain, headquartered in Atlanta. Employs 1000 with 650 exempt. Will seek all types of experienced exempt, including accounting/finance, sales, management, engineering (architecture, structural, HVAC backgrounds), and MIS (IBM). This office hires for all corporate positions, plus the reservations and data centers.

Procedure: Send resume to Manager of Employment,
3 Ravinia Drive NE, Suite 2000, Atlanta, GA 30346.
(404) 604-2000

HOME DEPOT

Profile: Atlanta-based retailer of home improvement and building materials supplies. Currently operates 230 stores in 21 states, and is expanding rapidly. Corporate headquarters employs 1700 and expects an increase. Recent grads are hired in accounting/finance and MIS (IBM 3090 and DG systems), although not always in an exempt category. College grads also hired into the management training program, along with non-degreed personnel. Experienced personnel are sought for accounting/finance and MIS, plus buyers, merchandisers and other personnel with home building products industry experience.

Procedure: Non-exempt, in-store positions are hired at the individual stores. For corporate staff positions, send resume to Director of Human Resources,
2727 Paces Ferry Rd NW, Atlanta, GA 30339.
(404) 433-8211

HOOTERS OF AMERICA

Profile: Atlanta-based, one of the fastest growing restaurant chains in the US, with 100+ units total, 30 company-owned. Headquarters employs 42 with one-half exempt, plus restaurant staffs here. Seeks both recent grads and experienced exempt in accounting/finance and management (has restaurant management training program for recent grads).

Procedure: Send resume to Director of Human Resources,
4501 Circle 75 Parkway NW, Atlanta, GA 30339.
(404) 951-2040

HOUSTON'S RESTAURANTS

Profile: Atlanta-based chain of full-service restaurants, operating 4 in Atlanta and 25 nationwide, and growing at 10% annually. Corporate office employs 50 with 35 exempt. Nearly all hires are for operations/restaurant management, recent grads and experienced. Corporate staff positions are frequently filled by promoting operations managers with the appropriate background (e.g., accounting/finance).

Procedure: Send resume to Director of Recruiting,
8 Piedmont Center, Suite 720, Atlanta, GA 30305.
(404) 231-0161

I B M

Profile: (Hiring is conducted through Employment Solutions Corp., an IBM subsidiary.) World leader in information technology, employing 5000 in Atlanta. IBM is currently in a well-publicized downsizing, and little hiring is anticipated in 1994. Most of IBM's hiring is for recent grads in technical sales and MIS-related positions. Accounting/finance is handled in NY headquarters, and although there are special programs for MBA's, they too are not in Atlanta. Engineering grads are hired to go into MIS, not engineering. Although IBM prefers to promote from within, and thus hires relatively few experienced exempt, there are special needs in MIS and for sales backgrounds from competitors or other IBM system experience. All exempt hiring for Atlanta and the Southeast passes through this office.

Procedure: Call job info line and reply as directed, or send resume to Central Employment,
3200 Windy Hill Rd, East Tower, 2d Floor, Marietta, GA 30067.
(404) 835-9000 (press 1 for job info line)

INBRAND CORP.

Profile: Atlanta-based firm that manufactures and markets disposable incontinence items. Employs 300 with 60 exempt. Seeks both recent grads and experienced exempt in all disciplines when needed, but prefers to hire entry-level.

Procedure: Send resume to Human Resources,
1165 Hayes Industrial Drive, Marietta, GA 30062.
(404) 422-3036

INFORMATION AMERICA, INC.

Profile: Atlanta-based purveyor of on-line information from public and private records. Employs 100 in Atlanta with 80 exempt. Most needs are for programmer/analysts and systems managers (DEC VAX), entry-level and experienced. Also seeks experienced sales reps, staff marketing/product development personnel and client support reps. Has summer intern in marketing. (This office also recruits for positions other than Atlanta.)

Procedure: Send resume to Recruiter,
600 West Peachtree St. NW, Suite 1200, Atlanta, GA 30308.
(404) 892-1800

INSTITUTE OF PAPER SCIENCE AND TECHNOLOGY

Profile: University information and research service for the pulp and paper industry. Employs 150 with 75 exempt. Hires both recent grads and experienced exempt, mostly in chemistry, biology, and engineering (ME, EE, ChE, or pulp and paper).

Procedure: Send resume to Personnel Manager,
500 10th Street NW, Atlanta, GA 30318.
(404) 853-9500

JOHNSON YOKOGAWA

Profile: Atlanta-based joint venture company, supplys advanced instrumentation and control systems for continuous batch and discrete process industries; and is involved in the design, manufacture, sales, and service of industrial control products, and sales and support of Distributed Control Systems (DCS). Employs 325 in Atlanta (685 nationwide), with 200 exempt. Most needs are for engineers (ChE, EE, ME) with 3-5 years experience in process control instrumentation, control engineering, DCS engineering, and/or Process Control Sales/Marketing; experienced accountants, manufacturing managers and MIS (IBM and HP).

Procedure: Send resume to Manager, Employee Development and Recruiting,
4 Dart Road, Newnan, GA 30265-1040.
(404) 254-0400

K P M G PEAT MARWICK

Profile: Fourth largest CPA firm in Atlanta and one of the Big Six international CPA firms. Employs 400 total with 330 exempt, and expects an increase. Has three divisions: tax and audit divisions hire mostly recent accounting/finance grads and MBA's (no recent MIS grads). Consulting division employs 90 in Atlanta; seeks some MBA's (accounting/finance or engineering undergrad good) with some work experience, especially in health care or employee benefits.

Procedure: For tax and audit position, send resume to Director of Personnel; for consulting positions, send resume to M. C. Managing Partner. Both at, 303 Peachtree Center Avenue, Suite 2000, Atlanta, GA 30308.
(404) 222-3000

KAISER PERMANENTE
Profile: Nation's largest and Atlanta's largest health maintenance organization (HMO). Region office here employs 1300 with 450 exempt. Hires recent accounting/finance grads and experienced exempt with health care management backgrounds.
Procedure: Send resume to Human Resources,
            3355 Lenox Road NE, Suite 1000, Atlanta, GA 30326.
            (404) 233-0555

KEANE, INC.
Profile: Provides information systems and applications development consulting; purchased G E Consulting Services in 1993. Employs 70 in Atlanta, mostly exempt-level. Hires 20 experienced exempt annually (IBM mainframe, UNIX); seldom hires recent grads. This office also supervises staffing needs for other SE/SW branch offices (Dallas, Tampa, Raleigh, et al.).
Procedure: Send resume to Staffing Manager,
            2000 Gallaria Pkwy, Suite 400, Atlanta, GA 30339.
            (404) 850-7270

KIMBERLY-CLARK CORP.
Profile: Headquarters operations for Fortune 500 diversified manufacturer, supplying administrative support to several businesses. Employment is 1300 with 900 exempt. Hires mostly recent grads, mainly into research and engineering (ChE, EE and ME). Experienced needs are usually filled with transfers from other locations, but will have some openings for biology, chemistry and polymer backgrounds, including PhD's.
Procedure: Send resume to Human Resources Services,
            1400 Holcombe Bridge Road, Roswell, GA 30076.
            (404) 587-8000

KNOWLEDGEWARE
Profile: Atlanta-based, international corporation that builds, markets, and supports computer aided software engineering (CASE) tools, plus products to maintain and enhance current applications. Employs 850. Seldom hires recent grads, but will hire experienced exempt in accounting/finance, sales, technical sales support, customer support, product management, training and consulting, personnel, and administrative.
Procedure: Send resume to Human Resources,
            3340 Peachtree Road, Suite 1100, Atlanta, GA 30326.
            (404) 231-8575

KROGER SUPERMARKETS

Profile: Largest supermarket chain in Atlanta, with 30+% of market share. Operates 60+ stores in Atlanta area, employing 12,000 total and 300± exempt. This office recruits only management-level, mostly store management trainees and will hire 70 annually. Occasional need for engineers. No accounting or MIS here.

Procedure: Send resume to Recruiting Manager,
2175 Parklake Drive NE, Atlanta, GA 30345.
(404) 496-7400

KUPPENHEIMER MEN'S CLOTHIERS

Profile: Corporate headquarters for subsidiary of Chicago-based Hartmarx; manufactures, distributes, and retails men's clothing. Headquarters staff numbers 140 with 65 exempt, plus manufacturing. Hiring here is for corporate support, including accounting/finance, human resources, MIS (AS 400), advertising/media and merchandising/buying, plus manufacturing management; hires mostly experienced, but some recent grads. All store management hiring is conducted at the stores.

Procedure: Send resume to Human Resources Department,
5720 Peachtree Pkwy, Suite 100, Norcross, GA 30092.
(404) 449-5877

LANDMARK NETWORKS

Profile: Atlanta-based owner of The Weather Channel and The Travel Channel, employing 330 with 200 exempt.

Procedure: Send resume with cover letter stating area of interest, or call their job line and then respond to a specific opening.,
2600 Cumberland Pkwy, Atlanta, GA 30339.
(404) 434-6800; ask for job line and follow instructions

LANIER WORLDWIDE

Profile: Atlanta Corporate Headquarters for subsidiary of Fortune 200 Harris Corp., the largest electronics company headquartered in the SE. Sells and services copying systems, fax machines and dictation systems. Employs 1000 in Atlanta, one-half exempt. Most needs are for accounting/finance, R&D engineering, data processing and customer service. Recent grads should have some experience, e.g., co-op or summer jobs. No manufacturing here. Sales personnel are hired at the field offices.

Procedure: Send resume to Corporate Recruiter,
2300 Parklake Drive NE, Atlanta, GA 30345.
(404) 496-9500

LAW COMPANIES

Profile: Atlanta-based engineering and environmental consulting firm. Employs approx. 1000 in Atlanta, with 650 exempt. Most needs are for engineers

287

(CE, ChE, environmental, materials) and scientists (chemistry, biology, geology, hydrology, natural resources), recent grads and experienced.

Procedure: Send resume to Corporate Recruiter,
114 Town Park Drive, Kennesaw, GA 30144.
(404) 590-4600

LIBERTY MUTUAL INSURANCE COMPANY

Profile: Division office covering nine southeastern states, employing 200 with 80 exempt. Hires recent grads as trainees in underwriting, claims and loss prevention, and then promotes into upper management. No needs for experienced exempt.

Procedure: Each of the three areas has a recruiter. Send resume to Recruiter, [specify area],
200 Galleria Pkwy, Suite 550, Atlanta, GA 30339.
(404) 955-0003

LIFE OF GEORGIA/SOUTHLAND LIFE

Profile: Dutch-owned, Atlanta-based life and health insurance and data services company, employing 1000 with 400 exempt. Will need numerous recent grads and experienced personnel in Management Associate Program, underwriting, claims, accounting/finance, and MIS (IBM 3090 and PC's).

Procedure: Send resume to Personnel Department,
5780 Powers Ferry Rd NW, Atlanta, GA 30327-4390.
(404) 980-5710

LIFE OFFICE MANAGEMENT ASSOCIATION (LOMA)

Profile: Atlanta-based trade association that sponsors education, training, and research to promote life and health insurance companies. Employs 168 with 125 exempt. Seldom hires recent grads but recruits experienced exempt with specific backgrounds when needed, including writers and editors.

Procedure: Do not send resume. LOMA does not maintain resume files, so you must call first to inquire if there are current openings for your background.,
5770 Powers Ferry Rd, Atlanta, GA 30327.
(404) 951-1770

LITHONIA LIGHTING

Profile: Corporate headquarters for the nation's largest lighting firm, manufacturing all types of lighting fixtures for residential, commercial and industrial uses. Largest subsidiary of National Service Industries, an Atlanta-based Fortune 500 corporation. Employs 2200 in Atlanta, with 800 salaried. Hires recent grads as marketing and manufacturing trainees, plus 20+ experienced personnel in all corporate and manufacturing functions.

Procedure: Send resume to Corporate Manager of Human Resources,
1135 Industrial Blvd, Conyers, GA 30307.
(404) 922-9000

LOCKHEED AERONAUTICAL SYSTEMS COMPANY
Profile: Defense contractor that develops and manufactures aircraft; one of Atlanta's largest employers with 12,000 employees, including 5000 exempt. Seeks recent grads and experienced exempt in accounting/finance, manufacturing management, MIS and engineering (ME, EE, IE, AE; CE's with stress applications, not construction). Has co-ops in engineering.
Procedure: Send resume to Employment Manager,
86 S. Cobb Drive, Marietta, GA 30063-0530.
(404) 494-5052 - Employment Office; 494-5000 job info line

LOCKWOOD GREENE
Profile: Headquartered in Spartanburg, SC, this consulting firm is involved primarily in the design of large industrial projects. Also acts as engineers, architects, managers, and planners of major commercial, institutional, and industrial facilities. Employs 400 in Atlanta with 300 exempt. Hires recent engineering grads (ME, EE, CE and ChE—no IE), and engineers and designers with experience in the design of large industrial projects. Hires co-op engineers.
Procedure: Send resume to Recruiting Specialist,
INFORUM, 250 Williams Street, Suite 4000, Atlanta, GA 30303-1036.
(404) 525-0500; 818-8301 job line

LONDON AGENCY
Profile: Atlanta-based, commercial specialty insurance company. Employs 200 with 120 exempt. Seldom hires recent grads, but has needs for experienced underwriting and accounting/finance.
Procedure: Send resume to personnel,
6 Concourse Pkwy, Suite 2700, Atlanta, GA 30328-5346.
(404) 393-9955

LORAL INFORMATION DISPLAY SYSTEMS
Profile: Division headquarters for company that designs, develops and manufactures information display systems for military applications. Hires no recent grads, but will hire experienced personnel in accounting/finance, engineering (mostly EE), MIS (uses PC's) and manufacturing in a military electronics environment.
Procedure: Send resume to Director of Personnel,
6765 Peachtree Industrial Blvd, Atlanta, GA 30360.
(404) 448-1604

LOTUS DEVELOPMENT CORP., WORD PROCESSING DIVISION

Profile: Develops and markets a graphical word processor, Ami Pro. Employs 250, including 50 engineers, nearly all exempt. Seeks high-GPA recent computer science graduates and software engineers with applications development experience for Macintosh, MS Windows, UNIX X Windows, and OS/2 Presentation Manager, as well as customer support representatives, quality assurance engineers and experienced software sales reps. Has co-ops in computer science.

Procedure: Send cover letter indicating area of interest and resume to personnel, 1000 Abernathy Road, Atlanta, GA 30328.
(404) 391-0011

LOVABLE COMPANY

Profile: Atlanta-based maker of intimate apparel, employee-owned. Employs 500, 75 exempt, and expects an increase. Recent marketing grads are hired in marketing support, and exprienced exempt needed are in manufacturing management and MIS (AS 400).

Procedure: Send resume to Employee Relations, 2121 Peachtree Industrial Blvd, Buford, GA 30518.
(404) 945-2171

M C C PANASONIC

Profile: (Matsushita Communications Industrial Corporation of America) Facility that manufactures cash registers, cellular phones, pagers, and car stereos. Employs 800, 180 exempt. Most needs are for engineers (EE mostly), recent grads and experienced, employed in either production management or design.

Procedure: Send resume to Personnel Manager, 776 Hwy 74 South, Peachtree City, GA 30269.
(404) 487-3356

M C C PANASONIC – RESEARCH AND DEVELOPMENT

Profile: Product design and development of cellular phones, pagers, car audio, digital business systems, and wireless business products. Employs 100, 85 exempt. Seeks engineers (ME, EE), especially with consumer electronics experience, occasionally recent grads).

Procedure: Send resume to Human Resources, 2001 Westside Pkwy Suite 260, Atlanta, GA 30201.
(404) 740-1485

M C I TELECOMMUNICATIONS CORPORATION

Profile: MCI is the nation's second largest long distance carrier and has several operations in Atlanta. Atlanta is headquarters for Business Services, and that group employs approx. 75% of the personnel here. They seek both recent grads and experienced exempt in accounting/finance, sales, and telecommunications, and there is a separate program for MBA's.

Procedure: Send resume to Human Resources,
Three Ravinia Drive, Atlanta, 30346-2102.
(404) 668-6000 – switchboard; 668-5122 – job application information;
800-274-5758 – job vacancies

MACY'S

Profile: Major department store chain, operating 8± stores in Atlanta. Macy's now maintains a limited support staff here. Store management, trainee and experienced, are hired here as well as at headquarters in NYC. All other positions are hired through headquarters.

Procedure: Send resume to Region Training Manager,
180 Peachtree St NW, Atlanta, GA 30303.
(404) 221-7228

MAG MUTUAL INSURANCE COMPANY

Profile: Professional liability insurer to physicians and hospitals (malpractice insurance). Employs 80 with 45 exempt. Hires recent insurance grads and experienced insurance specialists (underwriters, claim adjusters, etc).

Procedure: Send resume to Human Resources,
P O Box 52979, Atlanta, GA 30355.
(404) 842-5600

MARTA (METRO. ATLANTA RAPID TRANSIT AUTHORITY)

Profile: Employs 3700 with one-third exempt, mostly at headquarters. MARTA will have limited exempt hiring in 1994, mostly in accounting/finance, administration, and staff support management. No engineering needs. Offers unpaid internships in MIS, personnel, and engineering.

Procedure: Send resume to Director of Personnel,
2424 Piedmont Rd NE, Atlanta, GA 30324-3324.
(404) 848-5544 for information; 848-5231 for information on hiring procedure and current vacancies.

MCDONALD'S CORPORATION

Profile: Regional office for McDonald's Corporation, directly responsible for company-owned units. Seeks mostly management trainees for their units, plus refers candidates to franchises.

Procedure: Send resume to Personnel Manager,
5901 Peachtree Dunwoody Rd, Suite 500, Atlanta, GA 30328.
(404) 399-5067

METROPOLITAN LIFE INSUR. — INVESTMENT INFO. DIV.

Profile: One of five departments that provide data processing and accounting/finance reporting support to the Corporate Investment

Division. Employs 325 with 250 exempt. Seldom hires recent grads, but will seek experienced exempt in accounting, MIS, and securities/brokerage.

Procedure: Send resume to Human Resources,
303 Perimeter Center North, Suite 500, Atlanta, GA 30346.
(404) 804-4600

MICROBILT CORPORATION

Profile: Atlanta-based subsidiary of First Financial Management Company (see listing), that provides data communications network (e.g., electronic mail, credit card terminals, loan origination, POS, electronic forms, electronic interfacing, etc.). Employs 500 in Atlanta, 450 exempt. Will hire exempt personnel in all areas, including accounting/finance, sales, engineering and MIS.

Procedure: Send resume to Human Resources,
6190 Powers Ferry Road, Suite 400, Atlanta, GA 30339.
(404) 955-0313

MITSUBISHI CONSUMER ELECTRONICS OF AMERICA

Profile: Manufacturing facility producing cellular phones and color televisions, employing 680. Seeks recent grads and experienced exempt in engineering (ME, EE), MIS (IBM) and purchasing.

Procedure: Send resume to Personnel Supervisor,
P O Box 299, Braselton, GA 30517.
(706) 654-3011

MOBIL CHEMICAL COMPANY

Profile: Manufactures and sells polyethylene (plastic films) and polystyrene (plastic foam) disposable products for consumer, industrial and institutional use. Consumer brand names include Baggies and Hefty. This manufacturing and distribution facility employs 800 total with 85 exempt. Hires few recent grads, but will hire experienced exempt in accounting/finance, sales, manufacturing and distribution management, and engineering (EE, ME, ChE). Also has occasional need for MBA's and in human resources.

Procedure: Send resume to Employee Relations,
P O Box 71, Covington, GA 30209.
(706) 786-5372

MOHAWK INDUSTRIES

Profile: Atlanta-based manufacturer of residential and commercial carpet, employing 90 at headquarters (30 exempt), plus 4000+ employed in manufacturing. Hq rarely hires recent grads, but some experienced exempt in accounting/finance and marketing are needed. Manufacturing personnel are hired at the plants, including the management trainees.

Procedure: Send resume to Human Resources,
1755 The Exchange, Atlanta, GA 30339.
(404) 951-6000

MUNICIPAL ELECTRIC AUTHORITY OF GEORGIA

Profile: Atlanta-based provider of electricity to 48 Georgia cities. Employs 100 in headquarters, 90 exempt. Does not hire recent grads, but will seek experienced accountants, engineers (EE mostly, some ME), economic development and marketing, and MIS (IBM).

Procedure: Send resume to Human Resources,
1470 RiverEdge Parkway NW, Atlanta, GA 30328.
(404) 952-5445

N C R — ENGINEERING AND MANUFACTURING/ATLANTA

Profile: Facility that designs, develops and manufactures integrated software and hardware computer systems for retailers. Employs 700, including 250 engineers, 420 exempt. NCR's corporate policy is to hire 95% recent grads and promote from within. Most of their needs will be for engineers (computer, ME, and EE) and computer science majors, plus a few general business grads. Offers co-ops summer internships for engineering (ME, EE, and computer), personnel, finance, and computer science majors.

Procedure: Send resume to Personnel Resources,
2651 Satellite Blvd, Duluth, GA 30136.
(404) 623-7000

N C R — U S GROUP SE DIVISION

Profile: NCR's domestic equipment marketing group, employing 15,000+ in the US and 1300 in Atlanta, 500+ exempt. Provides marketing and staff support for their Southeast sales organization. Hires recent grads for accounting/finance, marketing and MIS. No needs for engineers.

Procedure: Send resume to Personnel,
5335 Triangle Parkway, Suite 200, Norcross, GA 30092.
(404) 840-2740

N C R — WORLDWIDE SERVICE PARTS CENTER

Profile: Facility that handles national and international distribution of NCR parts. Employs 700 with 200 exempt. Hires mostly recent grads in engineering (EE), programming (NCR hardware) and purchasing (BBA best). Occasionally has need for experienced purchasing agents. [NCR is a division of AT&T.]

Procedure: Send resume to Personnel Administrator,
259 Highway 74 South, Peachtree City, GA 30269.
(404) 487-7000

N E C TECHNOLOGIES, INC.

Profile: Manufacturer of computer products, including monitors and CD rom, and assembles and tests automotive electronics for US auto manufacturer. Currently staffing within the manufacturing, warehouse, and technical areas. Employs 450 with 60 exempt.

Procedure: Send resume to Human Resources Department,
1 NEC Drive, McDonough, GA 30253.
(404) 957-6600

NAPA AUTO PARTS

Profile: Atlanta distribution center for Atlanta-based Genuine Parts Company, an automotive parts distributor and retailer. This distribution facility, plus the 29 retail stores in Atlanta, employ 475 with 160 exempt. Seeks management trainees for Executive Training Program, some recent grads but most with 3 - 5 years business experience (any field).

Procedure: Send resume to Personnel Manager,
P O Box 2000, Norcross, GA 30091.
(404) 447-8233

NATIONAL DATA CORPORATION

Profile: Atlanta-based data processing company within the computer services industry, providing data exchange, processing and telecommunications services to a variety of financial and corporate clients. Employs 1700, including 1000 exempt, and anticipates hiring 200 exempt annually. Recent grads are hired mostly as programmers and customer service representatives (BBA or liberal arts majors). Experienced exempt are hired in a variety of areas: customer service; programming and all types of MIS professionals (Tandem and Unisys); engineers (EE, EET and MET); accountants and financial analysts; sales representatives with experience in banking (cash management or credit cards especially), health care software systems and telecommunications. Has co-ops in MIS and staff marketing.

Procedure: Send resume to Director of Employment,
2 NDC Plaza, Atlanta, GA 30329.
(404) 728-2000; 728-2030 job info line

NATIONAL LINEN SERVICE

Profile: Atlanta-based division of Fortune 500 National Service Industries, also headquartered in Atlanta (see listing). This is the textile rental division and is NSI's second largest division, employing 750 (400 exempt) in Atlanta, which includes 4 plants + headquarters staff. Offers recent grads a Management Development Program that covers numerous corporate specialties, especially operations management and sales. Also seeks accounting/finance and experienced production/operations managers and sales representatives.

Procedure: Send resume to Manager of Personnel Administration,
1420 Peachtree St NE, Atlanta, GA 30309.

(404) 853-1000

NATIONAL SERVICE INDUSTRIES

Profile: Corporate headquarters for this Fortune 500 corporation, divided into seven divisions, which operate autonomously and handle their own hiring. Headquarters employs 110, and hires auditors and benefits specialists. (See listings for National Linen Service, Lithonia Lighting and Zep Manufacturing.)

Procedure: Send resume to Personnel,
1420 Peachtree St NE, Atlanta, GA 30309.
(404) 853-1000

NATIONAL VISION ASSOCIATES

Profile: Atlanta-based optical retailing chain with 250+ stores, mostly in Wal-Mart stores. Headquarters employs 75 with approx. one-half exempt. Hires both recent grads and experienced exempt in accounting, distribution, and MIS (AS 400).

Procedure: Send resume to personnel,
296 South Clayton St., Lawrenceville, GA 30245.
(404) 822-3600

NATIONSBANK

Profile: Fourth largest US bank, headquartered in Charlotte, NC. Atlanta is headquarters for General Bank division, employing 50,000 throughout nine states and DC. NationsBank is also the largest bank in Georgia, employing 5000+ with about 30% exempt. Seeks recent grads, mostly accounting/finance, management, and MBA's, plus experienced personnel (prefers financial services backgrounds) in accounting/finance, management, and MIS (IBM).

Procedure: Recent grads, direct resume to Manager of College Relations; experienced personnel, direct resume to Management Recruiting. Both at,
P O Box 4899, Atlanta, GA 30302-4899.
(404) 607-6157; job line: 491-4530 - non-exempt

NORDSON CORPORATION

Profile: North American Division Headquarters of Ohio-based Nordson Corp., a manufacturer of finishing and adhesive application equipment. This office provides marketing and technical support for several Nordson groups. Employs 400 with 180 exempt. Seldom hires recent grads, but seeks experienced exempt in sales, engineering (EE, ME), marketing specialties (analysts, product development, etc.) and technical training.

Procedure: Send resume to Manager, Human Resources,
11475 Lakefield Drive, Technology Park/Johns Creek, Duluth, GA 30136.
(404) 497-3400

NORFOLK SOUTHERN CORPORATION

Profile: Norfolk, VA-based railroad and transportation company, parent of Norfolk-Southern Transportation Co. (formerly Southern Railway) and North American Van Lines. Employs 1700 in Atlanta, 300 exempt. Hires mostly recent grads, although there are needs for experienced engineers (ME, EE, and CE) and MIS (IBM 3270 & Amdahl). Recent accounting/finance and MIS grads are hired for Atlanta positions. Recent liberal arts grads are hired mostly for sales, and engineers and business grads are hired for management programs; may be relocated after training. Opened new customer service center in 1993, but most hires will be internal.

Procedure: Send resume to Manager of Employment,
             125 Spring Street SW, Atlanta, GA 30303.
             (404) 529-1300

NORRELL CORPORATION

Profile: Corporate headquarters for the fifth largest temporary help company in the US. Operates 14 branches in Atlanta, 300+ nationally. Corporate staff numbers 350 with 50% exempt. Will hire a few recent grads and 30+ experienced exempt in accounting/finance, sales and sales management, and marketing. Has co-op in computer programming. No MIS.

Procedure: Send resume to HumanResources,
             3535 Piedmont Rd NE, Atlanta, GA 30305.
             (404) 240-3000

NORTHERN TELECOM ATLANTA

Profile: Atlanta telecommunications company consisting of Public Networks Products and Marketing, Private Networks, and Wireless Systems including Carrier and Cellular Networks. These groups are located at three area facilities in Stone Mountain, Norcross and Ravinia. In addition, the FiberWorld Conference Center for customers is located in Norcross. Overall Atlanta employment is 1600 with 60% exempt. Hires mostly EE's, along with a few accountants, marketing/sales professionals, and personnel from other disciplines, both recent grads and experienced, probably 50 annually.

Procedure: Send resume to Staffing Manager,
             1 Ravinia Drive, Atlanta, GA 30346.
             (404) 661-5000; 840-5501 job info line

NORTHWEST GEORGIA HEALTH SYSTEM

Profile: Formed in 1993 with merger of Kennestone hospital and two smaller hospitals. Four-hospital health care system employing 5500 with 30% exempt. Hires mostly medical personnel, especially nurses and therapists, plus some experienced accounting, administration, and MIS.

Procedure: Send resume to Human Resources,
             677 Church Street, Marietta, GA 30060.
             (404) 793-7070

OFFICE OF THRIFT SUPERVISION
Profile: Federal agency that regulates the savings and loan industry.   This office
             is one of five region headquarters and conducts on-site examinations of
             federally-insured thrifts. Employs 125 in Atlanta (250 in region) with
             100 exempt. Most hires are recent accounting/finance grads to become
             examiners and loan analysts, although there are some needs for persons
             with banking or other regulatory agency experience. No MIS needs.
Procedure: Send resume to Human Resources,
             P O Box 105217, Atlanta, GA 30348.
             (404) 888-0771

OGILVY & MATHER
Profile: One of Atlanta's largest advertising agencies, headquartered in NYC.
             Employs 75 with 70 exempt. Hires a limited number of recent grads
             with experience or internship with an ad agency. Also hires experienced
             advertising professionals, and prefers ad experience for accountants. Uses
             Macintosh network. Offers several internships year-round for college
             advertising majors.
Procedure: Send resume to Personnel Manager,
             1360 Peachtree St NE, Atlanta, GA 30309.
             (404) 888-5100

OGLETHORPE POWER
Profile: Nation's largest power generation and transmission cooperative, based in
             Atlanta. Employs 550 with 400 exempt. Seldom hires recent grads, but
             seeks experienced accounting/finance, engineering (EE, IE mostly; few
             ME) and MIS.
Procedure: Send resume to Human Resources,
             2100 East Exchange Place, Tucker, GA 30085-1349.
             (404) 270-7600

OHMEDA MEDICAL ENGINEERING SYSTEMS
Profile: Atlanta-based company that manufactures and sells hospital medical gas
             delivery systems. Employs 140 here (70 exempt) + hires for the 30 field
             sales personnel located throughout the US. Occasionally hires recent
             grads, but most needs are for experienced engineers (ME, EE).
Procedure: Send resume to Human Resources,
             2850 Northwoods Pkwy, Norcross, GA 30071.
             (404) 448-6684

OKI TELECOM

Profile: Manufacturer of cellular mobile phones and automotive electronic products. Employs 730 with 200 exempt. Most needs are for engineers (EE, IE, ME and software), both recent grads and experienced.

Procedure: Prefers that you not send resume until you have called the Job Line, then respond to a specific opening.,
437 Old Peachtree Rd, Suwanee, GA 30174.
(404) 995-9800; 822-2701 Job Line

OXFORD INDUSTRIES

Profile: Atlanta-based, Fortune 500 apparel manufacturing and marketing company, mostly for private and contract labels. Has manufacturing facilities throughout the Southeast, including several close to Atlanta. Corporate staff numbers 220, 40% exempt. Hires mostly recent grads in accounting/finance, manufacturing management, and computer science (AS 400).

Procedure: Send resume to Manager of Human Resources,
222 Piedmont Avenue, Atlanta, GA 30308.
(404) 659-2424

PACTEL CELLULAR

Profile: Subsidiary of Pacific Telesis and provider of cellular communications services to businesses and individual users. Employs 300 in Atlanta, 100 exempt, and growing rapidly. Currently does not seek recent grads, but may later. Will need experienced exempt in accounting/finance, sales (any successful background ok), management, engineering (mostly EE's to design and construct networks), customer service and marketing. MIS handled at California headquarters.

Procedure: Send resume to Human Resources Manager,
4151 Ashford Dunwoody Rd, Atlanta, GA 30319.
(404) 257-5000; 237-5000 x 7306 job line

PAMECO CORPORATION

Profile: Headquartered in Atlanta and the nation's largest wholesale distributor of commercial refrigeration and air conditioning equipment and one of the largest producers of high energy friction materials and components. Employs 75 at headquarters, all exempt. Seeks both recent grads and experienced exempt in accounting/finance, sales, management, personnel and credit/collections, although all may not remain in Atlanta.

Procedure: Send resume to Director of Human Resources,
1000 Center Place, Norcross, GA 30093.
(404) 798-0600

PANASONIC (MATSUSHITA ELECTRIC CORP. OF AMERICA)

Profile: Southeast region sales and service office, employing 300+. Nearly all hiring is for experienced consumer and industrial sales representatives.

Procedure: Send resume to Recruiter,
1854 Shackleford Court, Norcross, GA 30093.
(404) 717-6700

PENNEY, J. C. AND COMPANY

Profile: Region headquarters for the nation's fourth largest retail chain, specializing in soft lines. Only recruiting here is for store management, especially recent grads to enter training program. All accounting and MIS is at corporate headquarters in Dallas, TX.

Procedure: Much entry-level hiring is done through campus recruiting, but resumes are accepted also. Send resume to,
715 Peachtree Street NE, Atlanta, GA 30302.
(404) 897-5500

PENNEY'S CATALOG DISTRIBUTION CENTER

Profile: One of six national distribution centers, employing 1700 with 100 exempt. Almost all hiring is for Management Trainees in operations and distribution, and generally hires 6+ each year. Prefers to promote from within and thus seldom hires experienced exempt.

Procedure: Send resume to Employment and Personnel Relations Manager,
5500 South Expressway, Forest Park, GA 30050.
(404) 361-7700

PEPSI COLA

Profile: Bottles and distributes Pepsi Cola brands of soft drinks. Employs 450 here, with 90 exempt. Hires both recent grads and experienced exempt for accounting, operations management and engineering. MIS is handled at corporate headquarters in NY. Offers summer internships in operations management.

Procedure: Send resume to Director of Human Resources,
1480 Chattahoochee Ave, Atlanta, GA 30318.
(404) 355-1480

PEPSICO EMPLOYMENT PLUS

Profile: Provides recruiting and sourcing services for PepsiCo's three restaurant subsidiaries – Pizza Hut, KFC, and Taco Bell. Recruits solely for restaurant operations management, both recent grads for trainee positions and experienced restaurant managers. Hires 100+ annually.

Procedure: Send resume to Personnel,
1395 Marietta Parkway, Building 300, Suite 108, Marietta, GA 30067.
(404) 429-7770

PIZZA HUT – GEORGIA MARKET OFFICE

Profile: Third largest fast food chain in the world, subsidiary of Pepsico, Inc. Operates 170 stores in metro-Atlanta and south Georgia. Most hiring here is for store operations and management, probably 30 recent grads and 125 experienced.

Procedure: Send resume to Human Resources,
7094 Peachtree Industrial Blvd, Norcross, GA 30071.
(404) 903-1140

PLANTATION PIPELINE CO.

Profile: Atlanta-based, interstate pipeline transporter of liquid refined petroleum products. Employs 118 in Atlanta, 70 exempt. Seeks mostly recent grads in accounting/finance and engineering (CE, ME, EE), and seldom has needs for experienced exempt.

Procedure: Send resume to Senior Personnel Analyst at,
945 East Paces Ferry Road NE, Atlanta, GA 30326.
(404) 364-5880

PORTMAN COMPANIES

Profile: Atlanta-based parent company of internationally renown architect John Portman. This office handles commercial real estate design, development, management and finance. Human Resources Department acts as a clearing house or liaison with various departments, and refers resumes to the appropriate hiring source. Most experienced exempt positions are very specialized, and they rely heavily on in-house job postings, referrals and personnel agency contacts. Recent grads are hired in accounting, plus there are often needs in their marketing department for journalists and communications majors.

Procedure: Send resume to Human Resources,
225 Peachtree St NE, Suite 201, Atlanta, GA 30303.
(404) 614-5252

PRICE WATERHOUSE

Profile: International Big 6 CPA firm, employing 300 (250 exempt) and with three divisions: tax, audit and consulting. Audit and tax divisions hire mostly recent accounting and tax grads and MBA's; consulting division hires 30 annually, mostly experienced exempt and some recent grads (including MBA's) in MIS, CIS, or accounting. Uses IBM systems and software.

Procedure: For audit and tax divisions, send resume to Director of Human Resources,
50 Hurt Plaza, Suite 1700, Atlanta, GA 30303
(404) 658-1800.
For consulting division, send resume to Human Resources Manager,
3200 Windy Hill Road, Suite 900 West, Marietta, GA 30067.
(404) 933-9191

PRIMERICA FINANCIAL SERVICES

Profile: Atlanta-based company selling term life insurance and mutual funds. Employs 1300 here with 525 exempt. Seeks recent grads in accounting, management, journalism, and liberal arts for customer service positions. Seeks experienced exempt in accounting/finance, MIS (IBM), and insurance specialties.

Procedure: Send resume to Corporate Recruiter,
3120 Breckinridge Blvd, Duluth, GA 30199-0001.
(404) 381-1000; 564-6100 job info line

PRINTPACK, INC.

Profile: Atlanta-based, nation's fourth largest converter of unprinted, unlaminated packaging film. Employs 575 here with 250 exempt. Hires a few recent grads for sales training and seeks packaging degrees for management training. Most hires are experienced exempt with 3-5 years experience in sales (industrial or packaging), manufacturing management and engineering, accounting/finance and MIS (IBM and HP — prefers manufacturing experience).

Procedure: Send resume to Corporate Recruiting Manager,
4335 Wendell Drive SW, Atlanta, GA 30336.
(404) 691-5830

PRUDENTIAL PROPERTY AND CASUALTY CLAIMS

Profile: Region claims office handling six SE states. Employs 80 here with 20 exempt. Hires recent grads for claims trainee positions; no experienced needs.

Procedure: Send resume to personnel,
3150 Holcombe Bridge Rd, Norcross, GA 30071.
(404) 441-6100

RACETRAC PETROLEUM, INC.

Profile: Corporate headquarters for retail gas and convenience store chain, one of Atlanta's three largest privately held firms. Headquarters staff numbers 150 with 50 exempt. Hires a few recent accounting grads, but most needs are for exempt (and non-exempt) personnel in accounting/finance, marketing, purchasing, legal and MIS (AS 400 and PC's), and engineering/design.

Procedure: Send resume to Personnel Manager,
P O Box 105035, Atlanta, GA 30348.
(404) 431-7600

RESOLUTION TRUST CORPORATION (FDIC)

Profile: East Region office of the liquidation division of Federal Deposit Insurance Corp, selling off defunct S&L's. Currently reorganizing and downsizing, and thus not accepting applications. Very difficult to contact in person.

Vacancies are advertised on Tuesday in the Wall Street Journal and on Sunday in The Atlanta Journal-Constitution.

Procedure: Best effort is to call the phone recording below and if openings occur, instructions for their application procedure will be explained.,
245 Peachtree Center Avenue NE, Suite 1100, Atlanta, GA 30303.
(404) 225-5708 (recording)

RICH'S DEPARTMENT STORES

Profile: Corporate headquarters for one of the largest department store chains in Atlanta, and division of Federated Department Stores. Employs 7,000 in Atlanta. Most recent grads are needed for their Executive Training Program, which encompasses all facets of the corporation. Experienced exempt hired are retail professionals and MBA's for sales support group. Most MIS functions are handled by SABRE Group (see listing). Accounting/finance at Cincinnati headquarters only.

Procedure: Send resume to Executive Recruitment Staff,
223 Perimeter Center Parkway, Atlanta, GA 30346.
(404) 913-5176

RITZ-CARLTON HOTELS

Profile: Atlanta-based chain of luxury hotels, operating 30 world-wide, including 2 in Atlanta. Headquarters staff numbers 100, with 50 exempt, plus hotel staffs. Recent grads are hired into non-exempt positions, most often by an individual hotel, then promoted into exempt positions in management or corporate headquarters as neded. Seeks experienced exempt with hotel background.

Procedure: Send resume to Human Resources,
3414 Peachtree Rd NE, Atlanta, GA 30326.
(404) 237-5500

ROBINSON-HUMPHREY COMPANY

Profile: Full-service financial services firm, specializing in the southeast region, selling institutional and individual investment opportunities. Corporate headquartered in Atlanta, and subsidiary of Smith-Barney Shearson, a Primerica company. Employs 600 in Atlanta. Recent MBA grads are hired as Corporate Financial Associates and recent undergrads (usually finance) are hired as Corporate Financial Analysts, a two year training program. More often, recent grads are hired for non-exempt administrative positions (research; sales, trading, and operations assistants) to learn business basics first; they are not hired as brokers, unless they have three years prior sales experience. Broker training program available for individuals with 3+ years sales or entrepreneurial experience.

Procedure: Send resume to Director of Human Resources,
3333 Peachtree Road NE, 7th Floor, Atlanta, GA 30326.
(404) 266-6656

ROCKWELL INTERNATIONAL — TACTICAL SYSTEMS DIV.

Profile: Major defense contractor, manufacturing high-tech components, including the AGM-130 Standoff weapon system. Employs 900 with 400 exempt. Hires recent grads and experienced engineers (EE), plus experienced exempt in accounting/finance and DOD backgrounds.

Procedure: Send resume with cover letter indicating job objective and areas of expertise to Human Resources--Employment,
1800 Satellite Blvd, Duluth, GA 30136.
(404) 476-6474 HR dept; 476-6300 main switchboard

ROLLINS, INC.

Profile: Corporate headquarters for diversified service corporation, including Orkin Exterminating Company and Rollins Protective Services. Employs 500 with 200 exempt, and will hire 50± exempt annually. Recent grads hired are usually entry accountants. Seeks experienced personnel for typical corporate headquarters types: sales, accounting/finance, insurance administration, distribution, MIS (IBM mainframe using Cobol; VAX/VMS using C); etc.

Procedure: Send resume to Human Resources Department,
2170 Piedmont Rd NE, Atlanta, GA 30324.
(404) 888-2000; job line: 888-2125

ROSSER INTERNATIONAL

Profile: One of Atlanta's largest architectural/engineering firms, employing 350 with 250 exempt. Parent company of Lowe Engineers, an environmental and hazardous waste engineering company. Hires both recent grads and experienced exempt in accounting/finance, administration, and engineering (all types, including architecture).

Procedure: Send resume to Human Resources,
524 West Peachtree St. NW, Atlanta, GA 30308.
(404) 876-3800

RUSSELL, H. J. & COMPANY

Profile: Fourth largest minority-owned business in the US, headquartered in Atlanta. Has eight subsidiaries, primarily in real estate, construction and communications. Employs 500 in Atlanta office, with 40% exempt. Hires few recent grads, except for their interns. Experienced personnel hired include accounting/finance, property management, construction engineers, management services (e.g., personnel, PR, administration, etc.) and MIS (AS 400).

Procedure: Send resume to Human Resources Director,
504 Fair Street SW, Atlanta, GA 30313.
(404) 330-1000

S I T A

Profile: French headquartered telecommunication/data processing company, employing 300 in Atlanta, 250 exempt. Hires a few recent grads, but mostly experienced exempt in various positions – customer support, administration, operations, and technical.

Procedure: Send resume to Human Resources,
3100 Cumberland Circle, Suite 200, Atlanta, GA 30339.
(404) 850-4500

SAAB CARS USA

Profile: US corporate headquarters for Swedish car company, relocated to Atlanta in 1992. Hq employs 100 with 60 exempt. Does not hire recent grads, but seeks experienced exempt in accounting, finance, and automotive marketing. No needs for engineering or MIS.

Procedure: Send resume to Human Resources,
4405-A Saab Drive, P O Box 9000, Norcross, GA 30091.
(404) 279-0100

SABRE GROUP

Profile: Atlanta-based information processing division of Allied/Federated department stores, parent of Atlanta-based Rich's department stores and others. Employs 1400 with 750 exempt. Nearly all recruitment is for MIS, recent grads and experienced. They operate four IBM 3090's.

Procedure: Send resume to Personnel,
6801 Governor's Lake Pkwy, Bldg 200, Suite 500, Norcross, GA 30071.
(404) 448-8900

SAFECO INSURANCE COMPANY

Profile: Major full-lines insurance company employing 315 in Atlanta, 185 exempt. Hires recent grads, preferably with some professional work experience (insurance not necessary) for training programs in underwriting, claims and marketing.

Procedure: Send resume to Personnel,
P O Box A, Stone Mountain, GA 30086.
(404) 469-1111; 879-3357 job info line

SALES TECHNOLOGIES

Profile: Atlanta-based subsidiary of D&B that designs, develops, installs, markets and supports software to improve productivity of large corporate sales forces. Employs 400 in Atlanta, all exempt. Nearly all exempt needs (about 50 each year) are in MIS, some recent computer science grads, but mostly for experienced UNIX and MS-DOS systems professionals and experienced C programmers.

Procedure: Send resume to Human Resources,
3399 Peachtree Road NE, Suite 700, Atlanta, GA 30326.

(404) 841-4000

SCHLUMBERGER INDUSTRIES, INC. — ELECTRICITY DIV.

Profile: Division headquarters, manufactures electrical measurement and control products for use by the public utility industry. Employs 225 with 190 exempt. Will hire 7-10 recent grads annually, mostly engineers (EE, computer engineering and computer science) for marketing applications, software, firmware and hardware design. Also seeks 5 experienced personnel in the same areas, plus sales engineers.

Procedure: Send resume to Personnel Department,
180 Technology Parkway, Norcross, GA 30092.
(404) 447-7300

SCIENTIFIC ATL. — BROADBAND COMMUNICATIONS GROUP

Profile: Largest division of Scientific Atlanta, manufactures and sells hardware for the cable TV industry. Employs 1500 in Atlanta with 525 exempt. Most recent grads hired are electrical engineers and MBA's. Experienced exempt needs will be for accounting/finance, sales, engineering (EE) and marketing. Offers internships in engineering and marketing. No MIS needs here.

Procedure: Send resume to Staffing Manager,
P O Box 105027, Atlanta, GA 30348.
(404) 903-5000

SCIENTIFIC ATLANTA — CORPORATE HEADQUARTERS

Profile: Employs 150, with 100 exempt. Provides corporate staff support functions for divisions. Most hires are in finance, MIS (DEC VAX and IBM 3090) and human resources, usually experienced but some recent grads.

Procedure: Send resume to Human Resources Dept.,
P O Box 105600, Atlanta, GA 30348.
(404) 903-4000

SCIENTIFIC ATLANTA — ELECTRONIC SYSTEMS DIVISION

Profile: Division that manufactures remote sensing ground stations and support equipment, and supplies electronic instruments and control systems for telecommunications, industrial, and government applications. Employs 300 with 180 exempt. Most needs are for engineers (EE, Physics, ME and CS), plus accounting/finance and sales; hires recent grads and experienced exempt.

Procedure: Send resume to Human Resources Director,
P O Box 105027, Atlanta, GA 30348.
(404) 449-2000

SCIENTIFIC ATLANTA — NETWORK SYSTEMS GROUP

Profile: Manufactures and markets high-tech telecommunications equipment and systems world-wide. Employs 350 with 150 exempt. Most recent grads hired are electrical engineers; experienced exempt may be needed in sales, marketing, and engineering (EE).

Procedure: Send resume to Human Resources, Mail Code 31-B,
            4356 Communications Drive, P O Box 105027, Atlanta, GA 30348.
            (404) 903-5000

SCIENTIFIC GAMES

Profile: Atlanta-based corporation that is the world's largest printer of lottery tickets for state-operated lottery games. Employs 75 in headquarters (mostly exempt), plus 200 at their new manufacturing facility. Most needs are for programmers (Stratus) and experienced gravure printers for manufacturing.

Procedure: Send resume to Director of Personnel,
            1500 Blue Grass Lakes Pkwy, Alpharetta, GA 30201.
            (404) 664-3700

SIEMENS — ATLANTA AREA SERVICE CENTER

Profile: Manufactures commercial switchboards and panelboards. Employs 225 total with 27 exempt. Hires recent engineering grads (EE and ME), and has a co-op engineering program. Hires experienced exempt in accounting, engineering (EE and ME), MIS (Prime) and materials management.

Procedure: Send resume to Personnel Manager,
            2140 Flintstone Drive, Tucker, GA 30084.
            (404) 493-1231

SIEMENS — CIRCUIT PROTECTION AND CONTROLS DIVISION

Profile: Manufactures and sells low voltage electrical distribution equipment for commercial, industrial, and residential uses. Hires a few recent grads, plus experienced personnel in accounting/finance, engineering (all types) and marketing analysis.

Procedure: Send resume to Employee Relations--Circuit Protection and Controls Division,
            3333 State Bridge Road, Alpharetta, GA 30202.
            (404) 751-2000

SIEMENS ENERGY & AUTOMATION — CORP.HEADQUARTERS

Profile: Headquarters employs 200, 60 exempt. Hires recent grads in accounting/finance, engineering (mostly EE, ME and IE), MIS (need CS degree) and management. Has two-year Management Training Program in accounting/finance or engineering: employee is given four six-month assignments and then permanent assignment, based on results of temporary assignments. Will also seek experienced exempt in same areas, although most engineers are hired at division level (see other Siemens listings). Has need for German bilingual applicants, and offers exchange program with German locations for technical and management personnel.

Procedure: Send resume to Corporate Personnel Manager,
P O Box 8900, Atlanta, GA 30356.
(404) 751-2000

SIEMENS — SALES/SERVICE

Profile: Handles hiring of sales and service personnel. Has a few needs for experienced sales and sales management personnel with electrical/electronic manufacturing and marketing backgrounds, but prefers to hire recent engineering grads (EE mostly) for their Sales and Service Engineer Training Program.

Procedure: Send resume to Sales/Service Employee Relations Manager,
3333 State Bridge Road, Alpharetta, GA 30202.
(404) 751-2000

SIEMENS — SYSTEMS DIVISION

Profile: Manufactures AC and DC variable speed drives, programmable control products, industrial systems, and power systems. Employs 340 with 235 exempt. Most hires are for engineers (EE and electrical related), both recent grads and experienced.

Procedure: Send resume to Human Resources,
100 Technology Drive, Alpharetta, GA 30202.
(404) 740-3000

SIMMONS COMPANY

Profile: Atlanta-based manufacturer of bedding, with three facilities in Atlanta employing 300 total, 200 exempt; corporate staff nunbers 130 with 110 exempt. Seeks recent grads for sales and management trainees, and experienced exempt in accounting/finance, sales, marketing, management, engineering (IE, ME mostly) and MIS (AS 400). This office hires for headquarters and the research center; manufacturing has their own personnel department.

Procedure: Send resume to Corporate Recruiter,
1 Concourse Parkway, Atlanta, GA 30328.
(404) 521-7700

SIMONS-EASTERN CONSULTANTS

Profile: Atlanta-based, multi-discipline design and consulting firm, specializing in the design of industrial manufacturing facilities. Employs 600 with 400 exempt. Most personnel needs are for engineers and designers (CE, ChE, ME, EE and Pulp and Paper), some recent grads but mostly experienced.

Also hires some experienced exempt in accounting/finance, MIS (DEC VAX) and personnel. Has co-op program for engineering students.

Procedure: Send resume to Personnel,
P O Box 1286, Atlanta, GA 30301.
(404) 370-3200

SMITH, W H USA

Profile: US Corporate Headquarters of British conglomerate. Owns and operates 300+ retail gift shops located in airports and hotels nationwide. Employs 110 in Atlanta, with 50 exempt, plus managers and sales associates in several stores in Atlanta. Hires experienced exempt in accounting/finance, distribution, marketing and MIS (DG system), plus retail specialties (buying, merchandising, etc.).

Procedure: For Store Management, send resume to Regional Manager; for other positions, send resume to Human Resource Department,
3200 Windy Hill Road, Suite 1500 West Tower, Marietta, GA 30067.
(404) 952-0705

SMITHKLINE BEECHAM CLINICAL LABORATORIES

Profile: Largest clinical laboratory in the world. Employs 900 in Atlanta, plus 400 additional in SE, mostly medical and laboratory specialists. Most needs are for clinical and medical technologists (entry-level and experienced), and certification is required.

Procedure: Send resume to Personnel,
1777 Montreal Circle, Tucker, GA 30084.
(404) 934-9200; 621-7450 job line

SNAPPER POWER EQUIPMENT

Profile: Atlanta-based manufacturer of outdoor power equipment (mostly for lawn and garden), and division of Atlanta-based Actava Group (formerly Fuqua Industries). Employs 1300 with 150 exempt. Hires numerous recent grads in all areas, accounting/finance, sales, manufacturing, engineering and MIS (AS 400)--sometimes in non-exempt positions to learn business from the ground up, and then be promoted into exempt-level. Hires experienced personnel in all areas, especially manufacturing backgrounds.

Procedure: Send resume to Personnel Department,
P O Box 777, McDonough, GA 30253.
(404) 954-2500

SOLVAY PHARMACEUTICALS

Profile: Clinical research and development center for major pharmaceutical firm, employing 400 here with 300 exempt. Most hires are in pre-clinical and clinical research, and some in MIS (DEC VAX and HP 3000), generally with experience but occasionally a recent grad.

Procedure: Send resume to Human Resources Department,

901 Sawyer Road, Marietta, GA 30062.
(404) 578-9000

SONY ELECTRONICS
Profile: Sales office employing 150, 75 exempt. Hires no recent grads, but seeks experienced sales and sales support personnel with background in magnetic tape, electronics or video equipment.
Procedure: Send resume to Personnel,
3175 Northwoods Pkwy, Norcross, GA 30071.
(404) 263-9888

SONY MUSIC ENTERTAINMENT INC.
Profile: Facility that manufactures audio tape cassettes and musical video cassettes. Employs 1150 with 110 exempt. Exempt needs for manufacturing IE's and EE's, and finance.
Procedure: Send resume to Human Resources,
P O Box 1528, Carrollton, GA 30117.
(404) 836-2000

SOUTHERN COMPANY SERVICES
Profile: Provides engineering, information resources, accounting/finance, PR/communications, and other administrative services to subsidiary electrical utilities throughout the Southeast, including Georgia Power, Alabama Power, Gulf Power, Mississippi Power, and Savannah Electric and Power. Employs 1200 (600 in MIS-related) with 850 exempt. Hires recent grads (3.0 GPA preferred) and experienced exempt in the above disciplines.
Procedure: Hires heavily through campus recruiting. Experienced exempt should check first with their Job Hot Line, then respond to a specific opening. Send resume and cover letter indicating the position for which you are applying to Human Resources,
64 Perimeter Center East, Atlanta, GA 30346.
(404) 393-0650; 668-3464 Job Info Line

SOUTHERN ELECTRIC INTERNATIONAL
Profile: Engineering and consulting firm that builds, owns and operates power plants; subsidiary of Atlanta-based Southern Company. Employs 100 in headquarters, 90exempt. Seeks some recent grads, but mostly experienced exempt in accounting, engineering (EE, ME, ChE) and MIS.
Procedure: Send resume to Personnel Manager,
100 Ashford Center North, Suite 400, Atlanta, GA 30338.
(404) 261-4700

SOUTHTRUST BANK OF GEORGIA, NA

Profile: Birmingham-based bank, operating 85+ branches in Atlanta, employing 1300 with 400 exempt. Hires recent grads and experienced exempt in management and accounting/finance. MIS only at HQ in Alabama.

Procedure: Send resume to Human Resources,
2000 RiverEdge Parkway, Atlanta, GA 30328.
(404) 951-4000; 951-4010 job info line

SOUTHWIRE

Profile: Corporate headquarters for the nation's largest wiremaker. Employs 2500 at this location, with 500 exempt. Will hire co-ops, recent grads and experienced exempt in all areas, including accounting/finance, sales, management, MIS (Unisys A series) and especially engineering (EE, ME, ChE and IE). Offers co-op programs in engineering, MIS, metallurgy, accounting, and chemistry.

Procedure: Send resume to Professional Employment,
1 Southwire Drive, Carrollton, GA 30119.
(404) 577-3280

SPIEGEL

Profile: Telephone catalog ordering center for major retailer, employing 450 in Atlanta, mostly non-exempt. Hires recent grads as customer sales representatives, often non-exempt. Has no needs for experienced exempt. Hires temps for Christmas season.

Procedure: Send resume to Personnel Administrator,
6050 Oakbrook Pkwy, Norcross, GA 30093.
(404) 441-1288

SPORTSTOWN

Profile: Atlanta-based retailer of sporting goods, with 22 stores total, five in Atlanta. Employs 600 in Atlanta, 70 at headquarters. Hires recent grads as Manager Trainees, but prefers some retail experience. Seeks experienced exempt in retail management and operations, plus accountants.

Procedure: Send resume to Human Resources,
680 Engineering Drive, Suite 50 (Technology Park), Norcross, GA 30092.
(404) 246-5300

SPRINT CORPORATION

Profile: Third largest long distance telephone carrier, employing 2000 in Atlanta, 900 exempt. Personnel with experience in telecommunications or other large systems (e.g., computers) are needed for marketing and sales positions, plus engineers with network communications experience and MIS (IBM system) professionals.

Procedure: Send resume to Staffing Manager (they respond to all resumes),

3100 Cumberland Circle, Atlanta, 30339.
(404) 859-5000; 859-8397 Job Information Line

STAR ENTERPRISE
Profile: SE region office for joint venture of Texaco and Aramco to market
            Texaco products. Employs 150 with 100 exempt. Currently
            reorganizing and anticipates limited hiring in 1994. Previous hiring
            included recent marketing grads, plus some construction-related engineers
            (CE, BC). Seldom hires experienced exempt. Accounting and MIS in
            Houston.
Procedure: Send resume to Manager of Human Resources,
            333 Research Court, Norcross, GA 30092.
            (404) 903-1500

STATE FARM INSURANCE COMPANIES
Profile: Office that consolidates all support operations for State Farm policy
            holders in Georgia. Employs 1350 with 525 exempt. Prefers to hire
            entry-level and then promote up; thus, will seek many recent grads in
            accounting/finance and MIS, plus trainees for programs in underwriting,
            claims and administration (liberal arts or business).
Procedure: Send resume to Personnel Specialist,
            11350 John Creek Pkwy, Norcross, GA 30198-0001.
            (404) 418-5000

STEVENS GRAPHICS
Profile: Subsidiary of BellSouth, second largest printer in Atlanta, and prints
            mostly directories, catalogues, and business forms. Employs 400 with
            110 exempt. Hires recent grads for manufacturing management,
            engineering and MIS, and seeks experienced exempt in the same areas
            (printing experience preferred) plus accounting.
Procedure: Send resume to Human Resources Manager,
            713 Ralph D. Abernathy Blvd SW, Atlanta, GA 30310.
            (404) 753-1121

STOCKHOLDER SYSTEMS, INC.
Profile: Atlanta-based developer of software for the financial srvices industry,
            employing 330. Rarely hires recent grads, but will seek experienced
            exempt in accounting/finance, sales, engineering (software-related) and
            MIS.
Procedure: Send resume to Human Resources,
            4411 East Jones Bridge Road, Norcross, GA 30092.
            (404) 441-3387

SUN DATA

311

Profile: Atlanta-based remarketer of IBM midrange computers and services, employing 160 with 80 exempt. Hires part-time telemarketers and has occasional needs for experienced exempt in all areas.

Procedure: Send resume to Human Resources Director,
1300 Oakbrook Drive, Norcross, GA 30093.
(404) 449-6116

SUNTRUST SERVICES

Profile: Application Systems Division that handles programming operations for SunTrust Banks, Inc. (see separate listing above) and subsidiary banks, and employs 230, 60 exempt. Projected needs are for experienced MIS professionals as needed for replacements (IBM mainframe; Cobol, CICS, IMS).

Procedure: Send resume to Employment Manager,
250 Piedmont Ave, Suite 2000, Atlanta, GA 30302.
(404) 588-8877

SUPER CLUB MUSIC

Profile: (d/b/a Turtle's, Tracks, Rhythm and Views, and The Record Bar.) Atlanta-based retailer of records, tapes and videos, operating 300+ stores in the Southeast, including 60+ in Atlanta. Headquarters staff numbers 250 with 40 exempt. Hires experienced exempt and recent grads in management, accounting, MIS (AS 400 and RS 6000), advertising, and marketing.

Procedure: Send resume to Human Resources,
2151 Northwest Parkway, Marietta, GA 30067.
(404) 988-9805

SUPER DISCOUNT MARKETS, INC. (D/B/A CUB FOODS)

Profile: Corporate headquarters for franchise operator of eight Georgia supermarkets. Employs 1600 in Atlanta, 175 exempt. Hires 15± recent grads in supermarket management, MIS (AS 400) and accounting/finance. Seeks experienced supermarket management personnel. Will open three new stores in '94.

Procedure: Send resume to Director of Human Resources,
420 Thornton Road, Lithia Springs, GA 30057.
(404) 732-6800 (press 5 for personnel)

SYNCORDIA CORP.

Profile: Owned by BT (British Telecom) and headquartered in Atlanta, Syncordia markets data, voice, and image networking to multinational corporations. Currently employs 200 and anticipates an increase in employment.

Procedure: Send resume to Human Resources,
2727 Paces Ferry Road NW, Atlanta, GA 30339.
(404) 333-4600

T B S — CABLE NEWS NETWORK

Profile: Operates a 24-hour cable news gathering organization, which includes CNN, CNN Headline News, CNN International, Ckeckout Channel, Airport Channel, and CNN radio, and employs 1600 in Atlanta. Hires many recent grads annually for entry level positions as Video Journalist, but requires broadcast and/or internship experience. Applicants seeking on-air or correspondent positions need 5-7 years experience in television.

Procedure: Send resume to CNN Human Resources,
1 CNN Center, P O Box 105366, Atlanta, GA 30348-5366.
(404) 827-1500

T B S — CORPORATE HEADQUARTERS

Profile: TBS employs 2200 in Atlanta, 900 exempt. Hires experienced exempt in accounting/finance, sales (TV time sales and cable) and MIS. Also hires some accounting/finance grads in non-exempt positions, then promotes through in-house posting system.

Procedure: Send resume with cover letter including areas of interest and expertise to Human Resources,
1 CNN Center, P O Box 105366, Atlanta, GA 30348-5366.
(404) 827-1700, but do not call; no information is given by phone.

T B S — ENGINEERING DEPARTMENT

Profile: Provides engineering services all TBS companies and employs 200. Hires 8± recent BS and AS grads (EET mostly) to work in quality control engineering and maintenance. Also needs 8± experienced engineers annually, preferably with broadcast experience.

Procedure: Send resume to Engineering Training Director,
1 CNN Center, P O Box 105366, Atlanta, GA 30348.
(404) 827-1700

T B S – TURNER NETWORK TELEVISION (TNT) AND WTBS

Profile: TNT is the entertainment cable operation and WTBS is SuperStation Channel 17; combined employment in Atlanta is 450. This office conducts hiring for both operations, and seeks mostly recent grads or other entry-level personnel with TV intern experience, especially in the entertainment sector. Offers non-salaried internships for college juniors, seniors, and recent grads.

Procedure: Send resume to Human Resources,
1050 Techwood Drive NW, Atlanta, GA 30318.
(404) 827-1700, but do not call; no info is given by phone

TDS HEALTHCARE SYSTEMS

Profile: Atlanta-based company that develops, manufactures and markets hardware, software and services for comprehensive hospital information systems.

Employs 275 in Atlanta with 90% exempt. Seeks experienced exempt in accounting/finance, but all other hires (e.g., sales, MIS) should have clinical backgrounds.

Procedure: Send resume to Personnel,
200 Ashford Center North, Atlanta, GA 30338.
(404) 847-5000

TECHNICAL ASSOC. OF THE PULP AND PAPER INDUSTRY

Profile: Atlanta-based trade association employing 85 with one-half exempt. Most exempt needs are in communications and education, both recent grads and experienced.

Procedure: Send resume to personnel,
15 Technology Parkway South, Norcross, GA 30092.
(404) 446-1400

TENSAR CORPORATION

Profile: International, Atlanta-based company involved in the production and sale of geosynthetics for structural soil reinforcement technology. Employs 220 with 70 exempt. Nearly all hires are for civil engineers with soil improvement/reinforcement experience or for manufacturing engineers with polymer extrusion experience.

Procedure: Send resume to Personnel Manager,
1210 Citizens Parkway, Morrow, GA 30260.
(404) 968-3255

THE SYSTEM WORKS

Profile: Atlanta-based firm that manufactures plant performance systems to manage facilities and maintain equipment. Employs 195 with 175 exempt, and anticipates an increase. Seldom hires recent grads. Most hires are MIS-related in marketing, customer service, programming, and operations; has several systems – IBM, DEC. Some needs in accounting/finance.

Procedure: Send resume to personnel,
1640 Powers Ferry Rd, Bldg 11, Marietta, GA 30367.
(404) 952-8444

THE TRAVELERS COMPANIES

Profile: Insurance company handling all lines, employing 500 in Atlanta, 120 exempt, and hires approximately 5-10 positions annually. Seeks recent grads in accounting and for insurance training programs (risk management, claims, and underwriting); and experienced exempt in accounting/finance and insurance specialties, including employee benefits. Travelers' products are sold through independent brokers.

Procedure: Send resume to Human Resources,
P O Box 4416, Atlanta, GA 30374-0087.

(404) 393-7500; 246-7056 job info line

THOMPSON, J. WALTER USA
Profile: Third largest advertising agency in the world and one of Atlanta's largest. Employs 110 total with 75% exempt. Rarely hires recent grads, but will hire advertising professionals with 1+ years experience.
Procedure: Send resume to Personnel,,
1 Atlanta Plaza, 950 E. Paces Ferry Road NE, Atlanta, GA 30326.
(404) 365-7300

TOWERS PERRIN COMPANIES
Profile: Fifth largest international consulting firm, with three divisions: actuarial, insurance and general management. Employs 250 here, 180 exempt. Atlanta personnel office hires only entry-level, and seeks degrees in finance, economics, math and communications/journalism, plus MBA's. Experienced exempt are hired either through headquarters in NYC or by individual department managers here.
Procedure: Send resume to Human Resources Department,
950 E. Paces Ferry Rd NE , Atlanta, GA 30326-1119.
(404) 365-1600

TRANSUS
Profile: Southeastern common carrier and transportation service, corporate headquartered in Atlanta. Employs 800 here, 200 salaried. Hires recent grads and experienced personnel for accounting/finance, operations management, sales, MIS (AS 400) and technical school grads.
Procedure: Send resume to Employment Office,
2090 Jonesboro Rd, Atlanta, GA 30315.
(404) 627-7331

TREASURY DRUGS — RETAIL AND DISTRIBUTION CENTER
Profile: Withdrew from Atlanta market in 1993, selling most stores to Big B Drugs. Distribution center closed.
Procedure: Big B Drugs handles all hiring through headquarters in Birmingham, AL,

TRUST COMPANY BANK
Profile: One of three largest banks in Georgia in assets and subsidiary of Atlanta-based SunTrust Banks (see separate listing). Employs 5000 in Atlanta. Generally hires for more entry level positions than experienced. Recent grads are hired primarily from January through April, and those interested in a banking career can enter the Commercial Banking Training Program. Experienced personnel are hired all year, and there are needs in all areas, especially accounting/finance, MIS, banking professionals, etc.
Procedure: Send resume to Employment Manager,
P O Box 4418, Mail Code 019, Atlanta, GA 30302.

(404) 588-7199

TUCKER WAYNE/LUCKIE & CO.
Profile: Atlanta-headquartered and largest privately-owned advertising agency in Atlanta. Employs 145 in Atlanta, 60 exempt, and hires only experienced advertising professionals. Seldom needs accounting or MIS.

Procedure: Has no centralized resume distribution system, and each department head hires for his/her area only. Thus, send resume to a specific functional area (e.g., creative or research) or simply to the company and it will be directed to the appropriate person.,
1100 Peachtree St NE, Atlanta, GA 30309.
(404)347-8700

UNISYS CORPORATION – ATLANTA DEVELOPMENT CENTER
Profile: Research and development center that develops applications software and provides information services for the financial industry and for education (specifically libraries). Nearly all hiring is for MIS and computer science backgrounds, both recent grads and experienced, plus an occasional accountant.

Procedure: Send resume to Human Resources Manager,
5550-A Peachtree Parkway, Norcross, GA 30092.
(404) 368-6000

UNISYS — MARKETING REGIONAL HEADQUARTERS
Profile: Southern Region headquarters that directs sales of Unisys's hardware and software products and information services. Employs 525 in the Southeast with 425 exempt. Most hires are experienced computer sales reps, although there may be an occasional entry-level need.

Procedure: Send resume to Human Resources,
4151 Ashford Dunwoody Road NE, Atlanta, GA 30319.
(404) 851-3000

UNITED FAMILY LIFE INSURANCE
Profile: Atlanta-based life insurance company, employing 220 with 140 exempt at headquarters. Primary hiring is for entry-level positions, and thus frequently hires recent grads in service support (includes claims, customer service, etc.) and management.

Procedure: Send resume to Human Resources Department,
P O Box 2204, Atlanta, GA 30371.
(404) 659-3300

UNITED PARCEL SERVICE
Profile: UPS has corporate headquaraters in Atlanta and employs 1400 at that location. Although there are needs for experienced exempt, a career with UPS in all areas (accounting/finance, management, engineering,

personnel, etc.) often starts in an hourly operations position, such as sorting packages or driving a delivery truck, with promotion into higher positions when an opening occurs. These entry positions are generally filled at the district level, and you may wish direct your efforts there, rather than at the corporate level. Management positions at the corporate level are required to have a minimum of a bachelor's degree, with most requiring a master's.

Procedure: Two methods: (1) For entry-level positions, including part-time seasonal, UPS hires extensively through the Georgia Department of Labor, especially the offices in Smyrna and Decatur (see Public Agencies section). (2) Experienced personnel applying for Hq positions should call the Job Employment Line listed below and reply as directed, including the Job Code given. Resumes can be sent to ,
P O Box 468568, Atlanta, GA 30346.
(404) 913-6800 Job Employment Line; 913-6000 Corporate Hq; 662-3451 GA District Human Resources office

UPTON'S DEPARTMENT STORES

Profile: Corporate headquarters for this privately-held apparel chain, operating 32 stores in the Southeast, 13 in Atlanta. Corporate office numbers 180 with 110 exempt, and also conducts exempt-level hiring for local stores. Seeks both recent grads and experienced personnel (75+ each year) in accounting/finance, management, MBA's and MIS (AS 400). Also seeks experienced buyers, retail managers and personnel managers.

Procedure: Send resume to Director of Executive Development,
6251 Crooked Creek Road, Norcross, GA 30092.
(404) 662-2500

VON ROLL, INC.

Profile: US corporate headquarters for Zurich-based company that designs and builds industrial waste plants, employing 50 in Atlanta, 85% exempt. Most hires are for engineers (ME, ChE, environmental), both recent grads and experienced.

Procedure: Send resume to Recruitment,
3080 Northwoods Circle NW, Suite 200, Norcross, GA 30071.
(404) 729-0500

WACHOVIA BANK OF GEORGIA

Profile: Third largest bank in Georgia and subsidiary of Wachovia Corporation, headquartered in Winston-Salem, NC. Employs 5400 total in Georgia, with 2500 exempt. Will hire 100 recent grads each year, for all areas of the bank, and their management training class begins in June. Probably 100 experienced exempt personnel will be hired annually, again in all areas of the bank, and including those with banking experience. Some MIS (IBM) needed, although most is in NC.

Procedure: Send resume to Management Recruiting,

191 Peachtree Street, Atlanta, GA 30303.
(404) 332-5000

WAUSAU INSURANCE COMPANIES

Profile: SE region headquarters for sixth largest US commercial property and casualty insurance company, employing 338 in SE (175 in Atlanta) with 180 exempt. Seeks a few recent grads in business, accounting, and risk management, but most current needs are for experienced risk underwriters, environmental engineers, and sales reps.

Procedure: Send resume to Human Resources,
2987 Clairmont Road, PO Box 105067, Atlanta, GA 30348-5067.
(404) 633-1451

WENDY'S OLD FASHIONED HAMBURGERS

Profile: Fourth-largest fast food chain in the world, Wendy's operates 64 units in Atlanta. Atlanta office employs 50, all exempt-level. Plans to hire 25 recent grads and 125 experienced exempt into operations management. This office hires for Georgia and Mississippi.

Procedure: Send resume to Human Resources Representative,
375 Franklin Road, Suite 400, Marietta, GA 30067.
(404) 425-9778

WESTINGHOUSE REMEDIATION SERVICES, INC.

Profile: Remediates all hazardous waste sites except nuclear. Employs 280 with 150 exempt, and expects an increase. Hires no entry-level, but will seek experienced exempt with environmental engineering and environmental sales backgrounds.

Procedure: Send resume to Professional Staffing,
675 Park North Blvd, Bldg F, Clarkston, GA 30021.
(404) 299-4650

WINDSOR GROUP

Profile: Atlanta-based non-standard auto insurance and insurance services company, employing 375 here with 225 exempt, and has branches in Tampa and Oklahoma City. Hires recent insurance grads, plus BBA and accounting. Seeks experienced personnel in insurance specialties (auto claims, underwriters, adjusters, appraisers, etc.) and MIS (IBM ES9000, Cobol programmer/analysts, VM/VSE/ESA environment). Promotes heavily from within.

Procedure: Send resume to Windsor Group, Attn: Employment,
P O Box 105091 (located at 1300 Parkway Circle, Atlanta), Atlanta, GA 30348.
(404) 951-5599

WINN-DIXIE SUPERMARKETS

Profile: Division office and warehouse for largest supermarket chain in the SE, third largest in Atlanta, operating 62 stores here. Recent grads are hired mostly for mangement training positions (BBA best but others OK), plus a few accountants. Winn-Dixie promotes heavily from within, and thus seeks few experienced exempt. MIS function at Hq in Jacksonville, FL.

Procedure: Send resume to Human Resources Manager,
            5400 Fulton Industrial Blvd, Atlanta, GA 30336.
            (404) 346-2400

WOLF CAMERA AND VIDEO

Profile: Atlanta-based, largest camera retailer in the Southeast, operating more than 160 stores in 10 states. Employs 550 in Atlanta, including 140 at headquarters (60 exempt-level). Headquarters hires 10± exempt annually, mostly experienced accountants and other corporate staff types. All store managers start as sales personnel (non-exempt), then are promoted into management. No MIS or engineering needs.

Procedure: Obtain application form from any Wolf store and/or send resume to Personnel,
            1706 Chantilly Drive NE, Atlanta, GA 30324.
            (404) 633-9000

WORLDSPAN TRAVEL AGENCY INFORMATION SERVICES

Profile: World's second-largest travel reservations system, based in Atlanta, and employing 700. Seeks both recent grads and experienced exempt in all areas, and especially programmers (IBM), airline background ideal.

Procedure: Send resume to Human Resources,
            300 Galleria Pkwy, Atlanta, GA 30339.
            (404) 563-7400

YAMAHA MOTOR MANUFACTURING CORP.

Profile: Manufacturing facility that makes golf cars and water vehicles. Employs 450 with 320 exempt. Hires both recent grads and experienced exempt in accounting, manufacturing and engineering (mostly ME, some IE).

Procedure: Send resume with cover letter indicating the specific discipline for which you are applying, to Personnel,
            1000 Georgia Hwy 34, Newnan, GA 30265.
            (404) 254-4000

ZEP MANUFACTURING COMPANY

Profile: Corporate headquarters in Atlanta, third largest and most profitable subsidiary of Atlanta-based National Service Industries (see listing). Manufactures and sells specialty chemicals, cleaning agents and agricultural chemicals, primarily for the hospitality, health care and maintenance industries. Employs 300 in Atlanta, with 75 exempt. Hires recent grads in accounting/finance, sales, engineering (ChE and ME) and for operations (production/distribution) management training. Seeks experienced personnel in accounting/finance, sales, manufacturing management, distribution, engineering, MIS (HP), and laboratory assistants and chemists. Has co-ops in Chemical Engineering.

Procedure: Send resume to Manager of Employment,
1310 Seaboard Industrial Blvd, Atlanta, GA 30318.
(404) 352-1680

APPENDIX D:

ATLANTA PERSONNEL AGENCIES

The following is a list of Atlanta personnel agencies, all members of the Georgia Association of Personnel Services, followed by their area of specialization.

As I stated in Chapter IV, many good agencies are not members of the association, and so I urge you to follow my suggestions in choosing a personnel agency. Refer back to "Chapter IV, Tool #4: Personnel Agencies."

AAA EMPLOYMENT
2814 New Spring Rd, Suite 212
Atlanta 30339
434-9232
secty, sales, mgt, a/f, dp

ABACUS NETWORKS
3690 Holcombe Bridge Rd, Suite 100
Norcross 30092
446-1116
dp

AGRI-PERSONNEL
5120 Old Bill Cook Rd, Atlanta 30349
768-5701
agri, chem, eng, mfg, mktg, pharm, sales,
food

ANNE WILLIAMS & ASSOCS.
One Piedmont Center, Suite 120
Atlanta 30305
266-2663
legal, insur

ATLANTA TECHNICAL CONSULTANTS
2231 Perimeter Park, Suite 8
Atlanta 30341
454-8140
dp

BELL OAKS COMPANY
3390 Peachtree Rd, Suite 924
Atlanta 30326
261-2170
a/f, dp, eng, mfg, med, sales, mgt

BELLON & ASSOCS.
1175 Peachtree St NE, Suite 1920
Atlanta 30361
881-1153
attorneys

BEST AGENCY
2971 Flowers Rd South, Suite 143
Atlanta 30341
452-1732
generalist

BOREHAM INT'L
275 Carpenter Dr, Suite 309
Atlanta 30328
252-2199
secty, sales/mktg

BRADLEY-MORRIS
200 Galleria Pkwy, Suite 220
Atlanta 30339
612-4950
Jr. military officers, mfg, eng, oper

BRANDT & ASSOCS.
1010 Huntcliff, Suite 1350
Atl 30350
998-7802
insur

BROCK & ASSOCS
233 Peachtree St NE, Suite 303
Atlanta 30303
525-2525
a/f, bkpg, adm, legal, secty

BUSINESS PROFESSIONAL GROUP
3490 Piedmont Rd, Suite 212
Atlanta 30305
262-2577
eng (all levels), entry

CAREER DEVELOPMENT CORP.
1850 Parkway Place, Suite 925
Marietta 30067
426-5600
chem, dist, eng, fin, mgt, mfg, sales, r&d

CELLA ASSOCS
5028 Covington Highway, Suite C
Decatur 30035
288-0400
food (all levels)

CHANDLER CONSULTANTS
P O Box 741, Commerce 30529
577-2485
insur

COMMONWEALTH CONSULTANTS
4840 Roswell Rd, Suite C302
Atlanta 30342
256-0000
dp (all areas)

COMPUTER NETWORK RESOURCES
7000 Central Parkway, Suite 1010
Atlanta 30328
391-9009
dp

CONTINENTAL TECHNICAL SERVICES
400 Colony Square, Suite 200
Atlanta 30361
808-9996
eng, eng support

CORPORATE PERSONNEL
1148 Hampton Hall Drive
Atlanta 30319
252-3292
eng, mfg environment

CORPORATE SEARCH CONSULTANTS
47 Perimeter East, Suite 260
Atlanta 30346
399-6205
eng, sales (paper & box)

CORPORATE SOLUTIONS
5901 Peachtree Dunwoody Rd, Bldg A,
Suite 360, Atlanta 30328
396-1678
Acctg, secty, cust serv

C-PECK COMPANY
169 Interolocken Dr
Atlanta 30342
843-3183
Insur, mgt

DAVID C. COOPER & ASSOCS
400 Perimeter Ctr Terrace, Suite 950
Atlanta 30346
395-0014
acctg, fin

DSA - DIXIE SEARCH ASSOC.
5775 Peachtree Dunwoody Rd, # 200B
Atlanta 30342
252-8800
food (sales, mfg, retail/whol, hosp)

DUNHILL PROFESSIONAL SEARCH
340 Interstate north, Suite 140
Atlanta 30339
952-0009
mfg, eng, pkg, env, mat-mgt, QC

ERICH MAIER ASSOCS.
5200 Northside Drive, Atlanta 30327
956-8601
Pkg (sales, design, corr)

EXECUTIVE FORCE
2271 Winding Way, Tucker 30084
939-0484
dp (sales, supp, mgt)

EXECUTIVE RESOURCE GRP
927 Montreal Rd, Atlanta 30021-1334
298-0888
Health (upper lvel)

FINANCIAL RECRUITERS OF GEORGIA
5575-B Chamblee Dunwoody, Ste 340
Atlanta 30338
392-9441
acctg, fin

FLETCHER GROUP
233 Peachtree St, Suite 303
Atlanta 30303
525-4212
bkpg, acctg

FOCUS ENTERPRISES
3 Corporate Square, Suite 340
Atlanta 30329
321-5400
dp

HIRE SOLUTIONS
P O Drawer 671927, Marietta 30067
956-7278
generalist

HOWIE AND ASSOCS
875 Old Roswell Road, F-100
Roswell 30076
998-0099
dp, health, sales (med & dp)

HUDSON PERSONNEL/SEARCH, INC.
6151 Powers Ferry Road, Suite 540
Atlanta 30339
984-2414
credit, mktg, med, sales

HYGUN GROUP, INC.
3020 Roswell Rd, Suite 200
Marietta 30062
973-0838
environmental (all levels)

INSURANCE PERSONNEL RESOURCES
8097-B Roswell Rd, Atlanta 30350
396-7500
insur

ISC OF ATLANTA
300 Interstate North Pkwy, Suite 330
Atlanta 30339
952-2340
health, retail, commo, plastics, pharm,
envir, chem

JES SEARCH FIRM
3475 Lenox Rd, Suite 970
Atlanta 30326
262-7222
dp

JSA, Inc.
1000 Parkwood Circle, Suite 950
Atlanta 30339
955-2324
dp

LEADER INSTITUTE
2245 Dillard St, Tucker 30084
270-0990
eng, high tech, mfg, r&d, sales, mktg

LUCAS ASSOCIATES
• 1827 Powers Ferry Rd,
Marietta 30067
952-2775
• 5901-A Peachtree Dunwoody Rd, Suite
525, Atlanta 30328
901-5570
acctg, sales, Jr. military officers

MALCOM GROUP
P O Box 7811, Marietta 30065
565-5213
Insur

MANAGEMENT DECISIONS
1867 Independence Square, Suite 201
Atlanta 30338
512-0006
dp

MATRIX RESOURCES
115 Perimeter Ctr Place, Suite 1099
Atlanta 30346
393-9933
dp

McELROY & COMPANY.
1533 Brookcliff Circle
Marietta 30062
973-8626
transportation

MEDICAL & PHYSICIAN SEARCH
1401 Johnson Ferry Rd, Suite 328-N1
Marietta 30062
973-6277
health care management

MICHAEL ALEXANDER GRP
333 Sandy Springs Cir NE, Suite 131
Atlanta 30328
256-7848
acctg, fin

NPS OF ATLANTA
750 Hammond Drive, Bldg 15, #200
Atlanta 30328
843-3758
acctg, insur, secty

PACES PERSONNEL
245 Peacthree Ctr Ave, Suite 703
Atlanta 30303
688-5307
paralegal, exec secty

PATHFINDERS, INC.
229 Peachtree St NE, Suite 1500
Atlanta 30303
688-5940
secty

P.D.Q.S.
6151 Powers Ferry Rd, Suite 545
Atlanta 30339
850-6465
acctg, dp

PERSONALIZED MANAGEMENT ASSOCS
1950 Spectrum Cir, Suite B-310
Marietta 30067
916-1668
entry, food, hosp, mgt, retail, sales

PETERS ENGINEERING SERVICES
2155 Denson Lane, Marietta 30060
419-2594
environment eng (BS, MS, PhD)

PERSONNEL OPPORTUNITIES
5064 Roswell Rd, Suite D-301
Atlanta 30342
252-9484
insur, eng, mfg, secty

P J REDA & ASSOCS
1090 Northchase Pkwy So., Suite 200
Marietta 30067
984-3238
food (rest., hospitality, mgt), health

PLACEMENT RESOURCES
241 West Wieuca Rd, Suite 210
Atlanta 30342
843-3223
acctg, admin

PROFESSIONAL OPTIONS
5671 Peachtree Dunwoody Rd, Ste. 550
Atlanta 30342
843-6000
medical

RANNOU & ASSOCS.
1900 The Exchange, Suite 370
Atlanta 30339
956-8225
packaging (corrugated)

RETAIL EXECUTIVE PLACEMENT SERVICES
5901-A P'tree Dunwoody Rd, Ste 425
Atlanta 30328
396-9114
retail

RIDLEY, JAMES, INC.
4227 Keheley Rd, Marietta 30066
516-6590
attorneys

ROLLINS SEARCH GROUP
203 Parkway 575, Woodstock 30102
516-6042
insur (actuaries, dp)

ROWLAND MT. & ASSOCS.
4 Executive Park East, Suite 130
Atlanta, GA 30329
325-2189
Sales

SANFORD ROSE ASSOCIATES
3525 Holcombe Bridge Rd, Suite 2B
Norcross 30092
449-7200
Wireless telecom (sales, mktg, mgt, tech)

SEARCH ATLANTA, INC.
P O Drawer 674899, Marietta 30067
984-0880
full service

STERLING LEGAL SEARCH
5180 Roswell Rd NW, Suite 202
Atlanta 30342
250-9766
legal

SYMONDS & SMYTHE
P O Box 941635, Atlanta 30341
458-8234
chem, eng, health, insur, mortgage

TANNER PERSONNEL
3316 Piedmont Rd, Suite 170
Atlanta 30305
231-9303
medical

TECHNICORPS
2872 Woodcock Blvd, Suite 132
Atlanta 30341
455-8705
dp (progrmmers, systems analyst)

THOMAS EXECUTIVE SEARCH
713 Lanford Springs Drive
Lilburn 30247
381-1181
food, purch, distrib, acctg, fin, mgt

TOAR ENTERPRISES
545 Colonial Park Dr, Suite 202
Roswell 30075
993-7663
generalist

WHITTAKER AND ASSOCS
2675 Cumberland Pkwy, Suite 263
Atlanta 30339
434-3379
food industry - all areas

WINDWARD EXEC. SEARCH
58 South Park Sq, Suite B
Marietta 30060
425-6788
paper indus - eng, mgt, sales

APPENDIX E:

PROFESSIONAL AND TRADE ASSOCIATIONS

Do not underestimate the assistance available through these organizations. Most industries are represented by more than one association, and the following list is only a modicum of the total number of national organizations with Atlanta chapters. If your representative association is not included here, call the national headquarters and ask for the local contacts. Meeting times and places for many associations, plus for-profit job search seminars, are included in the Monday business section of *The Atlanta Journal-Constitution* in the "Weekly Planner" column.

Even associations that do not offer direct job assistance are often excellent network sources, especially at their meetings. I have spoken with many persons who found their jobs this way.

Remember that many of the officers and contacts are not paid, but have volunteered their time to help the association. Do not ask to have long-distance phone calls returned and avoid taking up too much of the volunteer's time.

I have included the names of the most recent officers here, but since they are elected for a limited time, they may have changed. If so, ask this past official for the new slate of officers. In case you are not able to locate the new officers, I have also included the phone number of the national headquarters. Call them, ask for "Membership Services," and then inquire the name and phone number of the current president for their Atlanta chapter or another city, if you are open for relocation.

List of associations and organizations included

Please let me know of other associations that I have not listed here and who offer job assistance, so that I can include them in future editions. I would also appreciate comments on how useful and successful they are for you.

Human Resources
American Society for Training and Development
International Foundation of Employee Benefit Plans
National Society for Performance and Instruction
Society for Human Resource Management
Working in Employee Benefits

Ethnic/Minority
National Society of Women Accountants
American Women's Society of CPA's
Financial Women International
National Association for Professional Saleswomen
National Association of Black Accountants
National Association of Female Executives
National Association of Insurance Women
National Association of Women in Construction
Black Data Processing Associates
National Black MBA Association
Women in Communications

Manufacturing/Distribution
American Production and Inventory Control Society
American Society for Quality Control
National Association of Purchasing Management
National Contract Management Association

Engineering/Technical/MIS
American Society of Heating, Refrigerating, and Air
    Conditioning Engineers
American Society of Mechanical Engineers
Association for Systems Management
Black Data Processing Associates
Georgia Society of Professional Engineers
Society of Logistics Engineers

Technical Association of the Pulp and Paper Industry
Advertising/Public Relations
Ad 2/Atlanta
American Institute of Graphic Arts
Atlanta Ad Club
Business/Professional Advertising Association
Creative Club of Atlanta
International Association of Business Communicators
Public Relations Society of America
Society for Technical Communication
Women in Communications
Accounting/Finance
American Institute of CPA's/Georgia Society of CPA's
American Society of Women Accountants
American Women's Society of CPA's
Financial Executives Institute
Financial Women International
Georgia Bankers' Association
Institute of Internal Auditors
National Association of Accountants
National Association of Black Accountants
National Association of Business Economists
Planning Forum
Management/Administration
Administrative Management Society
American Society for Public Administration
Association of Records Managers and Administrators
Georgia Society of Association Executives
National Association of Legal Secretaries
Professional Secretaries International
Medical
American Association of Occupational Health Nurses
Georgia Society of Hospital Pharmacists
Sales/Marketing
American Marketing Association
National Association for Professional Saleswomen
National Society of Fund Raising Executives
Society for Marketing Professional Services
Property Management/Construction
Building Owners and Managers of Atlanta
Women in Construction

Appendix E:

Professional and Trade Associations

Note: The following information is believed to be correct, except that the names of officers and contacts may have changed, as was stated in the earlier text. If the contact listed here is not able to assist you, call the national headquarters of your association and request the name of the current local president. In addition, I would greatly appreciate information on other associations not listed here and that offer job assistance for their membership. Send the information to
CareerSouth Publications
P O Box 52291, Atlanta, GA 30355.

AD 2 ATLANTA

Comprised of advertising professionals age 31 and under, including recent college grads. Meets at J W Marriott Hotel at Lenox Square on third Tuesday of each month at 6:00 for cocktails, followed by program; $7 for non-members. Primary career assistance is to help first job changers. Publishes monthly newsletter, but does not include job listings or seekers. Currently they have a Career Network Director that handles job and applicant match-up. They also sponsor a two-day Career Seminar in April of each year, mostly for recent grads, and an agency tour and workshop in the fall, mostly for college seniors. No charge for members, but must be a member to participate ($65/yr). For more information on career services, contact the Career Network Director, Kevin Beerstecher at (404) 915-5113 (home). For other information, write
P O Box 18829, Atlanta, GA 30326.
Or call (404) 264-6223 This is their answering service. Leave your name, phone number, and the person you wish to contact, and they will return your call.
President: Brandy Wood @ *The Atlanta Journal-Constitution* @ 526-5300

AMERICAN ASSOCIATION OF OCCUPATIONAL HEALTH NURSES

Corporate headquarters in Atlanta. Publishes monthly newsletter that includes both job openings and job seekers, usually five of each; for a copy, call Christy Roof, Communications Specialist, at 262-1162. Maintains a file for interested employers, and applicants are coded to preserve anonymity; listing information must be received by the fifth of the month prior to

publication. Cost is $100 for companies and non-members, but is free to members. Does not meet monthly; rather, has large, national meeting in April and smaller, leadership conference in September. Employment information board is available at both meetings. For information, contact Melody Hughes, Public Affairs Assistant at
50 Lenox Pointe NE, Atlanta, GA 30324.
(404) 262-1162 (Also national headquarters)

AMERICAN INSTITUTE OF CPA'S/GEORGIA SOCIETY OF CPA'S

Excellent source for CPA's and non-CPA's. Has seven chapters in the metro-Atlanta area, representing geographic areas, and each meets monthly; visitors are welcome. Georgia headquarters maintains a Job Bank file which includes job seekers and job openings. Membership is not required, nor is certification – there are many openings for non-CPA's. The Job Bank is updated monthly, with jobs deleted after one month; resumes, after six months. No charges for any of these services. For information concerning the various chapters and their meeting times and places, as well as for Job Bank information, contact Membership Services Coordinator, Carolyn Walter, at
3340 Peachtree Rd NE, Suite 2750, Atlanta, GA 30326-1026.
(404) 231-8676 x 815
Also publishes monthly newsletter which contains a classified ad section. Companies and individuals may advertise there for a fee of $30 for 50 words. To place an ad or obtain a copy of the newsletter, contact the Communications Department or ask for Casey O'Neal at the above address and phone number (x 814).

AMERICAN INSTITUTE OF GRAPHIC ARTS

The Atlanta chapter has 260 members, mostly creative and art directors and graphic designers, a few illustrators. The board of directors meets monthly, but the general membership meets bi-monthly, not on a specific date. Contact the president, Bob Wages, at
EM2 Design, 530 Means St NW, Suite 402, Atlanta, GA 30318.
(404) 221-1741
(212) 752-0813 – National Headquarters

AMERICAN MARKETING ASSOCIATION

The Atlanta chapter is one of AMA's largest, with more than 1000 members. Members are from marketing-related backgrounds, mostly research, advertising, planning, and analysis, with some sales reps also. Meets second Wednesday each month. Also has group called "Young Professionals," which meets monthly for career enhancement seminars. Publishes monthly newsletter, *Marketing Messenger*, which includes a

column for job openings and job seekers, and offers employment referral service (*must* be AMA member); for employment referral service information or to be included in the employment column ($30 for 40 words), called "Atlanta Market Place," contact Barbara Propst at 429-0565. For membership information, contact Hank Holderfield, Chapter Administrator, at
4500 Hugh Howell Rd, Suite 340, Tucker, GA 30084.
(404) 270-0619
(312) 648-0536 – National Headquarters
Note: The AMA has several affiliate groups representing the marketing functions in various industries, such as direct marketing, health care, insurance, *et al.* Call the Chapter Administrator for more information or to learn if your marketing specialty has a separate group.

AMERICAN PRODUCTION AND INVENTORY CONTROL SOCIETY

Membership comprised of companies and individuals engaged in manufacturing management and inventory control; current membership in Atlanta is more than 1000. Publishes monthly newsletter listing job openings and job seekers, and maintains a file for prospective employers. No charge. Membership is preferred, but not required. Has two group meetings monthly for dinner: Northside meets on second Wednesday and Southside meets on third Tuesday. Contact Jon Harvill, Placement Coordinator,
c/o Dunhill Professional Search, 340 Interstate North, Suite 140, Atlanta, GA 30339.
(404) 952-0009
President: Gary Bedford at 242-5459
(703) 237-8344 – National Headquarters

AMERICAN SOCIETY FOR PUBLIC ADMINISTRATION

Members are public service and government employees. Does not include job openings in their newsletter, since most government openings are posted elsewhere; or job seekers, since they have excellent networking at meetings. Sponsors an annual Job Fair with OPM every May. Meets monthly on the third Wednesday for lunch at 12:00. Contact either Ms. Lou Sissom, President, with the Gwinnett County Tax Office @ 822-7338.
(202) 393-7878 – National Headquarters

AMERICAN SOCIETY FOR QUALITY CONTROL

Membership comprised of quality control administrators, including governmental, manufacturing, administrative, etc.; Atlanta chapter has 1200 members. Meets monthly, usually for dinner on the second Thursday, and non-members can attend. Publishes monthly newsletter for members, and often includes job listings and job seekers. Generally, however, all

employment assistance goes through one person who handles both job listings and job seekers, and also maintains a resume file. Membership is preferred, but not required. Send resume and contact Jim Shields, c/o BTG, 2364 Park Central Blvd, Decatur, GA 30035.
(404) 981-3998
Chapter President: Sandi Reynolds at 494-2055
(414) 272-8575 – National Headquarters

AMERICAN SOC. FOR TRAINING AND DEVELOPMENT

An educational society of personnel trainers and performance managers, both corporate and consultants; Atlanta chapter has 1200 members. Meets for dinner and program; time and location varies and is announced in the monthly newsletter. Has Job Hotline for members only, that includes information on current job openings. For information, including monthly meetings and membership application, contact the Executive Director, Carol Teja, or write the ASTD office at
4514 Chamblee-Dunwoody Road, Suite 327, Atlanta, GA 30338.
(404) 668-9963
(703) 683-8100 – National Headquarters

AMERICAN SOCIETY OF HEATING, REFRIGERATING AND AIR CONDITIONING ENGINEERS, INC.

Society headquartered in Atlanta, and publishes monthly magazine with classified section in which individuals may at their own expense include a classified ad. Headquarters may be contacted regarding membership and monthly meeting dates, but does not conduct any employment assistance. Local chapter publishes monthly newsletter which lists both job openings and synopses of job seekers, available free to members only. Meets second Tuesday monthly at Sheraton Century Center at 5:00 for social hour, dinner, and program. To receive the newsletter and submit your synopsis, contact Dan Finkelstein at 419-7533.
President: Ben Coe with Hibble, Peters and Dawson @ 455-7707
Treasurer: Martin Keller with Atlanta Gas Light Company @ 584-3777
National office: 1791 Tullie Circle NE, Atlanta, GA 30329.
(404) 636-8400

AMERICAN SOCIETY OF MECHANICAL ENGINEERS

Has 1500 members in greater Atlanta. Publishes monthly newsletter, but currently does not include job openings or seekers. Coordinates job referrals through Dallas, TX region office, which does maintain job bank for members only; call Judy Cobb at (800) 445-2388. Maintains resume file for prospective employers and announces job openings at meetings. Meets first Monday each month, except summers. Contact Terrel Beckham, chapter chairman, day; 1573 Twelve Oaks Cir, Snellville, GA 30278

(404) 497-7760 day; 978-8471 evening
Employment Coordinator: Rhual Guerguerian, 2110 Wenlok Train, Marietta 30066, (404) 928-3716
Chapter secretary: Cindy Kromer at 740-7404
(800) 445-2388 – Southern region office
(212) 705-7722 – National Headquarters

AMERICAN SOCIETY OF SAFETY ENGINEERS

Members are individuals whose employment, education and experience are safety-related. Meets second Monday each month all year. Publishes monthly newsletter which contains both job openings (from companies and personnel agencies) and job seekers; membership is not required to receive newsletter or to attend meetings. For information, contact Dan Williams @ 836-6576.
For newsletter, call Bob Weir, (404) 529-2618.
(708) 692-4121 – National Headquarters

AMERICAN SOCIETY OF WOMEN ACCOUNTANTS

Publishes monthly newsletter that includes job seekers and openings, but without individual or company names. Local membership is preferred, but not required, especially for individuals relocating to Atlanta. Their service is not available to personnel agencies. Meets on the second Monday of each month for supper, a speaker and then the business meeting. Yearbook is published for members, that includes companies and job titles of their membership. Send resume and references to Barbara Beagles, chapter president, at c/o Dynatron/Bondo Corp, 3700 Atlanta Industrial Pkwy, Atlanta 30331.
(404) 696-2730 office; 943-8918 home3
(312) 726-9030 – National Headquarters

ASSOCIATION FOR SYSTEMS MANAGEMENT

Membership tends to be more experienced information systems professionals. Atlanta chapter has 200+ members and meets on the second Tuesday monthly at 5:30 for social hour and networking, followed by dinner and speaker at 6:30. Visitors are welcome. For information regarding membership, meeting reservations and speaker topics, call 843-7088. No formal job assistance, but networking at meetings is acknowledged. Monthly newsletter contains ads from personnel agencies and local companies, but not job seekers. Contact Alan Sleeper, President, at (404) 393-9933, or
P O Box 467596, Atlanta, GA 30346.
Membership chair: Jennifer Burns @ 319-8234
(216) 243-6900 – National Headquarters

ASS'N. OF RECORDS MGRS. AND ADMINISTRATORS

Publishes monthly newsletter "Arma-gram," which lists job openings and occasionally applicants. A confidential file of job seekers is maintained, and applicants are notified before being referred to a company. Usually meets third Tuesday of each month for lunch and speaker, but may vary to accommodate exceptional speaker. No charge for service and membership is required. For information, contact Gerald Poe, Career Placement Chairman at

Georgia Department of Human Resources, Atlanta, GA 30334.
(404) 656-4366
President: Zona Walton with Federal Home Loan Bank @ 888-8122
(913) 341-3808 – National Headquarters

ATLANTA AD CLUB

Membership comprised of companies and individuals in advertising and advertising-related businesses. Has monthly luncheon on third Tuesday. Publishes monthly newsletter which includes employment columns "Positions Wanted" ($10 for members, $20 for non-members) and "Positions Available" ($20 for member companies and $50 for non-members); 30-word maximum for each listing. For information, contact Sandra Stockman, Executive Director, at 3988 Flowers Road, Suite 650, Atlanta, GA 30360.
(404) 458-3181

BLACK DATA PROCESSING ASSOCIATES

The Atlanta chapter has 140 members and is growing rapidly. Meets monthly on the third Wednesday from 7:00 - 8:30 pm, and then adjourns for an informal networking session close by. Has job coordinator who receives job openings and maintains resume file; to obtain job listings, call their Bulletin Board, 381-5245. Members can send resume to be circulated, and request to be added to the mailing list for the monthly newsletter, which lists job openings. For other information, leave a message on their voice mail service and your call will be returned.
President: Mr. Tony Dean at 436-9178.
Membership Chair: Millicent Fuller @ 289-5666
(404) 681-6025 - voice mail service, also includes general information, meeting dates and speaker, special events, etc.

BUILDING OWNERS AND MANAGERS OF ATLANTA

Membership consists of building owners, developers, managers, service companies, investors, and brokers. Meets for lunch and program usually on second Wednesday. Maintains resume file for prospective employers and

prints job openings when available in monthly newsletter. Membership not required. Contact Stewart M. Huey, Executive Vice President, 2786 North Decatur Road, Suite 240, Decatur,GA 30033.
(404) 508-0116; fax 508-0217
(202) 289-7000 - National Headquarters

BUSINESS MARKETING ASSOC.

(Formerly Business/Professional Advertising Assoc) Members are corporate marketing communicators, representatives of media, agency personnel, and industry suppliers (sales), that are involved in business-to-business marketing (generally not consumer marketing). Meets monthly (except summers) on second Thursday, for lunch and program. Maintains Professional Assistance Network (PAN) to help members with job search. Publishes quarterly newsletter, but does not list job openings or seekers. For information, contact the chapter president, David Avery, with Sawyer, Riley Compton, 1100 Abernathy Rd, Suite 800, Atlanta 30328.
(404) 393-9849
For membership info, call Karen Metts (president-elect) at 446-1400 x 219.
(703) 683-2722 – National Headquarters

CREATIVE CLUB OF ATLANTA

Members are creative advertising types: art directors, illustrators, photographers, copywriters, production, etc. Meets monthly, but time and place varies with speaker availibility. Publishes quarterly magazine, but does not include job information. No longer offers formal job assistance. Contact Sal Kibler, Managing Director, at P O Box 421367, Atlanta, GA 30342.
(404) 881-9991

FINANCIAL EXECUTIVES INSTITUTE

Membership comprised of senior financial executives – controllers, treasurers, VP's of finance and CFO's. Meets at 6:30 monthly on fourth Tuesday for dinner and speaker. Has "Member Career Services Committee" which serves as liaison with executive search firms, companies, and applicants, as well as with the national office job assistance program. Membership required. Contact Ron White, MCSC Chairperson,
(404) 451-8763
(201) 898-4600 – National headquarters

FINANCIAL WOMEN INTERNATIONAL

(Formerly the National Association of Bank Women.) Membership comprised of women in financial service industries. Atlanta chapter has 75 members. Offers no formal job assistance programs, but excellent networking system. Publishes quarterly newsletter, but seldom includes

openings or job seekers. Meets monthly, usually on the second Wednesday for dinner and program. For more information and to get into their network, contact Nancy Frenkel, President, c/o Gifford, Hillegass & Ingwersen, 1834 Independence Square, Atlanta 30338.
(404) 396-1100
Membership Chair: Janice Owens @ Metro Bank, 255-8550
(301) 657-8288 – National Headquarters

GEORGIA BANKERS ASSOCIATION

Represents all commercial banks in Georgia. Publishes bi-weekly bulletin which is distributed to all banks in Georgia, but not available to individuals. Job seekers can place a five-line ad at no charge in the bulletin. To list yourself, contact Dan Thomason, Operations Manager, at
Hurt Plaza, Suite 1050, Atlanta, GA 30303.
(404) 522-1501

GEORGIA SOCIETY OF ASSOCIATION EXECUTIVES

Represents the paid employees of more than 400 professional associations in Georgia. Send resume to their office, and it will be kept on file for 90 days for perusal by interested employers. Publishes monthly newsletter which sometimes lists job openings. For information, contact Sharon Hunt, Executive Director at
4500 Hugh Howell Road, Suite 340, Tucker, GA 30084
(404) 270-1248

GEORGIA SOCIETY OF HOSPITAL PHARMACISTS

Call Job Hot Line at (404) 508-1717 for current openings with contact data.

GEORGIA SOCIETY OF PROFESSIONAL ENGINEERS

Eighteen chapters in Georgia with 1700 members. Publishes bi-monthly newsletter that lists job openings. Maintains resume bank and refers resumes on file to interested employers. Has monthly meetings and major semi-annual meetings. Must be member to attend meetings and receive newsletter/MAGAZINE, and prefers membership in order to retain resume. For more information, including meeting dates and places, call Jackie Kimberly, Executive Director at (404) 355-0177. Or write
1900 Emery St NW, Suite 226, Atlanta, GA 30318.
(703) 684-2800 — National Headquarters

INSTITUTE OF INTERNAL AUDITORS

Members are auditors and accountants in private and public organizations. Grants the CIA designation. Averages 100 at monthly meetings on second

Monday, except summers and October (first Monday) at Sheraton Century Center at 5:00; visitors are welcome ($25, includes supper). Publishes monthly newsletter, but currently does not list job opportunities. Maintains resume file, and matches applicants and openings; no charge. Contact Walt Moser, job coordinator, at 827-7532.

c/o First Union Bank, Audit Dept.-9015, P O Box 740074, Atlanta, 30374
For other information, contact the chapter president, Roger Strout, at Georgia-Pacific Corp, 220-6377.
(407) 830-7600 – National Headquarters

INT'L ASSOC. OF BUSINESS COMMUNICATORS

Members are professionals in all areas of communications and public relations, working for corporations, as consultants or as freelancers. Members and non-members can participate in resume file and informal placement service by sending six copies of your resume and a confidential note to the placement coordinator summarizing years and areas of experience, and minimum salary requirements. Resumes are kept on file for three months unless renewed or removed. Publishes monthly newsletter, "Communicators Classified," that lists both job openings and seekers. The service is free to local members and employers, and costs $15 for non-members. All communication from job seekers except renewals is to be in writing. Ad will run only once unless renewed. Deadline is the 15th of each month. Send 40-word ad (plus contact data) + fee (if applicable) and resumes to Jean Peterken, 3455 Waters Cove Way, Alpharetta, GA 30201. For meeting and membership information, contact the Director of Membership, Anna Umphress with American Red Cross at 428-2695.
President: Ms. Lisa Lauterbach with Okula Communications, 438-2500
(415) 433-3400 – National Headquarters

INT'L. FOUNDATION OF EMPLOYEE BENEFIT PLANS

Local chapter is the International Society of Certified Employee Benefits Specialists. Members work in the field of employee benefits. Meets six times per year; call for dates and location. Has designated job coordinator who announces job openings at meetings or over the phone, including openings through personnel agencies, and who maintains a resume file for prospective employers. Membership is required. Contact Greg Marshall at 668-3876.
President: Mary Ann Hajdu with Coca-Cola at 676-2345
Immediate past president: Carol Hill with Towers Perrin Companies at 365-1898.
(414) 786-6700 – National Headquarters

NAT'L ASSOC. FOR PROFESSIONAL SALESWOMEN

Call Pat Poole at (706) 216-3864 for information.

NATIONAL ASSOCIATION OF ACCOUNTANTS

Atlanta chapter has 900 members and meets on the third Tuesday monthly, except summers, for social hour and dinner at the Marriott Perimeter. Has an Employment Director who maintains a resume file for employers' perusal, as well as an updated job list, rather than wait for the monthly newsletter; you can obtain the list by contacting Bert Erling, @ (404) 457-6969.

c/o Accountants 1, 1745 Old Spring House Lane, Suite 419, Atlanta, GA 30338.

Chapter president: Tom Moore, professor at Kennesaw State College, 423-6322.

(201) 573-9000 – National Headquarters

NATIONAL ASSOCIATION OF BLACK ACCOUNTANTS

Has monthly and quarterly newsletter that lists openings and job seekers, available for members only. Maintains "Job Bank" of resumes for interested employers. Meets third Wednesday each month, and printed agenda includes job openings. For information or to list, contact Cynthia Teddleton, Career Development Chairman, at (404) 679-1815.

President: Eddie Nesby with Reliance Electric @ 967-3381 x 210

(202) 682-0222 – National Headquarters

NATIONAL ASSOCIATION OF BUSINESS ECONOMISTS

Atlanta affiliate is "Atlanta Economics Club." Meets third Tuesday (except summers) for lunch and visitors are welcome; cost for non-members is $18. No formal job assistance, but excellent networking--the day I called they had just secured employment for someone! To tap into their network, contact Nigel Ogilvie, membership chmn with Office of the Comptroller of the Currency, at 588-4525.

President: Mr. Stacy Kottman with Federal Reserve Bank of Atlanta at (404) 521-8500

(216) 464-7986 – National Headquarters

NATIONAL ASSOCIATION OF FEMALE EXECUTIVES

NAFE has five Atlanta affiliates and more than 5000 members in Atlanta. For information on NAFE groups here and nationwide, contact Pat Poole, National Network Coordinator,

280 Blacks Mill Valley, Dawsonville, GA 30534.

(706) 216-3864.

(212) 645-0770 – National Headquarters

NATIONAL ASSOCIATION OF INSURANCE WOMEN

Three chapters in the Atlanta area: Atlanta, NE Atlanta and Cobb County. Membership is comprised of companies and individuals in insurance and insurance-related businesses, and includes both men and women. Each chapter has an Employment Chairman who announces current openings at meetings and will refer interested persons to existing openings. Monthly newsletter also includes current openings. NE Atlanta chapter meetings are held monthly on the second Thursday. For information regarding the NE Atlanta chapter, contact Geisel Grabel, Vice President and membership chairperson, at
P O Box 450905, Atlanta, GA   30345.
(404) 399-7169 office; (404) 962-8877 home

NAT'L ASSOC. OF LEGAL SECRETARIES

Several metro-Atlanta chapters. The Atlanta chapter meets second Monday evening for dinner and program. Has Employment Chairman, who announces current openings at meetings and will refer applicants to existing openings; has far more openings than applicants! For information, contact the Georgia State President, Donna Durrett @ 422-1776.
(918) 493-3540 – National Headquarters

NAT'L ASSOC. OF PURCHASING MANAGEMENT

Has more than 500 local members and meets second Thursday for dinner and speaker; membership is not required, but encouraged. Job help is informal, but very effective, and is handled by the local president. The national headquarters also sponsors a for-profit placement company, whose profits go to NAPM's education programs, and this agency maintains a list by state of job vacancies. For local openings and information, contact Don Fesko, the local President, at 608 Tree Mt. Pkwy, Stone Mountain, GA   30083. (Include a stamped, self-addressed envelope if you want job openings.)
(404) 786-9051 if out-of-state; in Atlanta, call (404) 593-6224.
For information from NAPM Services, contact Carol Jamison, P O Box 22165, Tempe, AZ 85282-2165.
(800) 888-6276 x3010

NAT'L ASSOCIATION OF WOMEN IN CONSTRUCTION

Membership comprised of women in construction-related positions and industries. Operates very successful Occupational Research and Referral Service, matching jobs and applicants. Also publishes monthly newsletter which includes job openings and applicants, and maintains applicant file for interested employers. Also offers information on EEO-related positions. National Headquarters has computerized Job Data Bank. Awards annual scholarship in Atlanta area. Meets first Tuesday each month at 6:30 for dinner, program and business meeting; membership not required. Important:

when sending resume, indicate WIC on envelope. Contact Laura Lovallo, Membership Promotions, at 640-6614, or write
c/o Kamtech, Inc., 1009 Mansell Rd, Suite J, Roswell, GA 30076
Chapter president: Lori Ann Olejniczak at 885-1500
c/o Glass, McCullough, Sherill & Harrold, 1409 Peachtree St NE, Atlanta
(817) 877-5551 – National Headquarters

NATIONAL BLACK MBA ASSOCIATION

Publishes monthly newsletter which includes job vacancies. Meets fourth Monday of each month. Has book of openings for perusal at these meetings and resumes are circulated to attendees. Non-members can attend two meetings at no charge, after which they are expected to join. For information, contact the local president, Patrick McElroy with AT&T @ 810-3350.
Membership Director: Arlene Moore at 325-3848
(312) 236-2622 – National Headquarters

NATIONAL CONTRACT MANAGEMENT ASSOCIATION

Has 160 members, involved in contracting with government and industry, mostly with DOD or defense industry. Meets third Tuesday (off summers). Publishes monthly newsletter that occasionally lists job openings, not seekers. Has Employment Chairman who maintains resume file and refers resumes to interested employers. Contact George Miller, Employment Chairman, c/o Scientific Atlanta, 3845 Pleasantdale Rd, Atlanta 30340.
(404) 903-2204
Chapter president: Paul Williams with Lockheed Aeronautical Systems @ (404) 793-0507.
(703) 448-9231 – National Headquarters

NAT'L SOC. FOR PERFORMANCE AND INSTRUCTION

Members are professionals in performance and instructional technology, with emphasis on increasing employee's performance and productivity; more emphasis on program design and instructional technologies, and less on platform instruction. Dues are $30/year. Meets third Tuesday of each month from 5:30 to 8:15, and much networking is done then; past Membership Chairman found her job this way! Cost is $14 for non-members; $10 for members. Informal job assistance among members, and monthly newsletter occasionally includes company openings. Contact current chapter president Bill Worth,
c/o Georgia State University, Vocational and Career Development, University Plaza, Atlanta, GA 30303.
(404) 651-2500
(202) 861-0777 – National Headquarters

NATIONAL SOCIETY OF FUND RAISING EXECUTIVES

Membership comprised of 200+ professionals in the non-profit fund raising industry. Offers annual conference and meets on the third Monday of each month. Events open to non-members. For membership info, call the national headquarters. Produces a periodic mailing of job announcements and maintains a resume file. Membership in NSFRE or $10 fee required to be included in Jobs Mailing. Mail resume only to Martha Scott, Services Committee Chmn at

Center for the Visually Impaired, 763 Peachtree St, Atlanta, GA 30308 (404) 875-9011

Chapter president: Ted Bayley with St. Joseph's Foundation at 851-5870

(703) 684-0410 – National Headquarters

PLANNING FORUM: THE INTERNATIONAL SOCIETY FOR PLANNING AND STRATEGIC MGT

Atlanta chapter has 90 members, mostly corporate planners and consultants, involved in financial planning, strategic management, and business development. No formal job assistance, but excellent networking. Meets monthly on second Monday, except during summer, at 6:15 for social hour and dinner at the Marriott Perimeter; visitors are welcome. Offers additional workshops and seminars. For information, contact the membership chairperson, Norma Wiley, at 446-1400 x278.

Chapter president: Manola Robeson with Business Management Solutions (404) 469-4738

(513) 523-4185 – National Headquarters

PROFESSIONAL SECRETARIES INTERNATIONAL

Awards designation "Certified Professional Secretary." Meets third Monday monthly @ 5:45 for social hour, dinner, and program at Terrace Garden Hotel in Buckhead. Has Job Placement officer who accepts job openings and places in them in monthly newsletter as well as announcing them at meetings; call Tava Kirk at the chapter phone number and leave contact info.

Pam Ellis - chapter president with D&B Software. Write her at 5720 Grove Point Road, Alpharetta, GA 30302. Or call (404) 239-2959 or leave message on chapter phone (605-7707).

PUBLIC RELATIONS SOCIETY OF AMERICA

Meets monthly on first Thursday for lunch. PRSA publishes a monthly newsletter and includes a section called "People Pointers," which lists job openings and job seekers for full-time, part-time, freelancing, and internships; lists an average of five openings and 25 job-seekers each month. Members of PRSA receive the newsletter free and can list at no charge, plus a file of resumes is kept for interested employers. Non-members can order a copy for $5, which also includes association information. Non-members can list in "People Pointers" for $25 and their resume also will be kept on file, and they will receive that monthly letter with their listing. The procedure is as follows: compose and send a 35-word synopsis of yourself, your resume and $25 fee (if applicable) to Denise Grant at 5108 Victor Trail, Norcross, GA 30071. Or call for information. (404) 449-6369

Important: Deadline for job listing is the fifth of the month preceding the monthly listing.

(212) 995-2230 – National Headquarters

SOCIETY FOR HUMAN RESOURCE MANAGEMENT

(Formerly American Society for Personnel Administration) The Atlanta chapter has 850 members and meets monthly, not always on the same day; non-members can attend two meetings, after which membership is required. Has Resume Referral Service that maintains a resume file for interested employers and publishes a list of job openings (average 20+ monthly) that is available at the monthly meetings or can be purchased from the chapter administrator, Beth Wright at 425-6624, or

P O Box 2032, Kennesaw, GA 30144.

(404) 552-7718 – Leave your contact info on recording.

To have your resume included in the Resume Referral Service, contact Chuck Staub with Norrell Corp. @ 240-3225.

President: John Fauré with Medaphis Corp. at 319-3300

(703) 548-3440 – National Headquarters

SOCIETY FOR MARKETING PROFESSIONAL SERVICES

Membership comprised of companies and individuals in architecture, engineering, planning, and construction, and who are responsible for marketing their organization's services; has 120 members. Offers Employment Opportunity Committee under Director of Development, that maintains file of job openings and applicants and acts as a "clearing house" for employers and applicants; contact Ellen Braswell at 352-3930 ($10 fee for non-members). Quarterly newsletter now includes job information in a "classified section" with job openings and job seekers; contact David Dennis at 604-9182 to be listed (membership required). Meets for lunch on the fourth Monday each month.

President: Ken Beckworth with Georgia Power @ 526-7305

Director of Development: Lori Langan @ 658-5900

(703) 549-6117 – National Headquarters

SOCIETY FOR TECHNICAL COMMUNICATION

343

World's largest association of technical communicators, and has 400 members in Atlanta. Meets third Wednesday monthly from 6:00 to 8:30 pm (no meal). Publishes monthly newsletter which lists job openings (including free-lance), not seekers, and is available for members and non-members at the monthly meetings. Has volunteer Employment Services Manager, who maintains a database of job seekers and job openings, available to members only. For more information, contact Mark Willis at 876-0785. Now has Telephone Information Line (404-612-7463) which not only gives meeting times and other association information, but also includes a "Job Line," listing available openings.
President: David Leonard, PhD, with IDC at (404) 751-9660.
(703) 522-4114 – National headquarters

SOCIETY OF LOGISTICS ENGINEERS

Promotes logistics education and tchnical activities. Atlanta chapter has 60 members and meets third Thursday for lunch at 11:30. Membership chairman maintains resume bank, and monthly newsletter lists job openings and job seekers. Headquarters has central job bank for members only, accessible with touch-tone phone 24 hours/day.
President: Paul Williams with Lockheed at 793-0507
Membership Chairman: Bob Shively wit Lockheed at 793-0534
(205) 837-1092 – National headquarters

TECHNICAL ASSOCIATION OF THE PULP AND PAPER INDUSTRY (TAPPI)

Corporate headquartered in Atlanta. Maintains a resume file for prospective employers. Publishes monthly magazine, *Tappi Journal,* which includes a classified ad section at the end, listing job vacancies. Occasionally, job seekers also include an ad, but there is a fee. Send your resume or call.
P O Box 105113, Atlanta, GA 30348.
(404) 446-1400

WOMEN IN COMMUNICATIONS, INC.

With 100± members, WICI meets second Thursday monthly, and alternates between lunch and dinner. Maintains a Job Bank, which matches job openings with job seekers; free for members, $10 for non-members. Publishes monthly newsletter, but does not include job openings or seekers. Contact and send resume to the Job Bank Chairperson, Sally Roberts at (404) 942-7321 (This is her home phone; leave message and she will return your call.) 7722 Pool Mill Rd, Douglasville, GA 30135
For general information, call the WICI office at (404) 237-5472
Chapter president: Katherine Breck @ 522-0022 (office)
(703) 528-4200 – National headquarters

WORKING IN EMPLOYEE BENEFITS

Mission is benefits education and networking, and members are from human resources backgrounds, consultants, and vendors. Has 160 members and growing. Meets third Thursday for lunch at 103 West restaurant. Has Job Bank coordinator that accepts resumes; monthly newsletter lists both openings and individuals seeking employment. Offers reduced membership fee for unemployed! Membership is elected for calendar year; thus, the following are 1993 officers who will refer you to current slate:

Linda Osborne - President, with The Wyatt Company @ (404) 252-4030; Laura Corrigan - membership chairperson @ 982-8991; Beth Riccio - Job Bank Coordinator with Johnson & Higgins @ 586-0007.

(312) 357-0830 - national headquarters

APPENDIX F: GOVERNMENT OFFICES

(1) U. S. (Federal) agencies

(2) State of Georgia

(3) Local counties and City of Atlanta

GOVERNMENT OFFICES

Federal:

Department of the Army Civilian Personnel Office
    See "Appendix C," the list of companies

Office of Personnel Management (OPM)
    75 Spring St SW, Suite 956, Atlanta, GA 30303-3309
    (404) 331-4315 for recorded message; 331-4531 for assistance

Largest federal agencies in Atlanta:
    Environmental Protection Agency
    345 Courtland St NE, Atlanta, GA 30365
    (404) 347-3486

    Federal Aviation Administration
    3400 Norman Berry Drive
    Routing # ASO-10
    East Point, GA 30344
    (Employs 1100 in Atlanta)

    Dept of Health and Human Services (including Social Security)
    101 Marietta St NW, Suite 1601, Atlanta, GA 30303
    (404) 331-2205

    General Accounting Office
    101 Marietta St, Suite 2000, Atlanta 30303
    (404) 332-1900
    Job announcement published each fall and applications are taken from
    September through April. Hires recent grads and experienced.

    General Services Administration--Southeast Region Office
    Note: This office conducts all hiring for the Southeast. Prefers to hire
    recent grads under the "outstanding scholar" authority, which requires
    graduation in the upper 10% of class or 3.5 GPA.
    75 Spring St SW, Room 388, Atlanta, GA 30303
    (404) 331-3186;   (404) 331-5102 Job Information Line updated each
    Tuesday

    Department of the Treasury--Internal Revenue Service, Atlanta District
    Office
    275 Peachtree St NE, Room 528, Atlanta, GA 30343
    (404) 331-6008

Department of Labor
1371 Peachtree St NE, Room 136, Atlanta, GA 30367
(404) 347-7692 Ask for "Chief of Employment Branch," currently Marilyn Vanne.

U S Forestry Service – Southern Region Office
1720 Peachtree Road NW, 7th Floor
Atlanta, GA 30309
(404) 347-2384

Federal Bureau of Alcohol, Tobacco and Firearms
2635 Century Parkway, Atlanta, GA
(404) 331-6436

General Accounting Office
101 Marietta Tower, Suite 2000, Atlanta, GA 30323
(404) 332-1900
(Moving to Century Center on Clairmont Road x I-85 in March, 1993.)

US Postal Service
3900 Crown Rd, Atlanta, GA 30304
(404) 765-7234

State of Georgia

State Merit System
200 Piedmont Ave, Room 418, West Tower, Atlanta, GA 30334
(404) 656-2724 - Two minute information recording, plus directions to their office.

Department of Audits
Financial Division: Hires mostly recent grads with accounting major or with 25 hours of accounting, probably 15 each year. Good GPA is important. Send resume to Director of Finance Division, 270 Washington St, Room 216, Atlanta, GA 30334.
(404) 656-2180

Performance Audits Division: Hires mostly MBA's and accounting grads, but also seeks a few economics and public administration grads; good GPA is important. Send resume to Director of Performance Audits, 270 Washington St, Room 602, Atlanta, GA 30334.
(404) 656-2006

Local

Atlanta, City of
Profile: Government for City of Atlanta, employing 8000+ and expecting an increase. Hires both recent grads and experienced personnel in accounting/finance, administration and MIS.

Procedure: Send your resume with Social Security Number and cover letter requesting to be placed on their mailing list for a certain job classification (*e.g.*, accounting, administration, engineering, etc.) and they will notify you of openings for which you can apply. If you are in Atlanta, you can go to their office and review the "Specifications List," which includes all current openings. Mail information or go to Employment Services Division, 68 Mitchell Street SW, Atlanta, GA 30335.
(404) 658-6164 to check on job information and resume status; 330-6456 for professional-level Job Hot Line.

Clayton County
Profile: Smallest of the five major metro-Atlanta counties, with 1600 employees. Publishes a Job Announcement List of current needs, which can be reviewed at their offices; they will not mail copies. You can call their office and ask if there is a job vacancy for your specialty, and if so, they will mail you an application form. Both recent grads and experienced personnel are needed.

Procedure: Contact or visit their office at
121 South McDonough St, Room 104, Courthouse Annex, Jonesboro, GA 30236.
(404) 477-3239

Cobb County
Profile: Third largest metro-Atlanta county and growing rapidly. Currently employs 4000 total. In a "normal" year, hires approximately 50 recent grads and 25 experienced exempt, primarily in accounting/finance, engineering (CE mostly) and MIS (Unisys, may change in late 1992), plus social work and urban planning. Seeks experienced managers in accounting and engineering. Considering a reduction-in-force in 1992.

Procedure: Send resume to Employment Manager,
Cobb County Personnel Department, 100 Cherokee St., Marietta, GA 30090-9614.
(404) 528-2544; 528-2555 job info line

DeKalb County
Profile: Second largest metro-Atlanta county, employing 5000+. All applicants are hired through the county merit system.

Procedure: Write for application from DeKalb County Merit System, 120 West Trinity Place, Decatur, GA 30030.
(404) 371-2331 - Job Hot Line

Fulton County
Profile: Largest metro-Atlanta county, employing 9000+. Has many openings in all areas. Must go to their office to review current job listing, then apply for employment. Most exempt positions require a proficiency test, which is given twice weekly.

Procedure: Go to their Personnel Office at 165 Central Ave SW, Atlanta, GA.
(404) 572-2382

Gwinnett County
Profile: For several years, Gwinnett County had been the fastest growing county in the entire nation, and is now the fourth largest metro-Atlanta county. Employs 2500, and expects an increase in hiring, both for recent grads and experienced personnel, especially civil engineers, accountants and other disciplines.

Procedure: Send resume to Personnel Department,
75 Langley Dr, Lawrenceville, GA 30245.
(404) 955-6506 - Job Hot Line; 995-6500 - information

About the author . . .

STEPHEN E. HINES has been involved in personnel recruitment and placement in Atlanta since July, 1970. He is the founder and owner of HINES RECRUITING ASSOCIATES, a professional-level personnel placement service, established in 1975. For more information, call (404) 262-7131, or write P O Box 52291, Atlanta, GA 30355.

The author wishes to thank the following for their contributions to this book:

Anne Kraft, whose presence is missed every day
Charlotte Taylor
Dick France
Raymond Lamb
Katie Baer
Jeffrey Smith
Ken Vaughn